New Library of Pastoral Care

Sin, Guilt, a~~nd F~~

New Library of Pastoral Care

NEW·LIBRARY·OF

PASTORAL·CARE

SIN, GUILT, AND FORGIVENESS

*The Hidden Dimensions
of a Pastoral Process*

Mary Anne Coate

First published in Great Britain 1994
Society for Promoting Christian Knowledge
Holy Trinity Church
Marylebone Road
London NW1 4DU

British Library Cataloguing-in-Publication Data

A catalogue record for this book is available
from the British Library

ISBN 0-281-04781-2

Typeset by Pioneer Associates, Perthshire
Printed in Great Britain by
The Cromwell Press, Melksham, Wiltshire

Contents

Foreword

The *New Library of Pastoral Care* has been planned to meet the needs of those people concerned with pastoral care, whether clergy or lay, who seek to improve their knowledge and skills in this field. Equally, it is hoped that it may prove useful to those secular helpers who may wish to understand the role of the pastor.

Pastoral care in every age has drawn from contemporary secular knowledge to inform its understanding of men and women and their various needs and of the ways in which these needs might be met. Today it is perhaps the secular helping professions of social work, counselling and psychotherapy, and community development which have particular contributions to make to pastors in their work. Such knowledge does not stand still, and pastors would have a struggle to keep up with the endless tide of new developments which pour out from these and other disciplines, and to sort out which ideas and practices might be relevant to their particular pastoral needs. Among present-day ideas, for instance, of particular value might be an understanding of the social context of the pastoral task, the dynamics of the helping relationship, the attitudes and skills as well as factual knowledge which might make for effective pastoral intervention and, perhaps most significant of all, the study of particular cases, whether through verbatim reports of interviews or general case presentation. The discovery of ways of learning from what one is doing is becoming increasingly important.

There is always a danger that a pastor who drinks deeply at the well of a secular discipline may risk losing a distinct pastoral identity and become 'just another' social worker or counsellor. It in no way detracts from the value of these professions to assert that the role and task of the pastor are quite unique among the helping professions and deserve to be clarified and strengthened rather than

vii

weakened. The theological commitment of the pastors and the appropriate use of their role will be a recurrent theme of the series. At the same time pastors cannot afford to work in a vacuum. They need to be able to communicate and co-operate with those helpers in other disciplines whose work may overlap, without loss of their own unique status. This in turn will mean being able to communicate with them through some understanding of their concepts and language.

Finally, there is a rich variety of styles and approaches in pastoral work within the various religious traditions. No attempt will be made to secure a uniform approach. The Library will contain the variety, and even perhaps occasional eccentricity, which such a title suggests. Some books will be more specifically theological and others more concerned with particular areas of need or practice. It is hoped that all of them will have a usefulness that will reach right across the boundaries of religious denomination.

DEREK BLOWS

Acknowledgements

This book has taken me longer to write than I had hoped, and I have come to realize that this is partly because the theme is potentially so huge. It has taken time to struggle with my material—first to organize it inside myself and then to try to communicate it in words—for the levels of experience, knowledge, and memory feeding into my thoughts were many and diverse.

Some of my sources have been inside me for many years; others I had to try to take in afresh. It is difficult therefore to identify them fully and exactly; although I have tried to acknowledge my written sources as fully and accurately as I can, there are still inevitably many possibilities for error and omission for which I apologize. The contribution of people, relationships, and past and present experience is even harder to itemize; and indeed by its very nature perhaps it cannot and should not be dissected or torn apart. So although I want to acknowledge and express my great gratitude to people, I hope I may be forgiven for not, here, teasing it out more exactly.

I would, though, like to thank in person Judith Longman and Derek Blows for their generous dialogue with my ideas, their constructive challenge, and their encouragement to persevere when sometimes I could not see the wood for the trees. Also Philip Law of SPCK and the editing and production team there for their patience and understanding with the constraints of trying to write creatively round a full-time job.

I have inevitably done my theme (and my sources) much less than justice for perhaps it is the theme of a lifetime. What I have written must stand, therefore, as *one* contribution, at *a* point in time and experience, to the exploration of what I sense to be timeless questions. Those who care to read these pages will come from their own place in time and experience which may blend in with *or* conflict with my own. My hope would be that in that meeting we can come to appreciate, *even just a little bit more*, the fullness and richness of that which I feel will always be, at heart, *mysterious*.

Mary Anne Coate
February 1994

Introduction

When I told some of my friends that I was planning to write a book on 'sin', their reactions verged on the ribald: 'that should be interesting anyway'; 'you'll have plenty of experience to go on'; 'you can do research with any of us, and we'll contribute.'

Underlying these responses were, I thought, several quite serious points. First, that 'sin', whatever we mean by it, is universal and quite natural. Second, the topic generates a sort of suppressed excitement, even fascination, which perhaps itself masks some sort of anxiety. Third, people seemed to think they knew immediately what was meant by the word, even though they were by no means all of a religious persuasion. This last I found interesting for, as I shall try to show in the course of the book 'sin' is a religious, even theological, term and has no strict meaning outside the religious frame of reference. Yet, it seems to have been hijacked into general currency. For this to happen, it must have tapped into an underlying human psychological or even sociological layer of experience. The word 'sin' must be 'standing for' something far more general and more deeply relevant to our human condition. We may not all call it sin, but something which some people call sin seems to be important to all of us.

I then found myself asking why it might be important to try to explore the whole area of sin, guilt and forgiveness, and I came to three tentative conclusions.

First, it is no academic matter. Many people, within and outside the various communities of faith, suffer from a crippling sense of guilt which they attach to their presumed misdeeds or to more fundamental deficits and deformities in their being. For many people this creates, as for George Herbert, a profound obstacle to the give and take of love:

> Love bade me welcome; yet my soul drew back
>   guilty of dust and sinne[1]

For some, the church's claim to forgive sin and to bestow peace 'works'; others can be reassured by another human being. But some people find no relief. It is certainly not a mere abstraction to ask what can be going on that 'forgiveness' works for some people in some situations and not for others; for it can make the difference between the vitality of life, or the experience of a living or actual death.

Others still are perplexed by the religious bodies who seem to set such importance on sin, and appear to be trying to inculcate a sense of guilt where previously there had been none. They can then see the whole religious dimension only as life-denying, destructive, and repulsive. This again is no light charge.

Second, I realized that there was—among others no doubt —a 'sin-shaped' gap in my earlier book on *Clergy Stress*.[2] I have only five indexed references to sin, and in all but one of them I use the word as a commonplace, and as if everyone reading the book will, of course, know exactly what I mean by it. I take sin almost for granted. Only once—when exploring the need for some people to rebel against the tradition in relation to the core of Christian faith—do I talk of 'profound "sin", whatever that word means?'[3]

There was, in that book, much *implicit* exploration of the area;[4] the nature of the relationship between guilt and sin, the sections on perfection[5] and falling short of perfection, and the longer passages on forgiveness and redemption.[6] Sin was not, of course, the main focus of my exploration—human stress was. Some religious writers would, I think, have wanted to say that one of the major causes of human stress is the sense and conviction of sin, but I chose not to explore it in that way then. At this point, it seems right to try to fill in that gap. Does that which we call our 'sinfulness' bear on the stress of our ordinary human lives?

Third, I encounter this area as a compelling mystery. It is a mystery that has its origin in the religious dimension, but seems to transcend it. To illustrate this let me juxtapose two snippets of experience from current everyday life:

A placard alongside the mainline railway from Scotland to Euston proclaims 'the wages of sin is death—prepare to meet thy God', as has many another placard or sandwich-board. We ignore these most of the time, but it can be a different story in huge revivalist meetings or in times of national catastrophe or even in the cruel mythology that has reared at least some sort of a head over the Aids threat. Sin and punishment for sin are given back a primitive power that can seem to threaten our very life and existence.

Or, consider the day-to-day news on the domestic and international scene: the carnage of the Gulf War of 1991 and its aftermath in terms of the devastation of the Kurdish people; the continuing violence and terror in Northern Ireland and Bosnia even as I write now in the autumn of 1993; the obstruction of relief work in Somalia and Angola. In the face of the so-called 'new world order', we are confronted time and again by what seems to be human nature in its darkest form—a nature that can stand by whilst others suffer, that does not seem to learn from experience, grow, and develop. In this confrontation, I am caught in a sense that I could well, with a part of me, describe as a sense of a sort of 'corporate sin'. The mixture of motives throughout and the result of it all in appalling human misery, suffering, and death is not something that any of us can escape or disclaim responsibility for. We may find it possible to anaesthetize ourselves by asserting our individual powerlessness in the face of corporate politics, or the activities of leaders far removed from us. But it *is* merely an anaesthetic, for:

No man is an Iland, intire of selfe—every man
is a piece of the Continent . . . any man's death
diminishes me because I am involved in Mankinde.[7]

If I am right in connecting this experience of human solidarity with a sense of sin, then I am beginning to raise the questions of whether sin is committed only against God or can also be against our fellow men, and of the relationship of sin to morality and human responsibility.

When I talk of a sense of sin, as in the paragraph above, am I really talking about guilt? At first I thought 'Yes'; I thought I could define guilt as that feeling (sense) that alerts us to the fact and presence of sin. 'I feel guilty about having done (or not done) so-and-so' is a familiar expression. On reflection, I think my definition over-simplifies things. For one thing, guilt is not only a feeling. It has an objective as well as a subjective aspect, as our legal system shows. The objective face of guilt seems to be equivalent to responsibility; if we are found guilty of an offence the judgement is that we did it—we are the person responsible. Nevertheless, it is the subjective face of guilt that tends to come most easily to mind; we *experience* guilt, we *feel* guilty. But even within the area of feeling things are not simple.

It is possible to feel guilty for no apparent cause. Some people feel more or less guilty for much of the time. Others feel little guilt when the reality of the situation indicates that it would be appropriate to do so. Feeling guilty can spur us to make amends, to redress a situation, but feeling guilty can also become an unremitting source of inner turmoil and torment. Like all feelings, guilt will not come and go at our will, and it is not always easy for us to reflect rationally upon it because it can become so much a part of us.

In the pages that follow I hope to be able to reflect—at least a little—on guilt, in order to explore its emotional and psychological basis, its more exact relationship to sin, and its place in the story of our relationship with God.

'Sin' and guilt together represent but half the mystery —the other half is enshrined in the words 'forgiveness' and 'redemption'. Forgiveness has ordinary human currency; most of us know what it is like to have been hurt and to try to forgive, or to hurt and hope another person will forgive us. But I am not sure that we can easily pinpoint what goes on in this very ordinary human act of forgiveness—is it a wiping out, a repair of damage to a relationship, a sort of forgetting, or what? And is it possible to extrapolate from this human experience some understanding of the forgiveness of God? Or should it, as some claim, be the other way round: the forgiveness of God is the prototype and source of our human experience?

Redemption has a human meaning as, for example, in

the buying back of items deposited at a pawnbroker, but has become a more clearly religious word; indeed it lies at the heart of the Christian tradition. I have begun writing this book at Easter time, which for the Christian re-enacts and commemorates the death and resurrection of the one who was described as 'the Lamb of God, who takes away the sin of the world'.[8] In poetry borrowed from the exilic period of the Old Testament and the prophet Isaiah the meaning of those events is proclaimed thus:

> He was wounded for our transgressions,
> he was bruised for our iniquities;
> upon him was the chastisement that made us whole,
> and with his stripes we are healed.[9]

This, we are to understand, is at least a part of what we mean by redemption and the very heart of the mystery. Christian atonement theology[10] has always oscillated between a subjective stance in which our redemption is brought about through our *imitation* of the example of Christ, and a more objective idea that *we cannot do it all by ourselves*. The powers of sin and death are felt to be too strong and overwhelming, and, therefore, the event of the death and resurrection of Christ is needed to contribute something to our struggle which makes it manageable and resolvable.

The heart of the mystery of redemption raises also the central question of the mystery of sin and forgiveness. *How* can we experience forgiveness? Can we stop castigating ourselves unmercifully for our falling short of our goals or for our repeated realization that 'the good that I would I do not . . . the evil which I would not, that I do'?[11] Can we free ourselves from guilt that persists despite our knowing it to be irrational and unfounded? Conversely, can we easily and on our own take responsibility for that which is indeed our own, face our true feelings whatever they may be, and feel a true concern for others rather than only ruthlessness with its inherent tendency to use and probably exploit?

Whether we think theologically, or whether we think psychologically, I think the answer here is a qualified 'No'. We need some help.

The liturgical acts of confession and forgiveness— whether corporate or individual—witness to the truth

xviIntroduction

that we cannot do it alone. Even the liturgy of the Jewish
Day of Atonement, and the ancient Israelite ritual of the
scapegoat cast out into the wilderness,[12] seem to be talking
both of responsibility—the responsibility to own the fault,
the imperfection—*and* the inability to deal with the burden
of responsibility without the help of another. The 'other'
is the formalized voice of absolution, the meditative taking
in of the gift of love from the cross of Christ, or the trans-
ferring of the burden to the lamb who is to be sacrificed.

The psychological story concurs. In a 'good enough'[13]
early environment, characterized particularly by the
quality of our relationship with the people most important
to us—normally parents—we can grow and develop as persons without too much restriction of our energies and
feelings. Where this natural provision has been inadequate
or limited—and it often is—we may need the help of
psychotherapy[14] in later life in order to re-discover parts
of ourselves that have got lost, frozen, or distorted. These
may emerge as good and creative, or as unrespectable
and sometimes destructive. The process of discovery
includes our taking responsibility for the 'us' we unravel
and, often, our necessary forgiveness—if we are to move
on—of those people who in the past have been the cause
of our pain, either intentionally or unwittingly and unconsciously. But this confrontation with more of ourselves
takes place within the therapeutic relationship. This
relationship aims to be non-judgemental. It seeks to understand and to allow a re-emergence of our true self in the
present. The distortions, conflicts, and deficits of past
relationships, and the strong feelings associated with
them, are often re-experienced as attached or 'transferred'
to the person of the therapist. There they see anew the
light of day, and if they can be emotionally understood
and re-evaluated, they can come to lose their stranglehold
on our present life.

These last two paragraphs beg nearly all the great questions of theological thinking and psychoanalytic and psychotherapeutic theory. The two disciplines do not correspond at many points; there is conflict between them,
and it is part of the purpose of this book to 'unpack'
them, assess the conflicts, and see which are resolvable,
and which must remain as points of difference. But they
have at least one fundamental point in common. The

mysteries of sin and forgiveness and of stunted or healthy human development and life are not phenomena which belong to the human being when alone and in isolation, but to the human being in relationship. Or so I believe, though I will be taking the exploration of this further.

But if sin and forgiveness essentially belong in relationships they will come to have an external social face as well as an internal private life. We perhaps see this best in the movement from sin as an inner state to sin(s) as acts or behaviour that are visible.

Some of the age-old 'sins', like sloth and gluttony, seem to operate mainly *within* people, but their effect extends to the people around us. Others, like anger, malice, and envy, operate more essentially *among* people. Where prohibitions concerning them have become normative for a society, we begin to talk of morality, though it is questionable whether we can just simply equate these two dimensions of righteousness—sinfulness and morality—immorality. The *mores* of a society can change, and can become harsher or more lenient than what is designated as sinful by a community of faith. Sin and morality may coincide when the motives and goals of society and the communities of faith coincide; alternatively society's *mores* may be motivated by economics, issues of social control and the like, whilst those of the community of faith may be more centred on purity, like-mindedness, altruism, threat to the sense of belonging . . . The social face of sin is unmistakably there, but how it relates to the *body* of society is not clear, though some exploration of this will form the last part of the book.[15]

It is the points at which the theological and psychological stories meet and interact that I want to be concerned with first. Here, unlike my writing in *Clergy Stress* when I was faced with a dilemma as to whether and how to separate the human, psychological, and religious dimensions and which should be primary,[16] I think the theological story comes first. Sin *belongs* in this story, and the theological longhand is the mother tongue.

Is this self-evident, or does it need justifying? To some it will be self-evident, others will not be so sure, and I shall need to return to this issue in Chapter 2.

Finally, I need to make two points that relate to the style of this book.

First, I have chosen, in Chapter 1, to illustrate my theme by the use both of figures from literature and *imaginary* people of today that I have made up. I used the same device in *Clergy Stress* in order to try to bring my material alive, but I then demanded that my readers should keep my imaginary people in mind, hold them through their reading of the book, and be able to refer to them and remember their life and life history whenever I made another reference to them. Some people found this not too hard to do; others have told me, either personally or through reviews, that this was asking a bit much. The imaginary people were bound to be more real to me, as I had created them, than to my readers. The task involved too much jumping around for the reader, both in the mind and more literally among the pages of the book. So in this book, though I have used the same device for the same reason—namely, to root what I am trying to say in actual experience rather than abstract thought—I intend that Chapter 1 will stand alone, and that reading the succeeding chapters should not overly tax readers' memory of it.

I am using the illustrations of Chapter 1 to create a 'climate' or 'atmosphere' of thought. I *have* referred to some of the illustrations later in the book, but I hope I have done so in a way that reintroduces them without putting overmuch strain on memory and continuity.

Second, in no sense can what I write be construed as a theological or psychological textbook on the subject. The theme is too vast, and the available source literature is too prolific to make that possible. The result will need to be seen and read as a personal, inevitably subjective contribution. For example, I have approached my theme from the point of view of the individual, and what goes on inside him or her. Were this book being written by a family therapist they might well have focused on the systems[17] in which individuals function rather than on the individuals themselves.

My hope is, therefore, that I will manage to articulate some of the questions that we all have on this subject, and provide, not necessarily some of the answers, but an idea of a way in which we are able constructively to approach the questions. I do not see this exploration as being of intellectual interest only, but as a relevant contribution to both the pastoral task of ministry, and the healing of soul and psyche of each one of us. If, at the end, the verdict is 'interesting, but so what?' then I shall have failed in the task I set myself.

For I believe that the constellation of sin, guilt, forgiveness, and redemption is concerned with our deepest human experiences—of love, hate, wanting, withdrawal, isolation. Such are their importance.

Notes

1. George Herbert, 'Love', in R. S. Thomas (ed.), *A Choice of George Herbert's Verse* (Faber & Faber 1967), p. 91.
2. Mary Anne Coate, *Clergy Stress* (SPCK 1989).
3. Coate, *Clergy Stress*, p. 111.
4. Coate, *Clergy Stress*, pp. 101–2, 154–6.
5. Coate, *Clergy Stress*, pp. 148–9.
6. Coate, *Clergy Stress*, pp. 116–23.
7. John Donne, 'Devotions 17', in *John Donne, Complete Poems and Selected Prose* (The Nonesuch Press 1962), p. 538.
8. John 1.29 (RSV).
9. Isaiah 53.6 (RSV).
10. See Chapter 5.
11. Romans 7.19 (AV).
12. Leviticus 16.15–22.
13. This phrase originates from the work and writings of the psychoanalyst Donald Winnicott. It refers primarily to the ability of a mother to adapt sufficiently adequately to the gestures, needs, and impulses of her baby, so providing an environment that facilitates the infant's emotional development.
14. For general reference see D. Brown and J. Pedder, *Introduction to Psychotherapy* (Tavistock Publications 1979), or A. Storr, *The Art of Psychotherapy* (Secker and Warburg, and William Heinemann 1979).
15. See Chapter 9.
16. Coate, *Clergy Stress*, pp. 5–7, 69.
17. For a helpful introduction to the ideas of family systems and other approaches to family work see John Burnham, *Family Therapy* (Tavistock Publications 1986).

ONE

Windows

─────────

I want to start this exploration of the mystery of sin, guilt, and forgiveness by attempting to look in on them, as it were, through *windows*. Some are but casement slots high up in the wall; others give more a broad view through a wide-angled bay. Still others are difficult to see through, for the stained glass which is their glory renders them opaque like a multicoloured mosaic. Slightly sinister barred basement windows with but half their height showing above ground level complete the scene. No one window shows the whole of the interior; different angles show a plethora of nooks and crannies, lights and shadows, but the totality remains obstinately just out of sight.

The Large Bay Window

It is 9.30 am on Sunday morning in the *Church* household. *Michael Church* is still at breakfast, a piece of toast balanced precariously between finger and thumb halfway to his mouth whilst his attention is momentarily caught by a headline in the Sunday paper. His wife, *Margaret,* is rushing around looking for the hair-drier, collecting cereal bowls and stray cups *en route* and depositing them in any spare spot in the kitchen. Alerted by the noise from upstairs she retrieves the hair-drier from where it is being used by *Mark,* aged nine, to dry off the protesting dog—the state of whose fur suggests a recent encounter with a muddy ditch. *Susan,* aged thirteen, is not yet up, and snuggles even further down the bed at the plea 'You've got ten minutes before we have to leave for church.' Downstairs, *Peter,* aged eleven is already well into an elaborate war-game which is taking up most of the hall space and has to be climbed over by all and sundry. Requests to 'Come and get ready, do' meet with a sullen

1

'Why should I—I don't want to go to church—it's boring sitting still for so long and I don't like the way the vicar's wife always tells me how fast I'm growing. And you always get talking to people at the end when you really don't want to at all, and it makes you bad-tempered when we get home and find there's nothing done for lunch.' 'He's about right there,' reflects *Margaret* rather ruefully, and marvelling not for the first time at how much her son sees through her.

10.30 am. The *Church* family take up most of one whole pew in the medieval parish church which sits four-square in the middle of a smallish town. They are rather near the front unfortunately, but there was nothing for it this morning—they only just arrived in time. Now the parish Communion is well advanced; the sermon has been and gone and *Margaret* has just breathed a sigh of relief at successfully negotiating her part in the shared intercessory prayers, but 'Why do I always seem to get landed with praying for the peace of the world? There never is any.' The presiding minister turns, somewhat ponderously *Michael* notices with a start—for they are much the same age and both putting on too much weight—and faces the people with a gesture of invitation.

> Let us confess our sins, in penitence and faith firmly resolved to keep God's commandments and to live in love and peace with all men.[1]

The congregation creaks to its corporate knees and responds obediently:

> Almighty God, our heavenly Father,
> we have sinned against you and against our fellow men,
> in thought and word and deed,
> through negligence, through weakness,
> through our own deliberate fault.
> We are truly sorry,
> and repent of all our sins.[2]

Michael comes-to halfway through with a start; he's been on automatic pilot, half-absorbed with the shadows of leaves outside darting about on the church wall—unaccountably they send him back to yesterday's foot-ball. He stumbles to find his place in the prayer, comes in at the wrong place and gets a knowing look from his daughter who is managing to look as if butter wouldn't melt in her mouth. 'Pity she's not like this always, the little rascal,' he thinks as he remembers yesterday's show of temper over a school sock that went astray at the crucial moment.

Margaret feels a tug at her sleeve and a not-so-soft whisper asks in *Mark's* unmistakable tones 'What's ne–ne–gligence —is it like ladies and gents?' *Margaret* can feel rather than see the people behind her snigger—'Why do children always show you up in the wrong place?'

A slight pause and the minister again turns to face the people and pronounces the words of absolution:

Almighty God,
who forgives all who truly repent,
have mercy upon you,
pardon and deliver you from all your sins . . .[3]

He has been saying these words week in and week out for the past twenty years and for much of the time he, too, is on automatic pilot, caught up in the onward movement of the liturgy. But today, as occasionally happens, he wonders 'What am I doing in these words and at this moment? What right have I?'

But the half-raised question must be dropped; the service quickly moves on to the Peace—the exchange of greetings throughout the congregation—and the clinking and shuffling that heralds the imminence of the collection and the Offertory procession.

The Eucharist moves nearer its climax with the great Thanksgiving prayer encapsulating and declaiming the story of redemption.

For he is your living Word,
through him you have created all things from the
  beginning,
and formed us in your own image.
Through him you have freed us from the slavery of
sin . . .[4]

The service continues with the remembrance of the Last Supper and the taking and blessing of the bread and wine—the sacred and solemn setting for the corporate re-offering of life and worship with which the prayer ends.

A silence, and into that silence come the familiar

words of the Lord's Prayer in which the children, now re-
galvanized into activity, join lustily, if slightly at their
own pace:

> Forgive us our sins,
> as we forgive those who sin against us.[5]

In the moments before the bread and wine is shared, the
minister speaks the threefold invocation of him whose
sacrificial life, death, and resurrection have just been
recalled and remembered:

> Lamb of God, you take away the sins of the world:
> have mercy on us.[6]

The Communion over, the service moves swiftly to its
conclusion. There is, as Peter had foreseen, the inevitable
delay with talk, greetings, gossip, and arrangements, and
then the family set off for home.

The reader may be wondering, at this point, at the sort
of family I have created. In one sense they are so ordinary
—in another they are too ordinary by half and may seem
to belong to a bygone age and not be representative of
our multicultural and multi-ethnic society, let alone that of
other countries. You may wonder also why I concentrated
on the service of the Eucharist—this, though of central
importance to Roman Catholics and some Anglicans, is
not so for other Anglicans and some if not most of the
Free Churches. In choosing as I have, have I not created a
caricature?

I hope not, for I had to start somewhere, and I wanted
to start here to make what I see as an important point.
Given a certain way of life, a certain context, sin does not
seem to impinge upon us much. *Michael* almost dozed off
in the confession; the priest was a little more aware—for
some reason that we are not told about—of his rather
extraordinary role as the bestower of forgiveness than
we gather he is on most occasions. The only person to
show some interest was *Mark* whom the long words
defeated. But his query might well have been our query if
we could let ourselves admit it; what quite is negligence?

What quite is negligence, and indeed what quite is sin?
Again the word is used as if we all know exactly what it
means. We get some clues; it appears to be something
that we do against God *and* other people. It is sin whether

we intend it with our full being or not, and regardless of whether we know quite what we are doing or cannot help it. It is apparently something that has us in thrall—even a sort of slavery—from which we need to be freed, and the Thanksgiving proclamation is just this: we are freed from it. The final clue is that the 'freeing' comes about in some mysterious way through the sacrificial life and death of Christ.

So, in at least three places the eucharistic worship focuses on sin, but for many of us most of the time it remains 'just a part of the service'. If this does not seem too strong a sentiment it is almost as if familiarity has somehow bred contempt. Confession and absolution are elements in most corporate and public Christian services—but the question remains; 'What do we, individually and corporately, make of them?'

In part the answer to this question must be that of course it varies what we make of them, and this is where the *Church* family is just one family among many, though I am suggesting that their reaction and participation in the service is not so unlike that of many others. But I called the Eucharist the 'Large Bay Window'. Why?

I used it in this way for two reasons. First, the Eucharist is a gathering of people who come from different backgrounds with different things on their mind. If we can imaginatively probe the inner thoughts of some more people at the service I have described we may be able to enlarge our picture. Second, the Eucharist is, in a sense, universal to Christendom. It may not be central to regular worship in all churches, but even so it is central in its *substance* to many—in countries throughout the world. The Eucharist in our English market town may feel and look rather different from, for example, the Mass in a Third World country, or the same service in an inner-city area of this country, or a Catholic or Orthodox celebration in Eastern Europe . . . The list could go on, but the heart and structure of the worship remains the same. Maybe it can and does justify being the 'large bay window'?

I want now to build on this and try to explore the possible thoughts and feelings of a selection of worshippers at this service in relation to what they bring to it and what relevance the concept of sin may have to them.

My selection is a creation of my own—others would inevitably paint a different picture. I think this matters not at all, as my purpose is to stimulate our thoughts and imaginations so as to widen the scope of our exploration.

The Multicoloured Stained Glass Windows

Pat and *John* have made it to church but only just, after yet another night of too much alcohol and yet another row—can their relationship last or not? Last night it was the same old accusations, the recrimination over the abortion that 'you made me have, because you said we weren't ready to settle down together and have a family. It's you that's not really grown up and isn't ready. Now I feel guilty in myself and can hardly look at you without remembering what you've done to me. It's no good. I don't think I can ever feel the same about you again—I can't forgive you.'

Stewart is in his late thirties and lives in the town, but commutes every day to one of the large cities where he works as administrator of a leading relief agency. Everyone notes his hard work and devotion; some may guess at his motives, but they remain guesswork for he will never talk and to the local people comes over as a pleasant but reserved and rather lonely man.

The only son of very 'respectable' parents, he knew himself to be homosexual from his school days. Unable to admit it to his family, unable therefore to show himself, publicly, within a loving relationship of the kind possible to him, he left home as soon as he could. *Stewart* found most of his companionship first in gay pubs and then in one-night stands, never realizing—for it was not known then—the danger in which he stood. At heart he believes he must be HIV-positive; he goes in fear and dread of the symptoms of Aids and shuns new relationships because he believes himself to be contaminated, though he has not been able to face having a test. 'It will endanger my insurance policies,' he says to himself, not without justi-fication. Deep down he is desperately afraid of the truth—not just for himself, though he does have a terror of ill-ness and possible death—but also for the shame he feels it would bring on his family.

He doesn't really know why he continues to come to

church, for it has condemned him for what he is and what he does, and he notes with a certain wry weariness the unending references to sin and sinfulness in the services. Sometimes they cause him to feel a mixture of bewilderment and resentment; most of the time he shrugs them off. Perhaps his continued churchgoing is part of the mask he needs to hide the awful truth from himself; perhaps he is hanging onto something, some hope of security and forgiveness. We cannot know, but he is there as usual this morning.

Sheila is fifty-six, unmarried and living alone since her mother died last year. Her father, a hard, driven, uncompromising man, died years ago from a sudden heart attack coming home from the office. She has always lived in the town and been a pillar of the church since she was very young, and in recent years has been prominent in many forms of church leadership: youth leader, diocesan representative, stewardship organiser . . . But her devotion has always stemmed from *fear*—fear of offending a harsh God whose love remains obstinately hidden from her.

Sin is a word that is all-too-familiar to her. Every night she measures herself against the dictates of the Sermon on the Mount[7] or the prayers in her well-thumbed copy of the writings of Thomas à Kempis,[8] and knows a despair that she always falls short and remains so utterly sinful. She tries repentance, confession, and more commitment, and yet she never feels at peace. A cross word here, an ungenerous or resentful thought there, or a smile lacking even under the most difficult circumstances; the daily imperfections come back to haunt her, and need repenting of not once but many times before sleep mercifully blots them out. No one would know; to everyone else she is the ever-present and ever-capable church warden, local councillor and the rest.

Matthew is the rector of this Anglican parish. His passing thoughts on pronouncing forgiveness to the people this morning were not in fact insignificant. For months now he has been going through a 'crisis of faith', plagued by doubt as to the meaning of it all, feeling unworthy as a priest and uncertain as to whether God does or ever did mean him to be one.

His ten-year-old daughter was attacked and nearly

raped on her way home from school one evening, and
since then he has been consumed by a rage he didn't
know he had in him. He feels rage at the man who did it,
rage at society that does not prevent these things, and
rage at his elder daughter who should have brought
her home, but had run off with her friends. *Matthew* is
bewildered at the estrangement the attack seems to have
caused with his wife, and he feels a near-hatred of the
God who allows such things to happen. Furthermore, he
cannot understand himself. He feels embarrassed with
his young daughter now and can't talk to her, certainly
not about the incident, but not even about the ordinary
everyday things of life. The easy companionship and
delight they shared in each other's company seems to
have gone for ever.

Yet he has had to go on ministering to other people,
preaching a God of love and forgiveness and feeling a
complete hypocrite. There has been no one for him to
talk to—other clergy and parents have sympathized, it is
true, but he has not dared tell anyone of the anger and
hate. He suspects that they would think that he should
not feel these feelings, but be able to 'turn the other
cheek'. Each day that passes he feels less of a priest and
more of a failure. The absolution means nothing to him
because though he is bewildered by his anger he cannot
actually repent of it—on another level it feels to him all
too justified.

Move now from this country town congregation which
seems so sleepy and 'respectable' but which turns out to
be harbouring all sorts of different things under the surface; look at one of the big cities, away from any church.
A group of teenagers—of all races and ages—are kicking a
football around on a piece of park-like ground. Half-time
is in evidence, as also are coke cans, crisp packets and the
like. When the break is over the game resumes with the
debris left on the side. Other breaks add to the mess until
finally interest wanes and the group prepare to disperse,
leaving their rubbish behind them. Not so the last three
or four; they are caught by an upright old lady who
shakes her walking-stick furiously at them and harangues
them thus: 'What do you think you're doing, leaving all
that mess? You're spoiling God's earth, spoiling it for
anyone who comes after you! You're nothing but little

hooligans, and your parents should have brought you up better.' All this produces is gales of laughter and muttered 'Silly old --- What does she think she's talking about anyway? All that stuff like we get at school assembly.'

The question here is: are the members of this group more than hooligans? Is being antisocial also a sin? In the old lady's frame of reference it almost certainly is, for God is her ultimate authority, but for the rest of us . . . ?

Many of us can probably remember incidents as children like being exhorted not to be greedy with the words 'God doesn't like greedy children', or 'Think of all the poor children in Africa/India . . . who don't have anything to eat, and there you are stuffing yourselves sick.' In all this there is a strange mixture of guilt-inducing devices and a use of ultimate authority, like that of God, to back up parental sanctions. Perhaps it is no wonder that many of us grow up confused about *who* minds what we do and with strange conflicting inner messages to ourselves. The *vocabulary* of sin may have slipped from us, or we may never have known it to start with, but something of its *substance* lives within us.

In yet *another family* in a northern inner-city area there is a battle royal raging.

'Why can't I go out to the cinema with my friends tonight? You can't keep me in; I'm getting old enough to do as I like.'

'As long as you are a member of this family and under this roof you are going to do what we tell you and observe our customs. Women and girls are not allowed by our religion to be out in public places.'

'But you don't really believe all that stuff do you—and anyway in this country everyone does it—all the people in my class at school, and they don't understand why you make me stay in.'

This is a Muslim family living in a city where there is a high concentration of people following the Islamic faith. Nevertheless, integrated schooling brings the children up against a more relaxed culture which the Muslim parents are fighting tooth and nail. What seems of minimal importance to the children is a near life-and-death matter to them. In this issue their religion is in conflict with the *mores* of the surrounding society in which adolescents of both sexes operate with few restrictions on their comings and goings. The situation is confusing and frustrating for the children and not particularly easy for the parents.

This last example shows yet another face of what we may choose to call sin. Here it is not so much what goes on in the inner life of an individual that is the issue, but the religious laws and customs of a group. Whatever the motivation for such laws—and this may be quite complicated —at least some of the answer is that the laws are perceived to be not just man-made precepts but instructions stemming ultimately from God himself. So transgression is not just against human custom, but also again divine will and authority.

The multicoloured stained glass windows have acquired quite a myriad of colours and hues, and raised yet more questions: the relationship between being sinful and being ill or mad; concern for the well-being of the planet we live on and that of our fellow human beings; and the issue of the laws of behaviour that are enshrined in the religious life of a whole group and which may not, it seems, be transgressed.

Do all these properly belong in the area of sin? We are not yet in a position to know this, but they certainly form a part of the picture we need to explore.

The Basement Windows

Let us leave aside for a moment the high casement windows, whose function it is to *shed light* on a dim scene, and go first to the basement, to those windows usually half above and half below ground level, often guarded by bars, and even in the most attractive garden flats sometimes having a slightly sinister feel about them.

Who or what lives in the basement? For some reason that I cannot as yet quite fathom, my thoughts go to figures from the past, from literature, rather than to creating real people in the present. Maybe this is because the great classical literature describes so well—and much better than I can—what I am trying to say; maybe it is because in part I am resisting this dimension in contemporary people and in ourselves . . . I am not yet sure.

I turn first to Dostoyevsky's *Crime and Punishment*[9] which chronicles in minute detail the inner dialogue and torment of one man, *Raskolnikov*, as he plans and executes the murder of a defenceless old woman—a moneylender. The antecedents of his act are complicated, connected as they obscurely seem to be with dark jealousies of his sister's forthcoming marriage; we trace the build-up through an appalling dream recalling a childhood incident of witnessing the battering-to-death of an old grey mare.

We can trace through Dostoyevsky's lines something of a man's conflict with the darkest parts of himself, from the moment of the conception of a terrible deed:

> And how could such a horrible idea have occurred to me? What a foul thing my heart is capable of, though! Yes, the chief thing is that it's so foul, so horrible, so disgusting, disgusting . . . And to think that for a whole month I . . .[10]

Here we have surely the disordered inner state—of *thought* only—not yet *deeds*. Is this what we mean by sin?

His torment intensifies and becomes more specific—the impulse grows, and yet there is still the instinctive repulsion against it:

> 'Good God!'—he cried—'is it possible that I will really take a hatchet, hit her on the head with it, crack her skull, slither around in warm, sticky blood, break the lock, steal and shake with fear.'

> 'But what am I thinking of? I know very well that I wouldn't be able to carry it out, so why have I been tormenting myself all the time? When I was coming downstairs yesterday I said to myself that the whole thing was foul and disgusting. Why, the thought of it actually made me feel sick and filled me with horror.'

Then there is a desperate prayer to be freed from the obsession:

> 'O Lord,' he prayed, 'show me the way and I shall give up this—this damnable dream of mine.'[11]

Raskolnikov experiences some hours or days of respite, but then the return of the torture—fed by a sign from outside—another's perception that the old woman was good for nothing but death: 'She is really wicked'—and then finally the last journey to the moneylender's house and the deed was done. We read then of the panic after the

act that produced a second murder, the maddened flight
from the scene of the crime, the illness that followed, the
tormented time when another man was arrested for the
murder, half confessions to the police as if wanting to be
caught and somehow eased of his torment. The great
novel goes on in matchless form to which no quotation
can do justice.

In *Raskolnikov's* agony we see a man in the grip of
torment. Driven by an obsession obscurely linked to a
mad part of himself in the recesses of his unconscious, he
is impelled to do the very thing he is, with another part
of his being and his plea to God, trying to resist. He
commits the act not without concern and not without
guilt, but neither of these can save him from it.

Move from Dostoyevsky to Shakespeare—to *Lady
Macbeth*. To many of us she conjures up the agonizing
sleepwalking scene at the end of the play when she is trying to purge herself of her crime:

> 'Out, damned spot! . . . What need we fear who knows
> it, when none can call our power to account? . . . What!
> will these hands ne'er be clean? . . . Here's the smell of
> the blood still: all the perfumes of Arabia will not
> sweeten this little hand . . . What's done cannot be
> undone.'[12]

Remorse and guilt like that of *Raskolnikov* are not truly
present here—they can only be implied in the restless
washing of the hands. Relief can only come through
suicide. Yet this was the woman whose ambition had
castigated her husband with shrinking from murder:

> 'Yet do I fear thy nature;
> It is too full o' the milk of human kindness
> To catch the nearest way;'[13]

Lady Macbeth said of herself in soliloquy:

> 'Come, you spirits
> That tend on mortal thoughts! unsex me here,
> And fill me from the crown to the toe top full
> of direst cruelty . . .
> Come, thick night
> And pall thee in the dunnest smoke of hell,
> That my keen knife see not the wound it makes,

Nor heaven peep through the blanket of the dark,
To cry "Hold, hold!"'[14]

Lady Macbeth does not want to take responsibility for that
which she first contemplates and then enacts. Yet in the
end she cannot escape from herself; neither can her more
tortured husband:

Methought I heard a voice cry 'Sleep no more!
Macbeth does murder sleep', the innocent sleep,
Sleep that knits up the ravell'd sleave of care . . .
Macbeth shall sleep no more![15]

For *Lady Macbeth*, suicide; for *Macbeth* nihilism and nothingness:

To-morrow, and to-morrow, and to-morrow,
Creeps in this petty pace from day to day,
To the last syllable of recorded time;
And all our yesterdays have lighted fools
The way to dusty death. Out, out, brief candle!
Life's but a walking shadow, a poor player
That struts and frets his hour upon the stage,
And then is heard no more; it is a tale
Told by an idiot, full of sound and fury,
Signifying nothing.[16]

Thus do these lines fill out the stark biblical statement
that 'the wages of sin is death.'[17] For these two characters
have no real concern, no true guilt and so, it seems, no
possibility of redemption.

Move again to another tragedy by Shakespeare, *Othello*,
and the machinations of *Iago*. In *Iago* we see a man
caught in the grip of what we might want to call evil,
plotting the downfall of his victims, safely, coolly, as a
detached observer from afar, showing us the darkest
aspect, perhaps, of human nature.

O! villainous; I have looked upon the world for four
times seven years . . . I never found a man that knew
how to love himself.

I hate the Moor . . . He holds me well;
The better shall my purpose work on him . . .
The Moor is of a free and open nature,
That thinks men honest that but seem to be so,

And will as tenderly be led by the nose
As asses are.
I have't; it is engender'd: hell and night
Must bring this monstrous birth to the world's light.[18]

Iago, like *Lady Macbeth*, is devoid of compassion, but worse, he seeks to use and pervert that which is good—in this case *Othello's* honest nature—into something bad, the insane jealousy which precipitates the final tragedy. Yet *Iago* is not seen to be involved—he is the arch-manipulator in one of the darkest of scenarios; to inflame another and yet stay detached oneself. There is no sense here of being in the grip of something he cannot help and would give much to be free from. There is only the *rejection* of love and almost the *revelling* in the dark and evil for its own sake.

The culmination point of such an inner state is well depicted in the work of a modern poet, in Ted Hughes' 'Hawk Roosting'. He depicts sadism born of a sense of omnipotence and concern for no one but self:

I sit in the top of the wood, my eyes closed.
Inaction, no falsifying dream
Between my hooked head and hooked feet:
Or in a sleep rehearse perfect kills and eat.

The convenience of the high trees!
The air's buoyancy and the sun's ray
Are of advantage to me;
And the earth's face upward for my inspection.

My feet are locked upon the rough bark.
It took the whole of Creation
To produce my foot, my each feather:
Now I hold Creation in my foot

Or fly up, and revolve it all slowly—
I kill where I please because it is all mine.
There is no sophistry in my body:
My manners are tearing off heads—

The allotment of death.
For the one path of my flight is direct
Through the bones of the living.
No arguments assert my right:

The sun is behind me.
Nothing has changed since I began.
My eye has permitted no change.
I am going to keep things like this.[19]

We see no chink in the omnipotence, no chink in the supreme self-confidence or self-seeking, no apparent possibilities for change; others exist only for his pleasure and as his prey. This must come very near to what Christian writing has framed as the sin that utterly destroys—what place can forgiveness and redemption have here?

What I am hoping we have now built up from all these 'windows' and vignettes is a mosaic-like picture *describing* the spectrum of attitudes, feelings, and behaviour that might come under the overall heading of sin and sinfulness.

We are left with:

The High, Clear Casement Windows

I would like to see the high, clear casement windows as enabling shafts of light to come to bear on the scene. If this does not seem to be stretching the overall image too far I would like to use them in the same way as before, but to describe situations and acts of *forgiveness* rather than *sinfulness*.

Sally and *Carol* are planning to meet for the first time in several months. Both in their late thirties, for a long time they were close friends as well as daytime work colleagues. Then there came a period of unfortunate gossip at work in which it seemed that *Sally* had accused *Carol* behind her back of being difficult to work with and of not getting through the work properly. There were some suggestions that alcohol was involved—that *Carol* was not always herself in the mornings or even after lunch. *Carol* for her part believed *Sally* to be holding a grudge against her since a time when they were both known to be keen on the same man. Insinuation followed insinuation, then there was an open blazing row and finally came a parting of the ways with *Sally* going off to a new and better job.

Over the months that followed each regretted the loss of the friendship. Away from the day-to-day pressure of the office, the accusations faded, diminished in size and began to look altogether less probable. *Sally* remembered that *Carol* had, at the time, been trying to recover from the loss of a parent. *Carol* thought from time to time how much she'd always envied *Sally* her bright open manner and her apparent ease of getting on with everyone. They still kept in vague contact through mutual friends. Would it be possible to be reconciled and renew the friendship? Yet each still feels hurt and wary and is approaching the meeting with caution.

In this situation what we might call mutual forgiveness is called for, but what might this involve? The hurt cannot be forgotten, and neither can some of the angry and cruel words they threw at each other. Would and could forgiving each other take them back to where they were before the estrangement had ever happened?

The detailed discussion of just these points is for a later chapter, but it illustrates—quite apart from any question of religious faith being involved—the all-too-familiar human situation where there has been a nasty, potentially fatal, breach of relationship, with much hurt on both sides. After so long it would be very difficult to sort out exactly who said what to whom and how much they were provoked and how justified or not it was. In any case will apportioning *blame* do anything to resolve the situation? The word 'sorry' seems to be called for, but what will this mean? Will forgiveness mean that they can return to being friends, forget what happened, or what . . . ?

Something of this situation is known to most, if not all of us; in the hardest case it can present us with an irresolvable problem. Sometimes we arrive at the 'I can forgive, but never forget' position—we can give *some* meaning to this. Yet is it satisfactory? What quite are we doing in the act of forgiveness, and what is the quality of a forgiven relationship? Does it also necessarily involve some sort of forgetting?

Forgiveness has, thus, a very human and well-known face, but it is also a word central to religious thought and practice. What *was* going on as *Matthew* faced his people on that Sunday morning and pronounced the words of absolution and forgiveness, not in his own name but in that of Almighty God? What happens to us, as human beings, if our sins are 'taken away' by the Lamb of God?

To some people the answer here is simple: *nothing* happens. The absolution is a form of words that for some other people somehow evokes a sense of relief and feeling good inside. It works in the same way as a human act of forgiveness can sometimes—but not invariably—making people feel all right inside and willing to try again with a relationship. For many of us most of the time the words of the so-called general Confession and Absolution—when confession is made in general rather than specific terms and within a fairly anonymous group setting—can almost pass us by.

But it has always been recognized that there are times when human beings both want and need to be more specific and personal, when they badly need to get things off their chest. Some people identify this as a religious need; others see it as a psychological need. Both dimensions make provision for trying to meet it, even though the resulting processes look rather different.

For many people, embarking on either counselling or psychotherapy essentially involves a sort of confession, sometimes all in a rush at the beginning, sometimes extended over a long period of time. There are few people who come to counselling or therapy who do not gradually, and often accompanied by a sense of shame and fear of being judged, bring into the open what they see as dark and shameful thoughts, actions, and feelings belonging either to their present or to their past. In this setting it is usually the very non-judgemental attitude of the counsellor or therapist that makes the revelations possible. Furthermore, in one very true sense it is often the act of admission that can enable the start of a process of taking more personal responsibility for feelings and actions. This helps people to see that they do not have to be caught in the stranglehold of past shames simply to repeat old behaviour patterns all over again in an unending circle.

Light that comes through the psychotherapeutic window is essentially that of a steady beam. It does fluctuate in intensity. Sometimes it brings great relief, but not usually in a once-for-all manner and it rarely produces an instantaneous change or 'cure'.

Things can be different in a religious situation.

Robert is sitting in a large hall, along with several hundred other young people, listening to one of the speakers at a much publicized evangelistic mission. The main speaker is well-known; the addresses have been mostly rather old hat—*Robert* is not quite sure why he is bothering to attend. He does not see himself as a fervent Christian, though he was brought up to go to church. He has come partly to please the people he lives with and partly because he had nothing better to do that night. The preacher has been talking about what he recognizes as 'orthodox' Christian teaching designed to show (or prove) the existence of God, the authority of the Bible, and so forth.

Tonight though the preacher is talking about Jesus Christ and the offer of a completely new quality of life to those who accept him as Saviour and Lord. He paints a picture of stark contrast between being held down in sin and the freedom and joy of life in Jesus. He cites some examples of things that might be holding people down— drink, extra-marital sex, bad temper, depression, uncomfortable peccadilloes from the past—and this with a vividness that somehow jogs *Robert* out of his complacency.

Is his life so good after all? He realizes that quite often he has no joyful feeling inside him, nor a sense of pleasure nor of where he is going in life. Suddenly it all seems rather grey. The preacher is compelling and *Robert's* hunger for what seems to be on offer grows.

The address ends with a renewed invitation to 'confess your sins and trust the Lord Jesus as Saviour and Lord', and in the extended silence that follows it feels to *Robert* as if something has exploded inside him. He 'sees', as it were, very clearly all his past life, in its murkiness and greyness, together with a taste of what could be his if only he could commit himself entirely to Jesus. He stumbles forward with many others and makes the act of confession and commitment, and at that moment his sense of joy, security, and happiness knows no bounds. He is 'saved' for ever, and he 'knows' with a great certainty the truth of all that before had seemed uncertain —that God, in Jesus, loves not just the whole world, but him personally.

I hope that people may be able to recognize *Robert's* experience as an inevitably limited description of 'conversion'—the experience that has hit people, from St Paul on, through the ages. Its essential ingredients seem to be the confession of unworthiness and a fervent trust in the saving power of God which sets in train a whole new level of subjective experience. My description has had to be halting, because I am not one of the people to whom it has ever happened; I cannot know it quite from the inside, and so must inevitably have done it less than justice.

Indeed one of the questions we may have about conversion is why it seems to happen to some people and not to others. It does not happen for the asking, either. Many people have testified to their—to them—total unpreparedness for the infusion of light. The same is true of most of those who have known more 'classical' mystical experiences, such as Julian of Norwich, Teresa of Avila and many others. The evangelical conversion experience and the mystical experience may often seem very different. They are couched in such different languages sometimes that they might not seem to belong to the same religious dimension. But I think they have this, centrally, in common: they both include a conviction of human littleness or unworthiness before the majesty and overwhelming light of God. To Julian the whole world became the size of a hazel nut;[20] to Teresa in her moments of great ecstasy God was forever and unmistakably 'His Majesty'.[21]

This may seem light years away from the painstaking uncovering of self that takes place in psychotherapy, and indeed perhaps here we have the disciplines at, apparently, their furthest apart. But there is a more 'middle' position.

It is 5.30 pm on a Saturday evening. In the presbytery of a large Catholic church in a big city *Gerald,* one of the priests, makes ready to go over to the church for the hour of confession time he is deputed to cover.

This is so much a part of his ministry that it comes as second nature to him. He cannot easily now remember the impact of the ordination service on him with its stupendous words 'whosoever's sin you do remit, they are remitted, and whosoever's sins you retain they are retained'. These words of great authority, this commission of great power, at the time made him feel immensely small, humble, and privileged. The reality over the years has somewhat tarnished the image. Hearing confessions is not always a labour of love—at times it can be very repetitive and boring. For his Anglican counterpart across

the city who is of a 'high church' persuasion, this state
may have taken longer to come about. He is not vicar of
one of the churches with a reputation for confessions, so
he does not hear so many as a part of his everyday routine.
However neither of them is in the mood tonight to wonder
at the magnitude of their calling; it is just a part of what
they are here for.

The modern Catholic church is light and airy this
summer evening. The first Mass of Sunday is due in an
hour's time so there are already servers and the sacristan
making ready the vestments. *Gerald* mutters an apology
as he reaches over and round them for his purple stole.
He reminds them he will need to consecrate more wafers
at the Mass to renew the Reserved Sacrament in the church
which is perpetually there for the adoration of the faithful
and the various sick communions that one of them takes
round the parish during the week. He walks over to the
area reserved for confessions—the old-style boxes were
removed some time ago and there is simply a prayer desk
and a chair with a shallow ledge in between. He notes
the three or four people already waiting for him, all, he
also notes, 'regulars'—probably nothing out of the ordinary tonight. He sits down, switches on a reading lamp
and waits.

Anne is the first in the queue. She comes to confession
most weeks. It is as much a part of her Christian life
as her weekly Mass and Communion. She walks over,
kneels down and the familiar ritual begins:

(Priest) May the Lord be in your heart
and help you to confess your sins with true sorrow.[22]

(Anne) I confess to Almighty God
and to you (my brothers and sisters)
that I have sinned through my own fault
in my thoughts and words
in what I have done
and in what I have failed to do;
and I ask blessed Mary, ever-Virgin
and all the angels and saints
and you (my brothers and sisters)
to pray for me to the Lord our God.[23]

The detailed confession that follows is relatively short: a loss of temper with the children once, too many cigarettes despite trying to give up, missed prayers on two nights, some thoughts about one of the men at work that she feels are incompatible with her married state . . .

We note the salient points of the ritual. Sin is to do with thoughts as well as deeds. It is our responsibility—'through my own fault'—and confession is made not just to God alone, but to his representative. This reminds us that sin is not just a private matter, but has some sort of public face.

Gerald knows his penitent well—knows her for a hard-working, even overworking mother and professional woman. The temper was almost certainly the result of tiredness, and the looking towards another man the desire for some relief from a marriage with a husband with a tendency to depression and to drink too much. However, in his experience of *Anne* it is very unlikely that her wishful thoughts and fantasies will ever go further than this. Sometimes he wishes in an unguarded moment that they would. He feels she has quite a hard life with three children and a full-time job which she must keep because her husband's work record tends to be rather unstable and from time to time he has needed a period of in-patient care in a psychiatric hospital.

He asks few questions, therefore, and says that she is perhaps harder on herself than God is, and suggests as advice a small time of relaxation each day. He knows, also from experience, that it will not be easy for *Anne* to follow this advice, but feels he needs to go on making the point. He asks her to say the Lord's Prayer as a penance—deliberately light—then

> God, the Father of mercies
> through the death and resurrection of his Son
> has reconciled the world to himself
> and sent his Holy Spirit among us
> for the forgiveness of sins;
> through the ministry of the Church
> may God give you pardon and peace.
> And I absolve you from your sins
> in the name of the Father, and of the Son
> and of the Holy Spirit.[24]

The rite concludes:

(Priest) Give thanks to the Lord, for he is good
(Anne) His mercy endures for ever
(Priest) The Lord has freed you from your sins. Go in
    peace.[25]

In the revised form of absolution given here the authority of the priest to forgive (or indeed not to forgive) is not
made explicit in the actual words used, but it is implicit
in the whole, and is explicitly re-affirmed in the introduction to the revision.[26]

The stupendous authority to forgive another's sins
in the name of God—muted in Anglican practice, by a
request by the priest *for* prayer in the recognition that
the person who absolves is also a sinner; the confidence
and assurance that something objective has happened—
sin *has* been put away, and the sinner *can* depart in
peace; these are hallmarks of the church's ministry of
forgiveness.

A moment's pause follows whilst *Anne* moves herself
clear of the confessional area and then her place is taken
by another, for the same ritual to be repeated.

Across the city in his Anglican church *Martin* is not
really expecting any call on his services this evening. He
keeps his Saturday opportunity for confession open,
mindful of the Anglican directive that people may wish
to unburden themselves to a priest in confession, but that
no one is obliged to. He settles himself in church in his
black cassock with a purple stole nearby and prepares to
read Evening prayer peacefully to himself.

He is surprised therefore when *Simon*, one of the
businessmen in his congregation, suddenly appears.
Well, almost in his congregation; *Simon* and his family
come off and on to church for they often go away for the
weekend. Nevertheless, *Simon* makes it clear that he has
not come just to walk round the church. He approaches
with a 'Vicar, I knew you'd be here at this time and I
wondered if I could talk to you.' *Martin* quickly puts
down his book, swivels round and indicates a place in the
pew next to him.

The story as it comes is sad and halting. *Simon* went
this week for the health check-up that his firm offers him
once a year. He noticed as they did it that they seemed

worried, and the very next day he was called to say that
they were very concerned about a growth they had
detected in his liver. They were very honest. They think it
may well be cancer and they want him immediately for
an operation. They said it was a large growth to have got
so far since the last time they saw him. *Simon* says 'I was
devastated. I've always been so well, yet I've had a terror
of being ill and perhaps dying. I've been wandering
around ever since unable to tell anyone, not even *Celia*,
my wife. I felt this evening I just must talk to someone.'

He goes on, 'In a way I think it's what I deserve, I've
not always been a good father and husband.' Silence
follows but *Martin* senses there is more to come. Then
even more haltingly comes the story of an affair,
recently ended but which had been going on for years,
and 'I don't think *Celia* ever had an inkling. She is always
so trusting. In her family it just would never happen.
That's almost what attracted me to *Janet*—she was more
exciting, knew about things and places and situations
that would have been completely foreign to *Celia*. I love
Celia, but at times I was getting bored, and she didn't
ever seem to realize this. Of late I've not made so much
effort with her and the family. I think they think I'm
remote and wrapped up in my work, and now I might be
going to die I feel guilty about them. Somehow I want to
get close again, and I don't know how to.'

Martin is not sure what is being asked of him. *Simon*
has chosen to come to see him here in the church. Is the
choice of venue because it is the only time he can be sure
of getting him without having to make elaborate appoint-
ments, or is there something more? The talk goes on, and
it becomes clear that there *is* something more—that
Simon's trouble of mind and heart and his guilty feelings
are what have brought him this evening quite as much as
the turmoil of his possible diagnosis. A confession has
virtually been made; *Martin* guesses that *Simon* does not
want or cannot make it more formal—he would not know
how—but wants something from *Martin* and God. So
finally *Martin* offers the words and prayer of absolution,
together with prayers for healing. *Simon* knows what he
wants to do, which is to tell his wife about the threat of
cancer. He feels strength enough now to go and do it.
After about an hour he goes away more peacefully than

he came, with an invitation to come back if at any time he feels he would like to.

In this encounter we see the connection—often felt, yet not always perceived rationally or with any degree of understanding—between sin, suffering, and punishment. Has the God who deplored *Simon's* adultery visited his illness upon him? This is a question that has plagued people since the days of St John's Gospel when Jesus asserted that the man born blind 'did not sin neither did his parents'.[27] Does sin inevitably bring punishment and suffering, and, worse, *if* there is pain and suffering does there mean there *must* have been serious sin?

We can wonder, too, what—deep down—*Simon* was wanting. Was he wanting only the chance to unburden himself to another human being whom he knew would be available at that time? If so, it would be valuable enough. Or did he, as seems to have happened, recognize that his distress went beyond this? Did he want 'direct' and personal contact with the God in whom he had only more or less half believed for most of his life? We cannot tell completely—perhaps *Simon* did not himself know when he approached the church. As he tells his story it becomes clear that he *is* making a connection between how he has been in life and how he would wish to be in case he has to leave it.

It is time to end this chapter. It will perhaps read almost as a 'hotchpotch' of human experiences and situations which more or less connect with the idea of sin—or rather with peoples' sometimes unformed and undigested ideas of what sin is. The questions it raises are immense—not least because we still have no real idea of what sin intrinsically is.

I want, therefore, to take the next chapters to try to trace the idea of sin from its religious roots, and explore the overlap that seems to have arisen in relation to our human feelings, psychological understanding and religious faith. I shall begin by *separating* the religious and the psychological and, true to my contention[28] that sin is originally and primarily a *religious* concept, I will tackle this religious dimension first.

Notes

1. *The Alternative Service Book 1980* (SPCK), Holy Communion Rite A, p. 127.
2. ASB, p. 127.
3. ASB, p. 127.
4. ASB, p. 130.
5. ASB, p. 142.
6. ASB, p. 142.
7. Matthew 5-7.
8. St Thomas à Kempis, *The Imitation of Christ* (OUP 1949).
9. Fyodor Dostoyesvsky, tr. David Magarshack, *Crime and Punishment* (Penguin 1951).
10. Dostoyesvsky, *Crime and Punishment*, p. 26.
11. Dostoyesvsky, *Crime and Punishment*, pp. 78-9.
12. William Shakespeare, *The Tragedy of Macbeth*, Act V, Scene 1.
13. Shakespeare, *Macbeth*, Act I, Scene 5.
14. Shakespeare, *Macbeth*, Act I, Scene 5.
15. Shakespeare, *Macbeth*, Act II, Scene 2.
16. Shakespeare, *Macbeth*, Act V, Scene 5.
17. Romans 6.23.
18. William Shakespeare, *Othello, The Moor of Venice*, Act I, Scene 3.
19. Ted Hughes, 'Hawk Roosting' in Ted Hughes *Selected Poems 1957-1981* (Faber & Faber Ltd 1982), p. 43.
20. Julian of Norwich, *Revelations of Divine Love* (Penguin 1966), Revelation 5, p. 67.
21. In, for example, 'Interior Castle' in E. Allison Peers (ed.) *The Complete Works of Saint Teresa of Jesus* (Sheed and Ward 1957), volume 2.
22. The Rite of Penance (Roman Ritual) (Mayhew-McCrinnon 1976), Section 43/5, p. 35.
23. The Rite of Penance, Section 58, p. 61. (This is taken from the section on the reconciliation of several penitents but suggested for this rite also.)
24. The Rite of Penance, Section 48, p. 44.
25. The Rite of Penance, Section 49, p. 44.
26. The Rite of Penance, Introduction, Section 6, p. 12.
27. John 9.2-3.
28. Introduction, and Chapter 2.

TWO

'Of Man's First Disobedience'
or
The Theological Story of Sin

━━━━━━

> Of Man's first disobedience, and the fruit
> Of that forbidden tree! . . .[1]

So runs the first line of Milton's *Paradise Lost*, and it has all the makings of a story. Indeed it *is* a reference to a story—the story told in Genesis 3. Adam and Eve, made in the image of their creator, are blissfully ensconced in the Garden of Eden. They till the garden and walk there daily alongside God. They have no fear of pain, disintegration, or death. Yet they disobey—through their own fault or beguiled by another?—the command that they should not eat of the central tree of the knowledge of good and evil. They are condemned to expulsion from the garden, to a life of unremitting hard labour, and to eventual return through death to the dust from which they were made.

This is the story of the source of what we come to know as sin. It is an ancient and mythological way of trying to explain the dilemma in which humankind finds itself.

Other writers root sin more firmly in human experience and flesh it out in human terms:

Sin as Conflict; Sin and Death. In St Paul's letter to the Romans we have this helpless cry:

> I can will what is right, but I cannot do it. For I do not do the good I want, but the evil I do not want is what I do.[2]

His helplessness increases and he begins to lose his sense of control over himself:

26

Now if I do what I do not want, it is no longer I that do it, but sin which dwells within me.[3]

How often have we experienced or heard something similar —'I don't know what got into me—I just couldn't stop myself doing or saying so and so . . .'

For Paul the conflict intensifies and finally he becomes almost desperate:

I delight in the law of God, in my inmost self, but I see in my members another law at war with the law of my mind and making me captive to the law of sin that dwells in my members. Wretched man that I am! Who will deliver me from this body of death?[4]

The fact that Paul goes on almost immediately to reiterate his faith in the saving power of Christ does nothing to detract from his anguish or the fact that he has associated the inability to do good with first, a sense of not being in control of himself, and second, with *death*. Sin, to Paul, is that serious.

<u>Sin and Suffering. Sin and Punishment. Suffering as Predetermined</u>. In John 9.2 we have the most obvious question to people of Jesus' time. Jesus and his disciples passed a blind man (whom Jesus later healed) and the instant question from the disciples was, 'Rabbi, who sinned, this man or his parents, that he was born blind?'[5] The obvious implication to the disciples was that someone must have sinned. Such suffering could only be in some sense a punishment for sin.

Jesus' reply, though refuting this idea, is hardly comforting, for he says that neither the man nor his parents sinned but the reason for his blindness was 'that the works of God might be made manifest in him'.[6] Jesus was apparently preparing the way for the healing that was to follow.

This is reminiscent of the dialogue that takes place between God and Satan in the first chapters of the book of Job from which it appears that Job is being used as a pawn in a trial of strength between the two of them; his suffering is predetermined by 'the gods'.[7] It is almost as if Satan is bored and needs something to do and God sets him a challenge which involves Job in much suffering, and much more protestation of innocence and faithfulness

against so-called friends who take him to task for the sin
they are sure he must have committed if he is suffering
so much.

Yet there is also in the book of Job a hint of the other side
of the question. Why do the wicked sometimes prosper?

> Why do the wicked live, reach old age and grow mighty
> in power? . . . They spend their days in prosperity, and
> in peace they go down to Sheol. They say to God, 'Depart
> from us! We do not desire the knowledge of thy ways.'[8]

This question must be asked because in a way the prosperity of the wicked confusingly contradicts the norm of
what people have been led to expect. It perhaps makes us
wonder if we are somehow wrong, and whether all our
attempts to bear the connection between sin and suffering
manfully are to no avail and indeed fruitless because it is
the wrong task.

<u>Sin as Fear, Sin as Separation, Sin and Ultimate Aban-
donment</u>. John Donne's ultimate sin was of fear, fear of
ultimate abandonment:

> For, I have more.

> I have a sinne of feare, that when I have spunne
>   My last thred, I shall perish on the shore;
> Sweare by thy selfe, that at my death thy sonne
>   Shall shine as he shines now, and heretofore;
>   And, having done that, Thou haste done,
>   I feare no more.[9]

This connection between sin and separation leading to a
sense of abandonment is found elsewhere. There is the
strange moment in St Luke's Gospel when Peter begs the
Lord to depart from him because he is a sinful man.[10]
Peter seems to sense intuitively that sin and holiness do
not mix. More starkly we see it in the separation of Judas
and Jesus, first at the last supper from which Judas sepa-
rates himself and goes out into the night[11] and then in his
final separation of death by suicide because he has
'betrayed innocent blood'.[12] Judas is abandoned by his
paymasters, the priests. We sense that he feels abandoned
by Jesus when he cannot respond to the greeting 'Friend'
in the Garden of Gethsemane.[13]

Moreover, we gather that it is not only *individuals* who become separated from and abandoned by God through sin. There is ample evidence throughout the Old Testament of the cycle: 'and the *people* of Israel did what was evil in the sight of the Lord . . . therefore the anger of the Lord was kindled against Israel and he . . .' (Judges 3.7-8; my italics). Israel's prosperity, even their survival as a nation, was inextricably linked to how God viewed their behaviour, and this was no light threat. Or at least this is the way the Bible portrays it. Another way would be to see the biblical writers as seeking an explanation for the undeniable facts of the fortunes of history in terms of periodic victories, defeats, conquests, and enslavements. Other peoples might have had other explanations for such events—for the children of Israel their understanding was inextricably invested in their relationship with their God.

So much is this the case that often the occasion of a corporate defeat or bad omen heralded the seeking of an individual scapegoat to bear the full impact of the separation. Somebody, somewhere must have provoked the wrath of the Almighty. We see this in the book of Joshua when the writer comes to the conquest of Ai.[14] A first onslaught resulting in the massacre of the Israelites was eventually laid at the door of a poor unfortunate who had stolen some of the spoils of war; he paid the ultimate penalty of death. An unfavourable first omen in the war between Saul and the Philistines assured Saul that sin had arisen.[15] A series of trials by holy lot revealed that Jonathan, his son, was the sinner because he had tasted some honey; he too would have died had not the people not interceded on his behalf. Even mercy in war could be a sin, as Saul found in his confrontation with the prophet Samuel over his initial sparing of King Agag of the Amalekites.[16]

The laws of sin and death as portrayed in the Old Testament were savage and absolute. The reality of the fact that they were mediated through other men—often great prophets but nevertheless potentially fallible—could not break the awesomeness and absoluteness of the chain, nor the visiting of the punishment on successive generations of a family or group in perpetuity.

Again other peoples might have explained the events

differently; for the children of Israel—given their religious tradition—they could only be explained in terms of
sin against their God who had adopted them and made
them his own unless and until . . .

Sin and Annihilation—the Wrath of God. Behind all this
lurks the 'spectre' of the mind of God. God, who in
Genesis 1.31 'saw everything that he had made, and
behold, it was very good', is the same God who in Genesis
6.5–7:

> saw that the wickedness of man was great in the earth,
> and that every imagination of the thoughts of his heart
> was only evil continually. And the Lord was sorry that
> he had made man on the earth, and it grieved him to
> his heart. So the Lord said, 'I will blot out man whom I
> have created from the face of the ground . . .'

The same God who creates can also annihilate, can make
as nothing. It is this indeed which make the issue so stark
and so threatening, for it appears that the God who gives
life can take it away again if we do not come up to
scratch, *and* we are dependent on this God for either outcome. If we were not so dependent then the threat would
not be so great. It is this interplay between God the creator and God the annihilator *and the sense we have that
we can, as it were, set God the annihilator into play* that
forges the inextricable connection between God and sin.
This sense seems to me to take sin beyond the relatively
controllable interplay between human beings and into
another realm. Whether the 'purely' human is as ultimately benign as this last sentence would suggest is
another matter. Sustained reflection on our own and
others' experience and a realistic reading of our news
suggests otherwise, but I still think that without the sense
of the *omnipotent* power of God, that which we call sin
would lose much of its power to threaten us.

We may therefore find ourselves *defining* sin as that
facet of our behaviour or our being which sets in motion
a certain threatening change in the activity and attitude
of God as this is directed towards us. Thus sin is, by
definition, a religious and theological term. By itself it
has no meaning. It needs the Other, the sense of God to
give it meaning. So sin roots itself firmly within the
theological story.

Sin—a Multifaceted Concept. There are many Biblical words and ideas translated by the English word sin. They include the Hebrew concept of 'evil imagination',[17] claimed to be implanted in all of us at birth; the idea of sin as transgression implying the idea of something—law, code, edict, prohibition—being transgressed or broken; and sin as falling short (of the glory of God)—see Romans 3.23. There is also that mysterious sin against the Holy Spirit which cannot be forgiven,[18] and which commentators have thought to mean that disposition or act of attributing the works of God to the devil. This is in fact the ultimate in perversity, calling good evil and evil good, or white black and black white. All these words have slightly different overtones; transgression implies something done or committed, falling short implies an omission or a deficit, whilst the sin against the Holy Spirit implies a grossly distorted judgement or perception. They probably contribute to the three dimensions of commission, omission or negligence, and distortion or enslavement that are picked up in various Christian liturgies

Sin and Sin(s). There is a further distinction to be made. There is a difference between sin and sin(s). St Paul and others often use the former—almost in a way personified: 'Sin which dwells within me'[19] and it seems to me to refer to a general condition of sinfulness. In this it is near to the 'evil imagination' of Old Testament thought. It is a general tendency which results in the commission of specific sins.

Of actual sins(s)—other than that against the Holy Spirit already mentioned—there are various lists given in the Bible and in Christian tradition. The lists vary through the Old and New Testaments and through history but the traditional seven deadly sins[20] comprise: pride, lust, avarice, anger, envy, sloth, and gluttony. These are also known as the mortal sins because if persisted in unrepentingly until death they are thought to lead us into the ultimate spiritual danger of permanent separation from God. Still another categorization was made in the early centuries after Christ of unforgivable sins or those for which penance could be done only once in a lifetime: these were adultery, murder, and apostasy (forsaking the faith).[21]

Right up to the end of the patristic period in the fifth century, the presence or commission of mortal sin was

judged almost entirely externally. If a person did something in the mortal-sin category it *was* a mortal sin, with
no regard to the circumstances in which it was done or
the motivation of the sinner in doing it. It wasn't until
the time of the scholastics, and in particular Aquinas and
Abelard, that the existing distinction between 'mortal'
and 'venial' (less virulent) sin became operative, along
the additional dimensions of circumstance and motivation.
A sinful act of the 'mortal' variety was judged to be so
only if committed with full knowledge of its seriousness
and deliberate intent; in other circumstances it might be
seen as being of the less deadly 'venial' kind. The same
process could operate in reverse, for sinful acts thought
objectively to be not too harmful. When committed under
certain circumstances of deliberate intent they could be
upgraded (or downgraded!) to the 'mortal' category.[22]

I cite all this to begin to show the complexities of the
problem. There is, in the theological story, a distinction
to be made between a sinful tendency and sins, and there
is, over time, an attempt to understand that sins are not
just sinful acts or omissions. The external circumstances
and internal intent can vary from person to person and
in themselves affect the gravity of the act.

Such then are some of the quite tremendous questions,
issues, and stories behind the deceptively simple narrative
story of Genesis 3. They are exemplified in the conflicts,
anguish, and torments of individuals and the interpretative
history of the people of Israel of the things that happened
to them. Perhaps the most difficult problem so far is not
about sin(s) (though we may need and want to explore more
about the complexities of circumstance and motivation)
but our understanding of sinfulness itself, and where this
can be said to have come from. It is here that ideas about
so-called 'original sin' and various mythological stories have
had their impact. The so-called 'Fall' story of Genesis 3 is
an attempt to externalize the issues and, as it were, lay
them out and look at them 'outside' us.

Like all attempts at externalization, the act of making
it can carry within it the hope that in so doing the problem
can therefore be solved. In this case we hope that we shall
somehow understand the whys and wherefores of sin
and so be able to cease from it. So a great deal of theological time and thought has gone into examining whether and

how the story in Genesis 3 does solve the problems of sin:
how or why we put ourselves in a position to invoke the
displeasure of God and risk his omnipotent response. And
it is to some exploration and discussion of this enterprise
through the ages that I now want to turn.

I turn to it because I have to if we are to begin to
understand the position we are in *today*—why, for example, Christian liturgy has come to take the form it has,
and what unresolved questions are present in the outward
forms of religious thought and practice, the liturgy, and
our own hearts. But I need also to set boundaries and limits
on this historical exploration because it is not meant to be
undertaken just for its own sake. Neither is this book meant
to read like a quasi-historical or theological textbook or
sourcebook. As an aid to exploring the theme I shall confine
myself to the biblical material, that of the formative period
of the early Christian communities and to such of the more
modern writers as seem to me to speak to the way I am
tackling the theme. This method is inevitably subjective,
but I hope it will be sufficient to identify the essential
issues and facilitate our exploration.

There seem to be three preliminary questions to address.

First, there is the danger of thinking that earlier writers spoke consistently on this theme—that they had a
position clearly and exhaustively worked out. This is in
fact far from the case.

Controversy sometimes forced more and more preci-
sion, as it did in the fourth-century battle that waged
between Augustine of Hippo and Pelagius on the nature
of human nature![23] Both men were motivated not by pure
theological thought alone. Each brought his personal
history, which is far better documented for Augustine via
his confessions and letters than for Pelagius. We know
little of the personal life of the latter except that he was
an English monk! They each brought also the environment
in which they lived. They may have been motivated by
ecclesiological, political, and sociological factors as well
by 'pure' concern for their theme. We need to beware of
assuming that in a controversy truth is *necessarily* more
closely approximated.

What conflict and controversy can do is to sharpen
and focus concentration on a theme, but that does not
necessarily remove contradiction and ambivalence. Many

of the Greek theologians, such as Athanasius and St John Chrysostom,[24] contained within their thought an idea of original sin as both a weakness *and* a depravity. This was the forerunner of Pelagius' and Augustine's divergence on the matter. But theirs and our 'fuzziness' may be helpful to us. Premature clarity may delude us into thinking we have arrived at some resolution when in fact we have not. *This may silence the ongoing questions which need to continue to live.* Furthermore the emotional and other consequences of enforced clarity of thought can be punitive and cruel—as many a child exposed to the clear views and principles of his or her parents would attest.

The questions that must be allowed to remain are: 'Is the fact that we tend to do wrong—that is sin—a *weakness* for which we deserve compassion and encouragement in our efforts not to give into it, or a *depravity* for which we ought to be punished?' and 'Is it what we *do* and *think*, or our very *being* that is somehow flawed and wrong?' These are hardly academic questions, as some of the vignettes in Chapter 1 show. The answers we give at any point raise or lower our self-esteem, isolate us from others or bring us into relationship with them, and leave us with a sense of being able to move forward or with a paralysing and profound sense of guilt.

The second issue has already arisen. It pertains to the *nature of myth, fairy story, and proverb.* It may seem clear to post-Darwinian humans that the Adam and Eve and creation myths are just these—myths. As such, they are stories that are intended to express symbolically some of the universal feelings and questions about human beings. They are not a literal account of how creation happened or how things went 'wrong'. But other myths and sayings persist. This makes for strange, conflicted, even bizarre ideas; the least rational of which seem to have a remarkable genius for survival and embellishment. 'Be sure your sins will find you out' is one such; 'Sin is contagious—you catch it like measles' is another. Martin Luther exhorted us: '*pecca fortiter*—sin bravely'.[25] The Holy Saturday liturgy proclaims 'O Happy Fault'[26]—the necessary precondition for the redemptive process. In fact on some rational or irrational level there is probably some truth in each of these phrases, but the proverbial form can become a hindrance to discovering what this may be. Familiarity of wording can bestow a quality of infallible pronouncement. Actually they are quick inroads to what is essentially a *mystery*—the interplay of what we know as good and evil, sin and forgiveness.

There seems to be an optimum place for a 'fence about a mystery'. Putting the fence too close—that is trying to force intellectual penetration of the mystery to its greatest depth can give a false sense of clarity and eventually lead to an arrogance. Put the fence too far away—protect the mystery from incursion and invasion—and it can become the peg on which the most glaring inconsistencies, unreality, and bizarre interpretations can be hung. I make this point because the mystery of good and evil is one that has defied resolution, and in my opinion always will. Because it has this mysterious core it is vulnerable to gross distortion and to the cruel consequences that can easily follow.

Third, we are in fact dealing with, *if not two mysteries, two aspects of the same mystery,* even though they must intertwine and overlap. In the mystery of sin are hidden the mystery of the nature of man and the mystery of the nature of God. I explored earlier—admittedly in rather an anthropomorphic way—how sin may be 'defined' as that which may make God react threateningly. In this 'definition' are encapsulated the great question and paradox: 'We have a God, whose nature we believe to be good, who created people in his own image; the creation then somehow "goes wrong". If people *truly* reflect God—*how can this be?'*

With these preliminary thoughts in mind, we can now begin to approach more systematically the theological contribution to the mystery of good, evil, and sin.

The intellectual problems associated with the origin of evil are immense. They have proved irresolvable to philosophers and theologians through the ages, and I am not sure how much we shall gain from trying to plumb them again here for their own sake. What I think is useful is that the various forms in which the problem or the 'solutions' have been expressed can be seen to bring different comforts or threats to our fundamental sense of being.

The *dualistic* view that good and evil are equal and opposite forces induces a great—and to some people an exceedingly threatening—uncertainty as to whether the positive can triumph or be overwhelmed by the negative.

This view proved no answer to philosophers contending that there must be 'something' behind and prior to the existence of good and evil.

The *monist* view is that good and evil are only aspects of something else. They only appear to exist. They have no real existence. Evil is only the absence of good. This view does violence to some peoples' experience of strong dark and opposing forces which seem to pull their being apart.

The mainstream *Judaeo-Christian* view does little, in my opinion, to resolve the essential difficulty. In essence it tries to keep God as a single principle or force who is both good and omnipotent. This *apparently* leaves no room for evil in God. What then happens is that evil appears at another point or in another order of creation and a *'split' between good and evil develops on the 'lesser' level.*

In Genesis 3, evil and the origins of sinfulness are located first in the serpent and then in the faulty will and judgement of Eve and Adam in following its counsel. In Genesis 6—an alternative 'Fall' story—it is some of the angels who fall and become evil Nephilim or giants who then intermarry with the human race and introduce their sinful fallenness to the earth. In both these stories there has been a intertwining of the act of 'Fall' with sexuality, or with marriage, or procreation which has had difficult consequences for Christian thought on these issues.

The other biblical sources of evil are the various Satanic figures—lesser than God yet allowed by God for God's and their own purposes. These include the beast in the book of Daniel, Satan in the book of Job, the Abomination of Desolation in the Maccabees, and the scarlet woman of the book of Revelation. Apart from the Satan in Job who is virtually personified in the text—as is Yahweh or the Lord—these figures are often neither quite man nor beast. Nor are they the 'principalities and powers' of the New Testament period and the various non-Christian Gnostic systems. They retain something of the bodiliness of *a* being.

Sometimes the 'split' is located even further 'down the order', as it were. We see this in the dichotomy that developed between the concepts of soul and body, or between things spiritual and things carnal, with the subsequent emphasis on the lusts and vices of the flesh which could then be either redeemed or disowned. But, despite variations in the imagery, in all of these biblical scenarios one thing is constant. Evil is removed to one step away from God himself—it shall not be seen to be *in* God. Yet, at the same time, evil must be allowed to exist and so must also have a place or 'person' from which to emanate. But in so far as these 'locations' are believed to *co-exist alongside or under God*, the displacing mechanism must compromise either God's goodness or God's omnipotence.

In none of these theories of evil does it seem to me that the essential difficulty and paradox is resolved. That we may decide that we *cannot* resolve it intellectually does not necessarily free us from the issue, for it is not perhaps one that we can 'choose' to let go or keep. Indeed I would like to explore in the next chapter whether our efforts in this direction do not perhaps correspond to different *psychological* ways of approaching and trying to rationalize the great threats we experience to our being. If the issue bothers us we shall have to go on struggling with it. If it does not then perhaps we shall find it increasingly irrelevant and so find we somehow 'leave' it.

Others may 'choose' also to leave the problem of human sinfulness. Indeed many of the old debates on this subject can seem rather dry, barren, and meaningless today, mainly because we no longer use the categories of thought in which they were conducted. Yet it is my contention that the liturgy still enshrines the thought of those old debates, and that to understand our liturgy we shall have also to understand something of them.

There is in the New Testament and in the works of later writers a strange mixture of interpreting the Genesis 3 story literally and allegorically. This oscillates, perhaps, according to the preponderance of underlying Platonic or Aristotelian ideas at the time.[27] On the whole, the Greek writers tended to allegorize the story and the Latin writers to take it more literally, though this distinction should not be pressed too far. In a strange way the difference does not really matter. What is important is that all the writers from St Paul onwards stressed the sense of solidarity between ourselves and Adam (whether literal or allegorical). According to how they interpreted the state and fate of Adam so they interpreted the state and fate of humankind. They tended to look at the story in a rather literal way even if they did not believe it to be a literal account of mankind's history.

For some writers, and particularly St Augustine,[28] Adam's first state was one of 'original righteousness'. He initially lived in unbroken communion with the creator in whose image he was made, until he tried to eradicate the gap between the creator and the created, taking to himself either the knowledge of good and evil or the gift of life. Other writers, notably St Irenaeus,[29] have no such sense of the glory of Adam; he was created primitive, though this probably referred more to a state of non-moral innocence than to the turmoil of raw feelings that the word 'primitive' usually conjures up for us today. For such writers as St Paul, the emphasis is not on any initial state; the story starts, as it were, with the act of transgression and this is then seen as the cause of our physical mortality.

For Paul, through our solidarity with Adam we henceforth partake of a condition of sinfulness;[30] we are potentially estranged from God. Whether ours and Adam's transgression is brought about by the Devil (alias the serpent), the powers of darkness, the operation of the 'evil imagination', or a misuse of a God-given and God-quality free will is not easy—in St Paul's work or that of anyone else—to tease out. It depends also on the views taken on the nature and origin of evil and the nature of God. But in every case the 'Fall' ensures a more complete separation of subsequent human nature from that of God; it widens the gap between creator and created and so preserves the purity of God's nature.

Other writers (and more notably, but not exclusively, the Western fathers) take this idea further and more literally. They pronounce that we have not only a tendency to sin, for we are solid with Adam in his fallen condition, but also that we must take upon ourselves solidarity with the *guilt* of his transgression. We are not only vulnerable and susceptible to doing wrong, but we are also adjudged guilty from birth for already having done it! We are not only originally sinful, but also originally guilty.

In its harshest form, this thinking says that a tendency to both sinfulness and guilt are communicated from generation to generation. The communication is automatic and involuntary and its 'vehicle' came to be seen as the process of procreation—consistent with one interpretation of Genesis 3 which emphasizes the theme of sexuality rather than the sin of pride, or wanting to be 'as God'. In this we see the tragic consequences of literalness taken to the ultimate. Sexual intercourse is the agent of procreation, therefore sexual intercourse potentially carries the taint.

The end of the process varies: Augustine takes the extreme position. In his thought mankind has become fatally compromised and *depraved*—that is, devoid of the capacity to choose the path of goodness or principle.[31] People would be damned and isolated from God, and bound to live a life of sin and wrongdoing, were it not for the rescuing 'grace' or loving-kindness of God. However, only certain chosen people will be offered grace *and* will have the ability to respond to it. Our own will can do nothing to influence this choice, except in so far as it is possible for us to pray to be saved. This is a strange idea, given our avowedly depraved condition and the likely expectation that we would not want grace nor recognize it when we saw it.

Pelagius, on the other hand, like Athanasius before him, thought that our tendency to sin was a *weakness*[32] rather than a *depravity* and that it is possible, by the exercise of our will, not to give in to it, but to live in increasing harmony with the love of God by choice and effort. According to Pelagius we can do something to alleviate our own condition; according to Augustine we are wholly dependent on the mercy of God.

The patristic way of talking may seem strange and perhaps almost meaningless to us today. In fact we continue to use a great deal of its imagery in the liturgy, but much of the time it passes us by because the issues it purports to address are not normally devouring us. If they are devouring us, as was the case with some of the people in Chapter 1, then the imagery may still pass us by because we cannot relate it to our tormented condition. If we can relate it, it may only serve to increase our torment, as was the case with *Sheila*, the pillar of the church whose sense of unworthiness and her imperfections was nightly reinforced by the Sermon on the Mount and Thomas à Kempis.

As 'enlightened' people of our time we 'know' that we do not believe in an actual first human pair called Adam and Eve, that we do not think of any sort of 'Fall' however it is represented, and that the idea that a guilt for what

has gone before us should continue to 'taint' us is prepos-
terous—particularly if it is thought to have something to
do with the process that produces us. Most of us do not
live daily with Augustine's final vision of humankind as
essentially a *massa damnata*, doomed but for the 'grace'
of God who somehow chooses to redeem *some* of us. Even
if we do sometimes think something approaching this—
when confronted by daily examples in the news of
appalling human acts—the implicit conclusion for most
of us most of the time is that we shall be among the elect
despite warnings in the parables of Jesus to the contrary.
Unless, that is, we are very severely depressed, or mad,
when we can experience just such fear or even certainty
of damnation. Fears such as these which flower in madness
do, though, tend to be exactly the ones that are played on
in a certain kind of evangelistic mission. Some people are
overtly vulnerable and susceptible to them. So are these
fears, in fact, so completely non-existent—at all levels of
our being—for the rest of us?

Many of us probably live as half-Pelagians—we do think
that with some effort we might be able to live fairly decent
lives, and we would not expect to be plagued daily with
guilt about our imperfections. But this armour-plating of
reasonable self-esteem and the good-enough life is not
always as watertight for us as we might most of the time
care to think. For many people the odd sleepless night or
the effect of a sudden reverse or failure in life can show
us otherwise.

For most of us the question of the love, grace, or loving-
kindness of God versus God's impotence or sadism only
comes up at moments of great personal or corporate
tragedy, but when this happens some of the old irrational
thoughts reappear. 'What have I done to deserve this?'
comes as a cry of anguish, guilt, and sometimes protest at
such times. It is perhaps also significant in this respect
that the Aids threat has been at times treated like a new
plague, and its victims both shunned as sources of con-
tamination and lumped with the sinners of old who by their
own misdeeds brought the suffering and tragedy upon
themselves.

We mostly do not think that the practice of infant baptism still implies primarily the need to counter some
quasi-magical transmission to newborn babies—through
the physical process of procreation—of an inherited and

potentially indelible sinfulness and guilt. Yet we still
echo regularly in the liturgy the words of the fifty-first
psalm: 'in sin did my mother conceive me'.[33] Sexual sins
are still heavily castigated in religious circles, and even
today I think there is still repression, distortion, and
devaluation of human sexuality in religious thought and
the communities of faith—as if it still somehow has a lot
to answer for.

On the other hand, we in today's circumstances are
probably most naturally attracted to follow at least some
of the thought—but not the whole, for he too was a man of
his time—of St Irenaeus who saw humankind as being born
individually and corporately primitive with a need and a
thrust to develop. For him the 'Fall' was a deviation from
an ideal development rather than a literal or symbolic
fall from grace or bliss. That idea seems to 'go best' with
our scientific and psychological 'know-how'. This religious and theological position is beautifully explicated by
Andrew Elphinstone in his book *Freedom, Suffering and
Love*:

> Man's earliest origin was not in some splendid perfec-
> tion of innocence and moral integrity in a far-off Eden.
> It was in a simple, undiversified cell stirring to the first
> tremor of livingness chronologically further away than
> Eden was ever supposed to have been. Our beginning
> was not in the heights but out of the depths, and human
> imagination is not equal to grasping the prodigious
> journey of selection and complexification which has
> brought that primeval speck to the physical and psy-
> chic intricacy of man with his technological skills and
> his morally self-conscious rationality.[34]

At a later point he describes further the primitive raw
material of this evolutionary struggle:

> Aggressive and defensive instincts—desires, needs, fear,
> anxieties and angers—were woven into the texture of
> his human make-up. They were essential to his sur-
> vival and their roots ran into the depths of his being
> and back down the long corridor of his ancestry.[35]

Of the 'Fall' he says:

> It was something that emerged as an inevitable corollary
> of the onward movement of evolution and psychic

progress at a particularly crucial stage in mankind's development . . . This was no fall from perfection, for there was no perfection and no height from which to fall. It was no tearing asunder of mankind's relationship with God, for he can have had only the most rudimentary awareness of the numinous. It can have brought no wholesome condemnation on man because he was groping his evolutionary way forward and learning, as child learns, a more exacting use of his evolutionary equipment. Above all, this was no cataclysmic moral tragedy, as Christian thought has felt obliged in the past to depict it, because through these events man was moving further into moral awareness, not away from it. It was the introduction to his quest for God, not the shutting of the door upon that quest; his baptism into the travail of entry into love, not his rejection of a supposedly existing capacity to love.[36]

I have quoted Elphinstone at length for two reasons. First, though I cannot agree with him intellectually at all points, I still find this book, which I read when it was first published in 1976, one of the most honest— intellectually and emotionally—and most moving explications of the dual mystery of sin and atonement that I have read, and I shall return to it later on in this present writing. I do not see any need, neither do I want to replace this synthesis with an inevitably lesser version of my own. Second, Elphinstone, so to speak, brings Irenaeus up to date, from the second to the twentieth century; and though I have almost certainly selected only part of Irenaeus' thought, that has always been the way by which I could link my reflections with the ancient sources and wisdom of the past. In some way which is not entirely clear to me this linking with the early origins of faith has been important, and to have been able to find 'back there' no common ground with my own experience would I think have undermined and invalidated both.

So, Irenaeus, Elphinstone, and myself concur in the dethronement of the ideas of 'original righteousness', and original innocence. But even as I write this the alarm bells start to ring, for I realize that the abolition of 'original righteousness' is not consonant with another strand in human experience.

It ignores the fact that many of us do sometimes seem

to hark back to or yearn for a blissful, carefree existence *as if it is something we have once known*. William Blake's 'Songs of Innocence' and 'Songs of Experience'[37] are classic in bearing witness to an 'innocent' state. More prosaically, the familiar extolling of the 'good old days', invokes the same theme. It is seen perhaps at its most extreme form in Tennyson's *The Lotus Eaters*:

> How sweet it is, hearing the downward stream
> With half-shut eyes ever to seem
> Falling asleep in a half-dream!
> To dream and dream, like yonder amber light,
> . . .
> To muse and brood and live again in memory,
> With those old faces of our infancy[38]

If the early fathers had not posited a state of original righteousness or bliss we might have had to invent one to do justice to all our experience and yearnings.

This must surely alert us to the importance of not taking on board only those aspects of the earlier and later theological thought which are comfortable to us. The foreign-sounding ideas that we unearthed earlier running through patristic thought may not be so intrinsically foreign after all—they may be resonating with some part of our experience that we discard at our peril. It is, after all, rather strange that we keep a liturgy with so much of this ancient imagery in it if we really believe it to be completely outmoded and to have nothing to say to us.

This of course is just the charge; that both the liturgy and theological thinking old and new are *not* speaking to us except on a subliminal level which some of us sometimes tune into and many of us often do not. At best, we can probably let ourselves be 'carried' by the tradition for much of the time, but the price of this may be that sin, confession, forgiveness, and atonement may go dead on us when we most need them. In this process either human beings may suffer painfully in their faith, or faith itself will become irrelevant and in the end die.

Part of the difficulty of the ancient thought is that it is so 'external' in form. It tends in its formalized way to approach God and sin as concepts we can study and be detached from rather than as processes and realities we

are engaged with and cannot objectify or make into 'things'.
In part this is because in the theological formulations and
in the liturgy we have the *results* of a systematic and relatively *public* process; we are not given the internal—and
sometimes passionate—thinking and feeling struggles of
the human beings who were individually or corporately
responsible for them. I felt I got into this 'external' way of
being as I tried to summarise five centuries of thought.
Perhaps this is inevitable, but the danger is of some 'split'
between doctrine and the religious community and between
intellect and feeling that can bring about a 'deadness' of
heart and spirit. Yet although the form and the language
may have become unhelpful—it may have to be changed
if it is to become revitalised for us, I do not think that we
shall make the right changes by *ignoring* the past and all
that has gone before, but rather by trying to *understand*
the past.

Second, some of the confusion seems to me to be about
whether what we call sin includes our actions, our thoughts
and our sense of being and identity—or only some of these.
In the famous passage of St Matthew's Gospel citing the
person who *desires* to commit adultery as in effect having
already done so,[39] the thought seems to be the same as the
deed. St Augustine's *massa damnata* seems to extend to
the whole of human beings; not only to their actions or
their thoughts. Though the church has always purported
to 'hate the sin, but love the sinner', the boundaries have
been blurred, and whole groups of people—such as
homosexuals—might be forgiven for wondering whether,
in the current state of church discipline, they are not in
fact being condemned for who they *are*. How possible is
it to separate a person from his or her thoughts and
behaviour? Even if we think we have made an intellectual
separation, can this be sustained on the emotional level?

There is a further question relating to those areas of
our being that we do not know about: our unconscious
selves. When we are not aware of some part of ourselves
what responsibility can we take for it? How far do
thoughts and actions that emanate from our more
irrational, unconscious aspects come under the umbrella
of sinfulness or goodness? It is possible that the ancient
thinkers did not have to ask this question, yet the saying
of Jesus on the cross, 'Father, forgive them; for they know

not what they do'[40] belies this. For our part we certainly cannot 'un-invent' our awareness of the unconscious, and so we must ask the question.

Furthermore still, can sin, which I have tried to define as being essentially to do with *God*, relate to our relationship and dealings with our fellow human beings; and if so in what way? The Lord's Prayer, 'Forgive us our sins as we forgive those who sin against us',[41] and Peter's question to Jesus, 'How often shall my brother sin against me and I forgive him—till 7 times?'[42] both certainly imply an affirmative answer to the question. Yet the affirmation may depend more upon the premise that human beings are made in the image of God than on purely humanitarian considerations.

Finally, there is the unique place in all this of the concept of guilt. It is hard to find in the theological story an explication of the relationship between sin and guilt. As I said in the preface, I was first inclined to think that guilt is the *feeling* that alerts us to the presence of *sin*, but found this to be far too simplistic and in any case patently not always true. Some people never feel guilty while others always feel guilty, and this is true in both the psychological and religious realms. Moreover, the treatment of original guilt by theologians, and the concept of the guilty verdict in any legal system, both suggest that guilt must have an objective as well as a subjective face. But the two get confused, in both the religious and the psychological dimensions. Guilt is a theme I want particularly to take up in the next chapter in the hope that if we can explore it psychologically this may help us understand it in its religious setting.

All these questions are complex, but they need to be teased out if we are to attempt to get nearer our stated goals of understanding more the internal meaning that sin can have for us, and exploring the far-from-academic issues of why it bothers us or does not bother us and how it does so. I think the theological story does pick up deep psychological truths, and because it does so it *can* speak to our human condition. The task for the next chapter, as I see it, is therefore to try to discern the psychological conditions, fears, threats, desires, and hopes for which the religious word sin can serve as a shorthand symbol.

Notes

1. John Milton, *Paradise Lost*, Book I, The Argument, lines 1–2, in *The Poems of John Milton* (OUP 1958).
2. Romans 7.18–19 (RSV).
3. Romans 7.20 (RSV),
4. Romans 7.22 (RSV).
5. John 9.2 (RSV).
6. John 9.3 (RSV).
7. Job 1.6–12.
8. Job 21.7–14.
9. John Donne, 'A Hymne to God the Father', in John Hayward (ed.), *John Donne: A Selection of His Poetry*, Penguin Poets (Penguin 1950), p. 177.
10. Luke 5.8.
11. John 13.21–30.
12. Matthew 27.3–5.
13. Matthew 26.50.
14. Joshua 7.2—8.29.
15. 1 Samuel 14.36–45.
16. 1 Samuel 15.3–33.
17. This idea is drawn from Genesis 6.5 and is explicated, particularly, in the rabbinic and apocryphal literature (for example, Ecclesiasticus 16.1–17, especially 14c.) For a discussion see N.P. Williams, *Ideas of the Fall and Original Sin* (Longmans Green 1927), pp. 59–70.
18. Mark 3.29.
19. Romans 7.17
20. There is, historically, more than one such list; this is used as the most traditional exemplar. For discussion see K. E. Kirk, *Some Principles of Moral Theology* (Longmans Green 1927), pp. 265–8, or Morton Bloomfield, *The Seven Deadly Sins* (Lansing, Michigan 1952).
21. For unforgivable sins throughout the first and second centuries, see, for example, Hippolytus, *Refutation of all Heresies* 9, 12, 20–6; Origen, *On Prayer,* 28.8ff. For full details of the patristic period see O. D. Watkins, *A History of Penance* (Longmans Green 1920), volume 1.
22. See St Thomas Aquinas, *Summa Theologica,* i,2 q 88 a2, or P. Abelard, *Scito Teipsum 15,* discussed in K. E. Kirk, *The Vision of God* (Longmans Green 1928), pp. 297–8, 540–3.
23. For a summary of early church doctrine and patristic references here, on following pages and in later chapters, see J. N. D. Kelly, *Early Christian Doctrines* (A. and C. Black 1958). This reference see Kelly, *Doctrines,* chapter 13, sections 5–7.
24. See Kelly, *Doctrines,* chapter 13, sections 2–3.
25. Martin Luther, *Letter to Melancthon,* Letters of Martin Luther, 1556, 1.345.

26. *The Sunday Missal* (Collins 1984), p. 383.
27. See, for example, chapters 5 and 6 of G. L. Prestige, *Fathers and Heretics* (SPCK 1940).
28. For summary, see Kelly, *Doctrines,* chapter 13, section 6, pp. 361-2.
29. St Irenaeus, *Against All Heresies,* 4,37; *Demonstration of the Apostolic Preaching,* 12.
30. See, for example, Romans 5.12-19.
31. See Kelly, *Doctrines,* chapter 13, section 6, especially pp. 364-6.
32. See Kelly, *Doctrines,* chapter 13, section 5, especially pp. 359-60.
33. Psalm 51.5 (RSV).
34. Andrew Elphinstone, *Freedom, Suffering and Love* (SCM Press Ltd 1976), p. 66.
35. Elphinstone, *Freedom,* p. 74.
36. Elphinstone, *Freedom,* pp. 68-9.
37. William Blake, *Collected Works,* (Penguin 1969).
38. Alfred, Lord Tennyson, 'The Lotus Eaters' in T. W. Moles and A. R. Moon (eds.), *An Anthropology of Longer Poems* (Longmans Green 1953), Choric Song V. 11 100-111.
39. Matthew 5.28.
40. Luke 23.34.
41. Luke 11.1-4.
42. Matthew 18.21-22.

THREE

The Inside of the Whale
or
The Psychological Undertones of Sin

Once upon a time, a long time ago, I was given a children's picture book of the story of Jonah and the Whale. You know the kind: big pictures, not very many words, easy on the eye and easy on small minds struggling with big ideas. It was also, I remember, most beautifully done. I cannot find it now to 'prove' whether what I am about to make of it is authentic or just my memory playing me false. Perhaps that does not matter anyway, because it is what I *did* make of it and obviously have 'stored' for many years that is important.

I carried away two particular pictures. The first is of the *outside* of the whale, a huge, smooth, dark grey-black mass broken up only by a large eye and a tail that looked a bit like the end of an aeroplane. As I went on looking it seemed to change into an elephant—an animal with which I was much more familiar from visits to the zoo. The double association confused me; they told me it was a whale, it looked to me like an elephant. I liked elephants, as most children do. They reminded me of large, familiar, teddy-bear-like objects that would be soft and pliable and could be cuddled up to. (I had never got near enough to the real thing to know the truth!) On the other hand, what little I knew of whales told me they were huge lumps that lurked ominously in the murky depths of the ocean which could suddenly set themselves in motion and heave dangerously up and down through the surface waves—things better kept well away from!

This, to me, sums up the position we reached at the

end of the last chapter. The religious 'object' called sin oscillates between being an elephant and being a whale in a confused and confusing way. It is big. It can be dangerous. Sometimes it is familiar, sometimes it strikes us as alien. Sometimes we think we know it, and can make friends with it, and even tame it. Sometimes it is a murky black shape that can lead us from our human homeland into the wastes of a dark, bottomless, and sinister ocean. Sometimes it humbles us, sometimes it damns us . . .

The second picture in the story-book that caught my imagination was of a rather bemused but not unhappy Jonah standing *inside* the whale gazing up and around at his surroundings. I cannot remember much more, except that the inside scene looked remarkably like a room in any house. It had nooks and crannies; protuberances to hold on to or sit on; different colours from pink to all shades of grey and blue; and, leading off it, what it seemed were lots of passages. There was a mixture of the familiar—it *looked* like a room—with a faint threat that it wasn't quite, with all these paths leading further into a darker innerness . . .

I remember turning the page rather too quickly away from this second picture, somewhat awed, partly reassured and partly a bit terrified. But I was somehow 'held safe' by the sense that Jonah—judging by the expression on his face—seemed to be standing up well to it. What I think it did do was increase my ability to hold together 'inside' and 'outsides'; I could dimly grasp that looking at them together and letting them 'mix' somehow made for a bigger, fuller picture.

The analogy cannot be pressed too far, but I find I am wanting to liken the inside of the whale to what I call the psychological 'inside' of sin. In this chapter I would like us—like Jonah—to stand up in it, walk around, explore and venture up some of the alleys, touch it and perhaps poke it around to see if it gives to our touch, and so begin to get a bigger picture of the whole thing.

We may inevitably be confronted with the questions 'Is it friendly? Is it alien? Can we tame it, or will it swallow us up?' But as a child, when I identified with the expression on Jonah's face, I managed better my curiosity, confusion, and anxiety about elephants and whales and insides and outsides. So I am encouraged by my experience to feel that the risk is worth taking. If the result is that we can fill out, make more malleable and flexible—though not necessarily more simple—our understanding of sin then it will have been a worthwhile exercise.

There are two ways of getting at this psychological inside of the whale. The first is through *describing* 'ordinary' human experience. The second is through trying to understand and make sense of it by drawing upon a body of *knowledge* which offers itself as a guide to doing just this. Both are necessary for reflective human beings who do not set themselves up as sole arbiter of their own and others' experience, but perhaps the most important thing is that the second shall be rooted in the first and *allow itself to be tested by the first*. It is no use building a beautiful edifice of psychological thought if we cannot relate it to what we as individual and ordinary human beings find that we actually think and feel. Psychological thought, like theology, is not infallible. Moreover, psychologists, like theologians, tend not to agree amongst themselves. So we cannot be absolved from the task of trying to digest what we take in and—after the manner of digestion—letting some of it be absorbed into us and some be discarded.

In order, therefore, to root my theological reflection in human experience I want first to return to Chapter 1 and the stories from literature and my imagination there outlined, and to enquire more closely into the human dilemmas presented to us. I am going to run through again the range of human experiences I tried to describe. I think and hope that every so often a fundamental and general question or issue will rear its head and 'ask' to be taken further. Where this happens I shall set it out and it will be underlined so that it is not lost to us.

There was the ordinary *Church* family—so ordinary in fact that I fear still they may come over as a caricature— and yet I think they do exist, in their hundreds. Sin did not really bother them much at all; it was part of the wallpaper. The only things that stand out are a child's query as to what 'negligence' in the General Confession means (and we may ask that too—what exactly have we neglected?) and the fleeting thought in the Intercession, 'There never is any peace in the world.' If we pause here for a moment this is rather a shocking thought. Why is there never any peace in the world, when we extol the virtue of peace so constantly? Human beings *say* they want peace; they pray for it earnestly and often, but it doesn't happen. In fact we find it very hard to live with each other either as nations or as smaller groups, as the warring couple also attending the service testify. We continue to hurt each other badly, even though another part of us says we do not want to.

Here is St Paul's dilemma in a concrete example. Why cannot we carry through to fruition our praiseworthy and altruistic desires and hopes?

We cannot, it seems, live at peace with *ourselves*, though the extent to which we suffer through this varies. Both *Stewart*, the homosexual parishioner, and *Matthew*, the rector, know this at first hand. Both have a shameful secret. *Matthew's* is in the realm of his fury and hatred at the man who attacked his daughter. *Stewart's* is the kind of person he is. Both feel isolated by their secret, and both fear that it could destroy their outer life and tear their inner being apart. Both 'solve' it by activity and in this achieve a shutting out. *Matthew* doggedly persists in his role as a clergyman, and *Stewart* overworks at the relief agency.

Yet the shutting out is not complete, for both men continue to participate in the life of the church. There, every so often, an odd phrase or nuance—in Matthew's case often pronounced by himself!—is virtually *bound* to remind them of their pain. There are other places and other situations where both homosexuality and fury might be better tolerated, but the two men are not taking this option. Matthew cannot for his livelihood is at stake; Stewart is choosing not to. So they retain a relationship with their pain and their anxiety by continuing to be exposed to a particular atmosphere and inevitable line of thought. When both of them are forced to stop and think fundamental doubts come up: 'Is this what I was made for? Was I really made for anything at all?'

The question is, what is making them feel so wretched? Is it solely because they feel at odds with themselves and their own ideals; or is it that they feel at odds with themselves partly because of the impact of *other people* upon them? Would *Stewart* feel so bad about his homosexuality if church teaching and some of society at large were not seeming to condemn it? Would *Matthew* handle his anger better if he was not continually being made to feel—by the precepts of his calling—that it is bad and that he should not be experiencing it? The trouble for both of them is that they have also become very isolated and are not able to talk to anyone about what they are and what they feel. Each therefore lives as a 'masked' person and so feels rootless and withdrawn from a genuinely personal and meaningful life.

A general question begins to emerge:

Why do we feel uncomfortable about certain things we do and think? Most of us will know and name this feeling as one of *guilt.* Is it because it offends our own ideal of ourselves and the 'nice' picture we may have built up of ourselves, or is it because it offends the sensibilities of other people to the extent that they may turn round and act against us? There are times, too, when we just feel uncomfortable and guilty; when there appears to be no external danger; when our vision of how we would like to see ourselves is not threatened; yet . . . all is not well and we sense it could get worse.

We come next to *Simon*, the businessman who is ill; indeed possibly his life is threatened. He cannot but connect this with an idea of being *punished* for the affair he has been carrying on behind his wife's back for years. He is tormented by the question, 'Is he suffering now because he has done something *bad*?' and it is clear that his instinctive answer is 'Yes'.

Illness, madness, and badness are difficult to disentangle. When we become ill is it that we have fallen prey to a weakness in our *body* system, to which by reason of heredity we are susceptible? That is one scenario. Or is the illness an inadequate and even dangerous way to solve an emotional problem because in our unconscious selves we know no other way, and does it also serve the purpose of condemning and punishing us for things we fantasize about, or know we have done, or for thoughts we have had? That is another scenario.

The interplay between body and mind is mysterious and complex. It lends itself to disturbing ideas and questions just because our body can seem to have a life of its own without reference to the rest of our being. It can seem to go frighteningly bad and frighteningly out of control. And when things are going badly wrong with that most intimate and personal part of ourselves—our body—we can think it is to give us what we deserve. We must either have done something specific to deserve it, or perhaps it is just showing up the incredible mess inside ourselves. We can die, but we know that is to be our end anyway. Our disordered body, as reflective of our disordered being, only tells us what we know and fear already; that we are condemned.

Furthermore, taken all in all, we seem to be singularly lacking in compassion for ourselves despite the fact that if we are Christian we are committed to and preach a God of compassion. We can also have a similar genius, that goes way beyond the rational and realistic, for tormenting ourselves for not reaching perfection. The perfection that we yearn for is always elusive—we never quite seem to do enough. The outsider is in a better position to take the longer and more gentle view, as the priest *Gerald* could with his penitent *Anne*. He could understand the pent up inner fury that issued in temper and the occasional looking and longing for another relationship as part of the stress and strain of her life with a mentally ill husband. *Anne* manages not to *act* on her desires, yet the feelings plague her. They conflict with some exacting standard deep within herself of which she always falls short. So also *Sheila*, the woman who has been a pillar of the church all her life, but knows no peace; she is never good enough, but for whom? For the God she turns to nightly, or for the exacting human father who was so harsh in his dealings with the family and with her especially so that she could never be sure whether she was loved or almost hated? Both these people are truly enslaved to a 'God' living inside them who is far more terrifying and exacting than the God outside that other people in their orbit seem to know. But for them—and this is the crux of the problem—the inside is *ruling* the outside. The God of fear and punishment inside is strong, and the God of love and compassion can make no real impact on them. They do not recognize such feelings in themselves. Their good deeds are as nothing for the 'bad me' lives on relentlessly, and they have no basis for thinking that God views them any differently.

> Here, in *Anne* and *Sheila*, we see the dilemma of the confusion between sin and sin(s). These people commit little in the way of sin(s), but the power of sin—the inner badness that afflicts them—is relentless and persecuting. There is little distinction between the sin and the sinner, for both are condemned.

Then we come to the area and mystery of the darkest reaches of human nature as we see them in *Raskolnikov, the Macbeths, Iago* and the *carrion hawk* of Ted Hughes' poem.

All have committed or are perpetrating murder, that most ancient sin of sins and crime of crimes. Yet their inner natures are not the same, and we dimly sense this in our reaction to them.

Raskolnikov ultimately cannot but arouse our compassion if we will let him. His own account of his tormented passage to murder—his fears, his dreaming sense of being taken over by something, partly from his past, that he does not understand and which part of him desperately wants to resist and cannot, his need for confession—tells us that we are listening to an essentially human being, but one who is very greatly troubled. We cannot in our fantasy rewrite the story, condone the act, or save him from the consequences. But I do not think that most people finishing reading *Crime and Punishment* have come to hate him. 'There but for the grace of God go I' is the more likely heartfelt cry. We intuitively recognize him as one of ourselves. In *Raskolnikov* it is possible to continue to see sin as an affliction and weakness. It is a terrible one, but one to which he does not consent with his whole being.

In my opinion it is the presence of his *guilt* that saves him for us and makes it possible for us to go on relating to him. The guilt of *Raskolnikov* keeps his humanity intact for us for we *recognize* it as what a human being who has done this thing *would* feel.

It is far harder not to separate ourselves from the *Macbeths*, and perhaps the reason for this is that we sense that they—*Lady Macbeth* in particular, and *Macbeth* as drawn into her orbit—feel no real guilt for their actions.

That this is so may not be immediately obvious for *Lady Macbeth* in her nightmare sleepwalk appears to be tormented by guilt—even to suicide. Her husband is drawn to a sense of nihilism and futility in all things and did seem to start from a different inside position from that of his wife. She indeed said of him:

> Yet do I fear thy nature;
> It is too full o' the milk of human kindness
> To catch the nearest way.[1]

He cannot resist and stand up to her. The point is, I think, that theirs is not a guilt like *Raskolnikov's*; it is not born of a sense of the wrongness of their acts and of unsuccessful desires and attempts to resist them. It is, if we call it guilt at all, a guilt without concern and without a human face. The *Macbeths* wanted something, and everything in their way was subsumed to their greed. That there were people in the way mattered not a jot; there was only greed and a sense of their own omnipotence—an inner sense of there being no limits to their power and what they could do or have, reinforced by the trappings of external kingship. Guilt when it does come—and perhaps we should not really call it by that name—is more like an enormous pricking of the bubble of omnipotence, for they cannot after all escape the consequences of their deeds. They are *not* God, and this realization comes to torment them. We from the outside world adjudge them guilty and they do indeed feel 'guilty', but these two uses of the one word are, I think, worlds apart, and span a gulf of kind, not degree.

In *Iago* and Hughes' *hawk* the omnipotence is clearer, and in *Iago* it is omnipotence working on destructive envy and a perversion of the good, the turning of it to bad—reminiscent of the sin against the Holy Spirit which ascribes the works of God to the devil. The very open nature of *Othello* which has made him lovable and is in such contrast to *Iago's* own dark secretive nature, is precisely that which is to be blackened and turned inside out so that *Othello* shall come to manifest *Iago's* dark and envious hate. Though something of *Iago* may well be in all of us, it is usually very hard for us to identify this to ourselves perhaps because of the element in him—that we both hate and fear—of cold and cruel manipulation, mixed with the desire to blot out and exterminate love—a love that he cannot share.

It is the element of *deliberate* and sustained reflection —*Iago* seems to know exactly what he is doing—which we also experience in the *hawk* in the top of the wood and of which the most terrible historical manifestation is arguably Hitler's planned extermination of the Jews in World War II, that strikes at us. The hate is extreme, undeterred, and by definition one-sided. The *hawk's* pride also is extreme for the subject himself is self-sufficient and perfect, or he thinks he is. There is no love, and it is this which for me gives it the quality of *depravity* rather than disturbance or weakness. It seems to be irredeemable, for what could ever pierce it? In the *hawk*—'I shall keep it like this'—no change is possible or desired.

It is surely no accident that the words I have found to describe the *Macbeths'* and *Iago's* behaviour—namely greed, envy and pride—are in fact three of the historical deadly sins.[2] As depicted in these people they make for a sense of ultimate separation and division between us and them, yet in a strange way I am acknowledging that the separation is *not* absolute; I realize that what they perpetrate I *could* know from inside, but I find that I *do not want to*. I want to keep the gulf between us because of what I might also find in myself if I acknowledged common ground between us. For I believe that the underlying forces and feelings are not completely foreign to us even though we hope that the actions to which they give rise may be.

I *could* say that if I knew more about what had happened earlier on in their lives to these people, perhaps I could understand and have compassion on them. But I talk to myself in this vein:

> Do I really *want* to understand them? Is it 'safe' to ponder that degree of hate? Could I get *fascinated* by it and inextricably caught up in it? Would it not be better to reject them, and deny the whole dimension they stand for?

As I write this last paragraph I find I am rather surprised at myself. I had thought I *was* able to accept the negative, believing that it can be integrated into our being rather than having to be exorcized and driven out, but another layer of perhaps unconscious reaction came off my pen. I find I both want to disown this dimension—which I think I have to call evil—and that at the same time I am vulnerable to it.

> If this is so for me perhaps it is also so for many of us. Here is sin at its most sinful and sin(s) at their most pernicious. Where do they come from?

We could say sin comes from the 'evil imagination';[3] we could say it comes from our early experience. I shall be wanting to return to this later in the chapter, but for the moment I want to go on with my *questionings*. Can there be understanding of and compassion for this dimension of our being, or is it deeply unforgivable? Does it stem from a deathly affliction deep inside all of us from which we are 'saved' only by the good fortune that someone chose to give us enough love that we should forever know what that word means—even if only dimly?

The *Macbeth/Iago* dimension is characterized by an absence of love; perhaps it was never born, perhaps it was blotted out. Yet of those who somehow have to blot it out we ask the further question, 'Had they any choice or was it something that happened to them without their knowledge or consent?' That would be Augustine[4] speaking in our time. Or, 'Is it something that we do all indeed know, but can have a choice as to whether to go with it or fight against it? When we do choose to fight against it *can* the battle be won?' That is Pelagius[5] speaking.

We are back at the issue of how free is our will. We can talk of a quasi-magical 'taint' that we have somehow inherited and cannot escape, or we can talk of a survival mechanism that somehow goes terribly wrong. What makes it possible for most of us to keep this darkest dimension at the level of fantasy, whilst others are driven to act it out? Indeed, it is perhaps just this *fear* of not being able to stop the one going over into the other that has led the religious world to say that fantasy, thought, and action are equally sinful.

These pages have been intended to *describe* at least some of the inside of the whale. It changes from being a fairly comfortable drawing-room which from time to time needs cleaning and redecorating, but which has reasonably good access to the outside world, to being a dark, chaotic, cavernous place subject to the influence of evil forces which threaten to infuse it completely by their presence so that the light which does filter through from outside is all but extinguished.

I have tried, like the Jonah of my picture book, to stand up inside the whale and look around and, where I have dared, touch. What I found I 'touched' were all the questions of original sin, original guilt and salvation, and they did not seem to me to be dry, irrelevant questions of the intellect. *Others'* gaze and exploration might well uncover different aspects and even make them want to deny that some of mine are real. This does not matter unless our inner landscapes are so far apart as to leave us without any common ground. If that happens no doubt the reader will stop reading!

But for those who wish to go on we now need another stage. I have isolated and outlined questions for myself; in a way I have the thing in bits. The theological story of sin is one way of struggling to put the bits together under the 'umbrella' of our relationship with God. But there is a psychological story—convergent, alternative, or parallel we do not yet know—and it also struggles for coherence, and it is to this second story that I now want to turn.

When I attempted to explore the psychological story of human development in *Clergy Stress*[6] I made three introductory points which it is pertinent to repeat here.

First, that we have both a conscious and unconscious part to ourselves, and the conscious part is but the tip of the iceberg.

Second, that the reason, in part, why a large part of our being is unconscious is that we fear it would be overwhelmingly painful to us if we had to experience it consciously. This is not the whole story, for no human being however aware and undefended and able to tolerate emotional pain and anxiety ever, in my opinion, manages to experience the whole of himself or herself. It would be literally too mind-blowing; we could not manage to pay attention to so much of ourselves *and* live, all at the same time. It is like contemplating astronomy and the universe; we cannot consciously experience for very long the great unending space, the nature of space and time and the concept of millions and millions of light years. Most

of us have to switch off from it in order to get on with the
more prosaic business of living. As with that physical
universe, so with the universe inside ourselves; we could
not deal emotionally with all of it all of the time. So we
use *defences* to make part of the reality of ourselves unknown to ourselves, and our well-being comes to depend
on an optimum and well-balanced level of *psychological
defences*. Too many and too high and we become
strained and rigid; too little and too low and we suffer
anxiety beyond that we can tolerate and something 'gives'.
The amount of defence we need and use is not, however,
the same for all of us.

My third point was that the basis for our own particular
pattern of anxiety and defence is laid down in our earlier
rather than later experience.

In this book, the focus is not anxiety that shows in
stress, but rather that dimension of human feeling and
experience that is to do with should and should not, good
and bad. But though the focus has changed the three
points remain valid.

Some people, through reviews, queried—as was likely,
since it cannot be 'proved'—my third point that it is
our early experience, particularly that of which we have
become unconscious that is crucial. They have reminded
me that there are ways of looking at ourselves other than
that summed up in the word 'psychodynamic'. Indeed
there are, and they may seem more pertinent than before
with this focus. So I think I should give some space to
'explaining' my persistence in holding on to a psychodynamic and psychoanalytical way of looking at things.
Of course I *cannot* explain it completely; in some ways all
I can say is that at this present time I 'believe' that this
approach makes most sense of experience to me. But if I
press myself further and attempt to say why I 'believe'
the following emerges.

The other contenders are *learning theory*[7] and the *cognitive approach*[8] (or the place of behaviour and thinking).
Learning theory posits that our behaviour is as it is
because we have learned it, and that this learning can take
place at any stage of life. The most important determinants
of the learning process are three. The first is simple: we
learn because we watch someone else who we take as our
model. That does in fact happen very early on in our lives

as any of us who have watched infants trying to imitate the facial expression of their mother know. The second is the extent to which different experiences become fused together for us; we learn, for example, that touching a hot stove and an unpleasant sensation we call 'burning' go together and the sensation is strong enough to stop us doing it in the future. The third is the extent to which other people reward or punish our efforts. If we are continually being shut out of the room for making a noise, or have our pocket money docked because we are greedy for sweets, then we are likely in time to change our behaviour.

This mechanism is the basis of the deterrent theory of punishment for adult crime; its correlate is that rewarding a piece of behaviour is likely to increase the likelihood of its happening. It is possible to see that even by this theory, early learning, when other people are very big in relation to our small selves, is likely to have a very powerful effect. But if learning theory was at the root of everything then we ought to be able to be educated out of our bad habits by a similar learning process to that which educated us into them—that is by teaching, by new associations, and by reward and punishment. We should also be able to discriminate between the models that we wish and do not wish to imitate, and to discard habits and even thoughts which are no longer useful to us. But this does not happen; we persist in old patterns.

Gerald's penitent continued to drive herself despite his suggestion that she should let up and be a bit kinder to herself. *Sheila* continued to be tormented by thoughts of her own unworthiness despite her life achievements or anything anyone else said to the contrary. *Raskolnikov* could not unravel—far less unlearn—the complicated chain of feelings and actions that led him into crime. It is as if something else, something more deterministic and less rational, is also working in us and our conscious will cannot override it. Learning theory by itself is too simple and furthermore it focuses on what we *do* and can minimize what we *think* or *feel* despite the fact that we sense that thinking and feeling loom large in us.

Cognitive therapists believe that we build up 'schemata' of thoughts such as: 'Suffering is due to sin', 'God will not love you if you are not good', or 'God will love you even if you are bad provided you admit your sin and throw yourself completely onto his mercy.' According to their theoretical understanding the power of thinking is paramount; we should be able to modify our schemata by testing them against external reality and dialogue with others. But again we find that often we cannot modify them. Furthermore, this way of approaching the issue cannot answer the prior question, 'How do these schemata get built up?' To some people that would not matter for it is not to them an important question; to others it matters a great deal.

In my opinion neither learning theory nor the cognitive approach are by themselves enough to take in our whole experience, though I am not saying by this that they play no part in an explanatory process. Their deficiencies make me return obstinately to the psychodynamic approach, aware, I hope, of its limitations, of the many questions it also poses and the fact that there are strong disagreements *within* this way of thinking. I use it because although it is not perfect it is the best I know.

But as with theology, so with the psychological theme. I cannot do justice to the weight and volume of thought and writing in a few pages, and my attempt to summarize and expound will therefore be selective and may be distorted. Nevertheless I shall take the risk.

The image of 'inside' and outside' is very pertinent here. In his early writing Freud[9] built up a picture of the 'inside' mental and emotional 'structure' of a human being. He saw us as being divided into three parts, *id, ego* and *superego*. The id was a seething mass of desires and instincts living deep inside us and not often allowed to see the light of day because it was too dangerous. It was thus largely unconscious and inaccessible to us. The ego was that part of this cauldron which *has* become organized and to an extent tamed by contact with the 'outside' world. The superego was that part of us which learns to observe, reflect on and criticize ourselves, and it exercises control over that which is or is not allowed to bubble up from the id.

Over time other people[10] have modified Freud's original concepts. Some have abandoned the ego and id terminology, and the term 'ego' stands for the *whole psyche* which then 'splits' into acceptable and accessible parts and unacceptable and inaccessible parts, or into life-affirming and life-denying parts. According to others, the ego is that part of the personality which relates to other people, or it represents that part of us that we think is subsumed under the subjective 'I'.

Confusion developed between the concepts 'ego' and 'self', and 'superego' and conscience. For some, notably Jung,[11] ego and self overlap but are by no means identical; the self is much more than the ego and it is mature whilst the ego is primitive. For others the ego belongs to a so-called objective study of stable characteristics in the personality—you could in theory study *it*—whilst the self comes from a more subjective world in which personality itself is a fluid concept which changes over situations and experiences. Conscience and superego also overlap, but conscience usually refers to conscious material, whilst the concept of superego goes beyond this into the unconscious dimension. The overlapping concept of the 'ego ideal' comprises a person's ideal of how he or she wishes to be; superego and ego ideal came to be distinguished along the lines that conflict with the former evokes guilt and with the latter shame, which then gives us two more words to define!

Such are the hypotheses about the structures inside us, but such an account of them can leave us feeling that they are as meaningless, falsely reified, and external as the theological concepts of the last chapter. They lack the sense that we are *in* the very 'thing' and experience we are trying to describe. Beyond a certain degree they become difficult to accept, for the language can only be analogical. We could not ever actually cut ourselves up and find an ego, a superego and an id! The fact that these early formulations were born of the avowedly empirical science of medicine no doubt contributed to their having this concrete flavour, but they have become foreign to our thinking in rather the same way as has the ancient language of sin.

Nevertheless, the same language also attempted an account of *how* these structures function. The balance between the ego and the id is said to be maintained by the operation of *defences*.[12] How defences work is partly determined by the nature and quality of the superego, and the stage of development reached. If the superego 'said' that greed, anger, or even love were not allowed then greed, anger, and love had somehow to be pressed out of consciousness, and kept out by the use of defences. Defence mechanisms[13] such as splitting, projection, denial, somatization and repression are used. Those defences requiring most mental organization are available only at later stages of development. The superego 'decides' what shall need to be defended against by a mechanism of *introjection*, or swallowing things in from outside. These are often parental wishes, injunctions, or prohibitions. The picture becomes more complicated since the superego itself can be subject to repression and facets of it become unconscious. More complicated still was the belief that the superego is not just a combination of actual parental figures writ large, because our own infant feelings also contribute to it and these may have themselves become distorted in the process. The energy for all this process was seen to come from the id, but since it must not be known to come from the id the energy is often self-attacking.

All this reads like an account of a rather strange 'closed system' and indeed the most important step forward in psychological thinking was the movement from structure to 'object relationship'.[14] This postulates that from the beginning we exist not as an isolated entity but in *relationship*—good or bad, satisfactory or unsatisfactory— with a person ('object' in the psychological literature). Winnicott said that the fundamental and earliest human unit was not an infant alone, but an infant and its mother.[15] When that relationship is in danger all is in danger. The relationship with the mother provides security, safety, survival, and meaning. (This is not unlike the position we reached over sin; sin alone is meaningless for it has existence only in relationship to God.)

Psychological and psychotherapeutic thinking came to be divided on the question of the right balance between universal, virtually innate feelings (notably of envy, destructiveness, attachment, and longing) presumed to exist in *all* infants, and the particular contribution to the strength and development of these of the actual early experience of any *one* infant. Freud himself oscillated on this issue as the controversy concerning whether memories of incest and child sexual abuse were fantasies or referred to actual experiences shows. Melanie Klein[16] focused on the universal, often unconscious, fantasies primarily of an aggressive nature which, she postulated, predominated over any individual historical experience.

Winnicott[17] through years of observation of many actual infants and their relationships with their mothers, took the 'middle' way. Winnicott's main contribution is the finding that when there is a 'good enough' early environment—that is when the mother is a good 'container' and can tolerate most of her baby's feelings—then the child moves of itself towards and through feelings and experiences of wanting attachment, wanting feeding, exploration, hesitation in exploring, *and* aggression. This behaviour is so natural that it can be called innate. The feelings are, however, liable to extremes of intensity; they become frightening to the infant, and then distorted if the mother cannot at that moment do what is necessary to make the baby feel that they are not overwhelming but can be progressively managed and integrated within his or her developing being.

For example, the experience of separation is one with which we all have to deal. Mother does go away, and we learn painfully that we cannot just command her back. Whether this piece of learning is unbearably terrifying for us or is manageable depends on such things as how long she is away and how she manages our distress. Similarly, the aggressive and devouring aspect of feeding—the desire and need to get all we want from our mother—can be pleasurable and exciting, but it can come to feel destructive to us if she cannot tolerate it or if we cannot get enough. If this happens something originally called 'wanting' becomes greed and somehow 'bad' and a source of pain for us; the rage engendered by this frustration can become too much for the infant emotional organization to handle.

For at this early stage we lack the capacity for reflection that can help us understand and tolerate what feels like extreme vicissitudes going on in us in relation to our well-being. We cannot, so to speak, get out of the universe, look at it from the outside and perhaps see there is a rhythm and a sense to it and learn that this stage will not last for ever. We are too much 'in' it for this and so it becomes 'mind-blowing' to us. We begin to fear that we shall be blown to bits, or sink in a black hole from which no communication from us to the outside world is possible, or fall through infinite and everlasting empty space.

I am writing in what *must* be analogy. None of us can actually remember what it was like to be a completely helpless infant. We can only reconstruct this, mainly through what comes up during psychotherapy and psychoanalysis at a later age. At this point it is already modified and distorted through the exercise of our intellect and the communicating, yet also constraining power of language. We have to speak by image and analogy; we cannot communicate direct reality. We have to make intuitive leaps between what we see to be going on with mothers and babies from the 'outside' and what *may* be going on 'inside' the infant.

Few, though, would be able to deny that something, and something fairly powerful, is going on. We have only to look at a child in a rage, or a withdrawn child after such an experience as being left in hospital, to see this.

Out of this maelstrom of experiences and feelings it is contended that we build up an 'inner world'.[18] This idea too is misleading for it is not a thing, in that it has no separate existence. It is a 'picture', but unlike my original picture-book it cannot be grasped and held. Yet having said that and acknowledged the limitations of analogy I would now like to treat it like the picture-book and open it and describe what I see. There are, of course, as many detailed descriptions of an inner world as there are people, and they may not fit together but some things may be constant enough.

We can see an inner world as having layers or rooms, some with staircases providing easy access from one to the other. Some, though, are like sealed apartments, and there are yet more passages leading to levels we cannot see. Some rooms seem filled with only energy: fire, ice, gas. Some are full of good things: food, warmth, welcoming arms. Nearer the top we think we can see people—cross people, happy people, stretching out and embracing people, turning away or hunched up people. Yet they are not quite people. Sometimes they have blanks for faces, or no real ends and beginnings. Sometimes they are midgets, sometimes they are giants. Some wear the clothes of our parents, sometimes both of them at once in a strange mixture, whilst some look like aunts, cousins, schoolteachers. Some look benign and caring; others look like ogres with misshapen limbs or even like devils with horns.

For any one of us at any time the scene in our inner world can look like an idyllic country homestead scene or like Leonardo's mother and child cartoon, or it can look like a scene from Hieronymous Bosch or Michelangelo's *Last Judgement*. It is not always the same, but for each of us, perhaps, there is a 'house style' that tends to be always reflected in the atmosphere, the colours, the aliveness or the deadness, the airiness or the sealed dankness of the rooms.

<u>I suggest that it is the presence and nature of this inner world of ours that contributes considerably to the way we conceive of and deal with sin and how we experience and handle the concept of God. The nastier the quality of our inner world and the more threatening the figures in it the more likely we are to resonate to the idea of sin as depravity and God as an implacable judge from whom we deserve and indeed receive little or no compassion.</u>

Furthermore, the psychological controversies about innateness, universal unconscious fantasies, and individual experience seem to me to be in tune with the theological question of whether original sin is a 'taint' we all inherit against whose power we have little chance. Are all our inner worlds more or less nasty in their most primitive and undeveloped form? If so, the inside of the whale is something we might all want to be delivered from.

In so-called 'normal' emotional and moral development this raw and primitive inner world gets modified and tamed. This we think happens in three ways: through the emergence of guilt and shame; through our own cognitive development which gives us the mental equipment which allows us increasingly to give a shape to and so master terrifying experience; and through the testing of our own internal experience by the reality of the outside world. I shall need to explore the latter two more when I come to my chapters on confession and morality. The first, the emergence of guilt and shame, belongs in this chapter, and I shall return to it shortly.

But I want first to suggest that there remain in all of us

areas that cannot easily be tamed, if at all. They remain unconscious and inaccessible to our self-organization. Hopefully they mostly lie dormant, but sometimes we seem to live as if we are ruled by them even if we are not sure what they are. Sometimes they erupt with or without resistance from the rest of our being. Sometimes they do not erupt, but neither does anything 'happen' that can change their nature. Their operation represents no true moral sense but only the laws of cause and effect and the retaliatory law of the jungle: 'Kill or be killed, fight or flee, annihilate or be annihilated.'

The worst excesses of human beings seem to me to come from the untamed and unmodified influence of this most raw and hidden area. Here we have the super-ego not as the guardian of moral precepts or judgements, but as a far more archaic God of the jungle, or as the harsh and uncompromising God of the Old Testament, motivated by omnipotence and capriciousness,[19] but without the ordered righteousness of the later Old Testament. The Old Testament God moves from being portrayed as a deeply primitive force—mediated through non-human taboos and orientated to conquest and destruction—to a righteous lawgiver whose utterances are orientated towards the survival and civilization of a people and the facilitation of harmonious living. In contrast, the archaic and untamed superego does not move.

Where there has been enough basic trust, where our earliest relationships have been of a good enough quality to 'contain' our early primitive feelings and experiences, this archaic part of our being is itself contained by us in later life; the more accessible part can be modified by the environment and our own thinking. Because of the continued presence in all of us of some sealed rooms or Bluebeard's chambers where the archaic still reigns supreme, the process of modification will never be com-pletely smooth; but if all goes well enough we come to see our shortcomings as a weakness with which we can more or less deal most of the time. Rumblings from our deep inside will probably not overwhelm us. Of such a psychological make-up is perhaps born the adult Pelagian position?[20] But where there has been gross failure in containment at an early age—when we so badly needed another to contain us—we sense the deep inside as threatening to our being and we are vulnerable to eruptions and to not managing ourselves in later life. Of this psychological position are perhaps born modern Augustines?[21]

I seem, therefore, to have arrived at the position of equating a sense of sin with the representation—in religious language—of that part of our inner world which, primarily as a result of our early experience, has built up patterns relating to our dis-ease with ourselves. In an attempt to be a little more precise I suggest that a sense of sin emanates from anxieties, threats, and conflicts in our inner world *and* defences against these. In later experience these contribute to what we call our moral sense, though I personally feel that they refer to more than the term 'morality' usually encapsulates, but at an earlier stage they are experienced as a source of non-moral threat or fear. This threat is a threat to the sense of our cohesion as a human unit. This perhaps tunes in to the theological and religious sense that the ultimate wages of sin are death and annihilation.

If we continue in this line of thought and go through the other phrases which have come to be associated with the result of sinfulness, then we can perhaps also see that they, too, have psychological correlates.

Omnipotence, Helplessness and Separation.

We have already seen that we need defences against the power and raw energy of our primitive, chaotic, and unordered selves. At a very early age there is not very much room for manoeuvre inside us—we have not got sufficiently developed mental equipment. Because of this, uncomfortable sensations and 'bad' experiences may have to be 'seen' by us as not belonging to us at all, but arising as it were from outside us, though the word 'see' suggests a more organized process than can possibly happen at that early stage. In psychological terms, though, we have to 'split'[22] ourselves and our experience, and project some of it out from us.

There is another phase that it is hypothesized that we all go through, namely 'omnipotence'. The intrinsic helplessness of our infant position means that we are in reality extremely dependent on our environment and another human being. We cannot manage the pain associated with any failure of the other and so have to deny our own helplessness and fantasize that we are in fact omnipotent, that we have all the power. We are the all-powerful being who can call up others at will simply by crying or beginning to show distress. Part of 'normal' development lies in our becoming able to move inwardly from this position to be confronted by the helplessness and the pain of realizing that the other is *separate* from us and cannot be controlled completely by us. She is not an extension of our own being.

We could suggest that the phase of infantile omnipotence corresponds with something in the story of Genesis 3 and the Garden of Eden. There it was the desire to know good and evil and partake of the tree of life—in short the desire to be as God—that provoked the 'Fall' and the consequent painful separation from God. We could therefore say that in part sin stands for defences against experiencing the painful feelings associated with the growth of separation and perceived abandonment. Though in the myth the omnipotence provoked the 'Fall', in psychological terms we would have to rephrase this. The growth in separateness is inevitable, and the desire and fantasy of omnipotence is the defence against it,

Fear and Alienation

At other stages when we have more mental equipment we do not have to expunge whole parts of ourselves. We can keep them inside, but at the cost of repressing them and make a split *within* ourselves rather than between us and the 'outside'. But in so far as whole parts of our being have to be repressed,[23] that is kept out of conscious awareness, our conscious being comes to function on three cylinders as it were, and in this sense we could come to see sin as a term used to express this state of alienation from the fullness of our being. As such it is again a defensive state.

Things are becoming complicated. From this perspective sin can represent *either* the tremendous forces within us against which we have to defend the integrity of our being, *or* the ways in which we do this defending. Neither of these is morally wrong in our usual definition of morality. The forces that threaten us could be seen as a source of nigh-intolerable affliction. Defences could be seen as weakness because they are not inevitably secure and can sometimes prevent large parts of our being from functioning.

Falling Short, Transgression

At a more developed stage, when we have more of a 'self', we can say that sin describes either our failure to live up to the injunctions of the conscious ego-ideal we are building up for ourselves or our transgressions against the partly conscious and partly unconscious prohibitions of that which has built up in us as our superego.

So Much for Sin—What of Our Sense of God?

At the earliest stage, when we cannot distinguish our-selves from our environment, and we are in reality very dependent on that environment, then God is both within and without us, and indeed almost is us. Our self and our mother, who in a strange sense, are also God to us, are indistinguishable from each other. Then our deepest fear must be of destroying and being destroyed, a fear of the annihilation of all that is. In the slightly more developed stage, the God (mother) is dimly known to be outside of us and 'other' to us. The deep fears are those of separation and of being abandoned. Later still, the primitive strength associated with the words 'destroy', 'annihilate', and 'aban-don' wanes. Our fear then is of offending the 'them'—parents and others. 'Them' may include God, who can be more definitely known now as outside us, but who, largely but not completely unbeknown to us, is reinforced by the God fashioned inside us through our experiences of the earlier stages. We can almost trace in this progression an analogue of the developments described in Genesis 1-3 from the undifferentiated void through the divided and differentiated creation to separateness, loss of the contaning security, and the consciousness of internal conflict.

On one level, these processes—if we are right in believing they do go on in us—take place whether we can put words to them to describe them or not, and whether we are conscious of them or not.

But the endpoint of Genesis 3 is a state of consciousness.

When Adam and Eve become conscious and know that they are naked they become *ashamed*.[24] For St Paul, writing a thousand years later, it was the advent of the law—of a set of prohibitions and injunctions—that made him conscious of sin, through his inability to fulfil its precepts.[25] And it is difficult to 'decide' whether the rise of consciousness is experienced as a 'good' thing or a 'bad' thing' for us. (I put 'decide' in quotes, because on one level it is irrelevant, for some development of consciousness is an inevitable for human beings.) Despite psychological theory 'saying' 'Consciousness is good for you', the awareness of their shame did not make it easier for Adam and Eve to understand and bear the consequences of their development. It made them want to run away and hide instead! The rise of consciousness of sin for St Paul made him feel more rather than less wretched, more rather than less helpless, and more in need of the rescuer that he found in Christ.

Shame and consciousness in this sense seem to be double-edged. They do not necessarily and automatically bring about the resolution of the disordered state, despite the claims of analytical psychotherapy for the beneficial results of increased consciousness.

Conscious feelings of *shame* develop when we fall short of our ego-ideal, which is one manifestation of the God inside us. We realize that we are not as we thought we were, but whether this puts us in a better overall place depends on whether this ego-ideal is realistic. If it is then feelings of shame may truly become a source for learning, changing, increased independence, and autonomy. But when the ego-ideal contains residual omnipotence or depends on a sustained denial of parts of ourselves— when it is too god-like and perfect in fact—then feelings of shame are likely to increase a sense of being exposed and vulnerable and of a fundamental alienation from ourselves and others for we have no means of resolving them. The need is rather for a modification of the ideal.

What applies to shame, also applies to *guilt*. The development of 'healthy' guilt may be equated with Winnicott's rise of concern.[26] Winnicott says that before a certain point of development the infant is ruthless. There is no guilt in the true sense of that word. Life is a series of more or less urgent needs which the environment must

fulfil. At a later stage the infant becomes concerned at
the effect his or her demands and feelings have on their
environment and particularly on the person of the mother.
Guilt before that point is not really concern but is the
sense of fear, rage, and threat engendered by frustration
of need or the lack of containment. As such it adds to our
disease rather than in any sense being part of resolving it.
It persecutes us.

Guilt at a later stage moves us on to concern for another
person and to begin to contain our own hostility and
frustration. We sense that we are related to the other in
both a positive and a negative way and we begin to tolerate
both. The story of Cain and Abel depicts the ruthless stage:
'Am I my brother's keeper?'[27] cries Cain and the vital element of concern for Abel is missing. Cain cannot grow and
make any true reparation for his deed, but is condemned
to wander the earth for ever. The rise of concern and
guilt requires some awareness of the other as separate
from us and as being able to be loved and hurt by us. It
involves the beginnings of personal responsibility. Only
that sort of guilt, which involves acceptance, containment,
and growing integration of hostile feelings into our being
can help us to grow. The 'guilt' feeling which is based on
fear will leave us stuck in suspicion, hostility, and threat
in relation to all that is not us. I think we shall see in the
next chapter that it is the capacity for developed concern
and guilt that makes forgiveness possible.

In summary, I have suggested that sin and sinfulness
have their roots in our very early experience and the
patterns laid down then. In so far as these experiences
are universal then sin is universal. If we or others talk of
'original righteousness' it seems that we are relating either
to a time of maximum defence against the turmoil of our
experience or to real experiences within that period when
things were good, so good that our every need and want
was securely met. Yet the one is a defence and the other
cannot last because of the development of separation
from the mother and the inevitable loss associated with
it. 'Original righteousness' is a misnomer, for righteousness does not really come into it; at the primitive stage of
development good and evil are not moral distinctions
but distinctions relating to quality of experience, for
example satisfaction or deprivation. Original 'bliss' may

therefore not be such a misnomer. 'Original guilt' must, I think, refer not to the more developed sense of concern, but to the earlier sense of persecuting threat or badness.

Against this background I would now like to look again at the seven so-called deadly sins'[28] to see if we can begin to understand how they came to be so adjudged. If we look at them in the context of early experience we can, I think, appreciate their life-and-death qualities, and see them all as being related to intolerable *fears*.

First, *pride*. I suggest that this relates to a state of omnipotence which as we have seen is extremely shaky and which, if persisted in, cuts us off from a mature and reciprocal dependence on another. Omnipotence persisted in must lead to ultimate isolation, and is forever vulnerable to its opposite—nothingness—erupting through. The feared opposite and 'punishment' of pride is annihilation.

Rather interestingly, *envy* and *gluttony* perhaps go together. Gluttony, or greed, is the ultimate end of wanting, wanting so much that the fear is that there will be nothing of the other left. Envy[29] is a wanting to which is added the need to destroy the provider and what is provided just because the wanting cannot be satisfied and the other has the good rather than ourselves. The fear lies in the neediness of the one who wants, but the desire to destroy perverts and poisons the supplies that could be had. That which could be good becomes bad. In this way envy also seems to be the root of the sin against the Holy Spirit—which attributes the works of a good God to the devil. Something good is made evil and destroyed. If we in this way succeed in destroying mother, the source of the good, God, or however we like to frame it, we cannot be forgiven; for there is nothing good left to hold, contain and forgive us. That good has become evil and henceforth is feared for it will work against us. The ultimate fear associated with gluttony is of scooping out and emptying the good source on which we depend. The ultimate fear accompanying envy is of perverting and destroying the good source on which we depend. In neither case can we go on living.

In the cases of *anger, sloth* and *avarice* perhaps the ultimate fear moves from that of ceasing to exist to that of separation and abandonment. Anger is perhaps the halfway house here, for there is still some sense that

anger may destroy the other. But even if it does not, even
if the other and ourselves are not destroyed, there is a
separation, even a rift between us which can feel to us to
be life-destroying. Sloth is the name I would want to give
to a state of withdrawal and apathy which, as long as it
lasts, will refuse to make contact with another and so cut
off the possibilities of nourishment and growth. It is not
itself death, but rather a kind of frozeness, and if we cannot come out of it or somebody cannot help us out it can
be as good as death for the most vital part of our being.

Avarice seems to belong to a later period of development when we are not so completely dependent and have
acquired the ability to withhold, and not to give. Again of
itself it will not kill us; of itself it may even token a healthy
desire for autonomy and independence. But it becomes a
separateness that is isolating because it is rigid and
forced. Only giving can bridge the divide, and persistent
avarice or withholding of gift is inimical to the growth of
love and concern. It is perhaps born of an insecurity that
one will not have enough to give and a fear of relating to
another because of what they might take, but if it goes on
forever it must lead to a loneliness of a death-like quality
—a state to which the *Scrooges* of this world bear witness.

Lust is almost the odd man out. It has come to be
focused in sexual desire and sexual possession, and it
is not immediately obvious why this should have happened. Perhaps its real root lies in possession, and the
need to possess rather than to be possessed, and it is in
some ways a conglomerate of all our desire and energy.
We could see it as the id run riot. Sexual power has perhaps become the working metaphor for it because of the
ubiquity of the sexual drive and the element of the giving
up of personal boundaries in the act of sexual intercourse.
The fear must be of desire gone mad inside us— could it
lead to our disintegration? It may later have come to represent our desire to intrude and possess what is not ours
to possess, such as the relationship between our parents.
Essentially it seems to be about devouringness, posses-
siveness, loss of control, loss of identity, and put in this
form the threat to our survival and well-being is more
obvious. Because all these things can become a factor in
adult sexuality, and because genital sexuality is one of the
most personally powerful human drives, the concept of
lust has become 'attached' to this part of us—so much so

that the root of original sin has also in myth become attached here. It is as if sexuality has become the barometer and the location of all desire and all potentiality for disordered desire.

We can therefore, if we are so minded, find psychological fears and mechanisms that may appropriately attach to each of the seven deadly sins so as to begin to give us an explanation of why they are so called. They do each present a fundamental threat to our being and they each arise ultimately in relation not only to ourselves but to another. On this basis too, sin will also have an unconscious as well as conscious dimension, for the most deadly of mechanisms are not usually known to us in their full strength and entirety.

I have in these pages attempted some sort of 'translation' of sin and sin(s) into psychological experiences focusing on those of childhood and infancy. I think that nothing else does justice to the universality, hiddenness, strength, and mystery of the origin of that which we know as sin. I am suggesting that our experiences in our earliest environment and earliest relationships are *analagous* to what theologians describe as sin, and furthermore that it is how we negotiate this early period that influences our later experience and understanding of sin. The question I have *not* tackled and will have to return to in a later chapter is whether the relationship between sin and certain psychological experiences is one of analogy or *identity*. Can we say that God, sin and the relationship between them are *like* our early environment and experience or do we have to go further and ask whether the sense of sin and therefore also the sense of God *derive from* that experience?

I am not answering that question now. All I am wanting to say at this point is that there is a 'human inside' to the concept and experience of sin that parallels parts of our human experience. When the language of sin and that of human experience tune in with each other and can extend into the depth of our being then sin recovers an authentic meaning for us. When there is no tuning in and no 'fit' then sin becomes other, external, and meaningless to us.

Yet the mystery of the nature and origin of sin and evil is but half the story. The rest is *forgiveness* and the growth of *love*, and it to these that we now need to turn.

Notes

1. William Shakespeare, *The Tragedy of Macbeth*, Act I, Scene 5.
2. See Chapter 2, Note 20.
3. See Chapter 2, Note 17.
4. See Chapter 2, Note 23.
5. See Chapter 2, Note 23.
6. Mary Anne Coate, *Clergy Stress* (SPCK 1989), especially pp. 52-3.
7. The literature on learning theory is vast and technical, but for a helpful introduction and summary see chapter 8 by Philip Evans in J. Radford and E. Govier (eds.), *A Textbook of Psychology* (Routledge 1991).
8. Originally developed in relation to the treatment of depression, the theory behind cognitive therapy has wider applications. See A. T. Beck, *Cognitive Therapy and the Emotional Disorders* (Penguin 1978), chapters 1-4; D. Rowe, *The Courage to Live* (Fontana 1991), chapters 1, 2 and 5; and D. Rowe, *Depression: The Way Out of Your Prison* (Routledge and Kegan Paul 1983), chapter 3.
9. The following may be of use as general references to psychoanalysis: C. Rycroft, *A Critical Dictionary of Psychoanalysis* (Penguin 1972); R. D. Hinshelwood, *A Dictionary of Kleinian Thought* (Free Association Books 1991); H. Segal, *Klein* (Fontana 1979); N. Symington, *The Analytic Experience* (Free Association Books 1986). For Freud's ideas, see Rycroft, *Dictionary*, pp. 38-40, 66, 160-1; S. Freud, *New Introductory lectures on Psychoanalysis* (1933), Standard Edition, volume 22 (Hogarth Press 1964), and S. Freud, *The Ego and the Id* (1923), Standard Edition, volume 19 (Hogarth Press 1961).
10. See Rycroft, *Dictionary*, pp. 38-41.
11. See C. G. Jung, *Collected Works* (Routledge and Kegan Paul 1953), volume 9, Part 11; and A. Storr, *Jung* (Fontana 1973), especially chapters 5 and 6.
12. See A. Freud, *The Ego and the Mechanisms of Defence* (Hogarth Press 1937), and Juliet Mitchell (ed.), *The Selected Melanie Klein* (Penguin 1986), chapters 1 and 2.
13. Some defence mechanisms are: splitting—unconscious separation of extremes of experience, e.g. 'good' and 'bad'; projection—seeing only in others characteristics which belong to the self; denial—unconscious distortion of unpleasant reality; somatization—conversion of unpleasant feelings into body symptoms; repression—unconscious 'forgetting' of experiences or aspects of self. For a summary of defence mechanisms, see D. Brown and J. Pedder, *Introduction to Psychotherapy* (Tavistock Publications 1979), pp. 25-33; and for some illustration and explication of them see Coate,

Clergy Stress, especially pp. 54–64.

14. Thinking about 'object relationship' developed particularly in the British school of analysts pioneered by Fairbairn, Balint, Winnicott, and Klein. See Rycroft, *Dictionary*, p. 101; Hinshelwood, *Dictionary*, pp. 363–73; and G. Kohon (ed.), *The British School of Psychoanalysis—The Independent Tradition* (Free Association Books 1986), pp. 20-2.

15. D. W. Winnicott, *The Theory of the Parent-Infant Relationship* (1960) in D. W. Winnicott, *The Maturational Processes and the Facilitating Environment* (Karnac Books and the Institute of Psychoanalysis 1990), p. 39. (First published Hogarth Press 1965.)

16. See Hinshelwood, *Dictionary*, pp. 32-8, 324-5.

17. See, for example, D. W. Winnicott, *Primary Maternal Preoccupation* (1956) in D. W. Winnicott, *Through Paediatrics to Psychoanalysis* (Hogarth Press 1975), chapter 24, p. 300; or *Ego Distortion in terms of True and False Self* (1960), in *The Maturational Processes*, chapter 12, p. 140.

18. A hypothetical construct used by most psychoanalytic thinkers. For some elucidation see D. W. Winnicott, *The Depressive Position in Emotional Development* (1954-5) in *Through Paediatrics*, especially pp. 272-3; or D. W. Winnicott, *Human Nature* (Free Association Books 1988), especially Part III, chapters 1 and 2.

19. See, for example, the story of Esau and Jacob in Genesis 27, or the folk-tale enshrined in Job 1-2.

20. See Chapter 2, Note 23.

21. See Chapter 2, Note 23.

22. This is a form of psychological defence, used when we cannot bear to experience our total feelings and unconsciously divide them. See Chapter 3, Note 13.

23. This is a form of psychological defence that makes some of our feelings or experience unconscious to us. See Chapter 3, Note 13.

24. Genesis 3.7-10.

25. Romans 5.13; 7.7-8.

26. See D. W. Winnicott, *The Development of the Capacity for Concern* (1963) in *The Maturational Processes*, p. 73.

27. Genesis 4.9.

28. See Chapter 2, Note 20.

29. Psychologically, the concept of envy was developed by Melanie Klein. See M. Klein, *Envy and Gratitude, and other works* (Virago Press 1988). For a helpful explication and illustration see Symington, *Analytic Experience*, pp. 271-4.

FOUR

Forgive and Forget
or
The Human Face of Forgiveness

'Forgiveness', unlike 'sin', has ordinary human currency—it is a word we all tend to use whether we are of a religious persuasion or not. It seems best, therefore, to begin to explore this theme from within this ordinary stance and then have another look at it through the spectacles of the theological and psychological dimensions.

I want to go back to some of the case studies of the earlier chapters, primarily *Sally* and *Carol*, *Pat* and *John*, *Matthew*, *Anne*, *Simon*, *Stewart* and *Sheila*. We may need reminding of them.

Pat, *John*, and *Matthew* live within the religious framework; indeed *Matthew* is the rector of the parish. *Pat* and *John* have something deeply unresolved between them and in their relationship—the abortion that *Pat* persists in saying that *John* made her have and about which she feels guilty, deeply resentful, and angry. She cannot forgive *John* and their relationship is degenerating into nightly battles featuring acrimonious exchanges and overmuch alcohol. *Matthew* is also caught in an unforgiving fury over the incident of the near-rape of his daughter. His rage would fly everywhere if he could let it; at the rest of the family who didn't protect the little girl from the ordeal, at the man who did it, and at himself for his awkwardness and sense of impotence in the face of the incident and its aftermath. He goes on preaching and pronouncing forgiveness in the name of the God he was ordained to serve, but on the human level he himself cannot forgive.

Sally and *Carol* do not, as far as we know, have any religious belief or framework. They are wondering if and

78

how to make up a longstanding and bitter quarrel in which each slandered the other at work, carried tittle-tattle, and ultimately could not bear the sight of each other until one of them changed job and they were not constantly forced to be in each other's company. They now feel rather sheepish about it all, and wonder how on earth they got into this position. Neither wants really to lose a friend for ever and they would like to try to make things up. Why ruin a decent friendship which has been going for several years before all this happened, and just *how did* it escalate so badly? But they are not sure how to attempt reconciliation. They suppose they had better meet, hopefully through the good offices of a mutual friend, but what will it be like and what on earth will they say to each other?

Furthermore, will it actually do any good? It is a risk to take. They might hurt each other more, but could they actually resolve it or even patch it up? They don't use the word forgiveness much, but they do know that somebody is probably going to have to say sorry to somebody and preferably both of them to each other.

What does forgiveness mean on the ordinary human level, and why is it important to try for it anyway? We can see why in the cases of *Sally* and *Carol*, and *Pat* and *John*. For both couples there is a relationship at stake; one has already broken down and the parties have a mind to try to renew it. The other—the closer relationship of actually living together in partnership—is in constant danger of breaking down. It hasn't happened yet, but it is only a matter of time before it does, unless something can be changed quickly.

We can also see why *Matthew* needs and wants to get back on to more real terms with his family. We are not told that there is any overt quarrelling going on, but we do gather that there is an inner rift in *Matthew* himself. He is not able to feel that he is himself with his nearest and dearest even if they are more or less unaware of this. He lives under strain and with a sense of isolation. It is not immediately clear what, if anything, he can do about his feelings towards the person who assaulted his daughter. There is no relationship between them. *Matthew* does not know the man, and neither does anyone else, for he ran off before anyone could get a good look at him and the police have so far been unable to come up with any results to their enquiries. *Matthew* is caught in a fury towards an unknown somebody it looks as if he may never set eyes on, who has no face and no shape for him. At least, not most of the time, but sometimes he conjures up inside his mind a face, an evil face, a face he'd like to smash to pulp. This inner face comes to torment him; it inflames and fuels his rage. He pushes it away and hopes for an inner calm and resignation, but to no avail—the face comes back and with it the all-consuming rage or sometimes a shivering ice-cold hatred.

Stewart, the gay man who works for the relief agency, is caught in another way. Not for him the fire of rage at the church and society who reject him and his homosexuality. For him there is only the way of withdrawal and isolation. In part this may be because of the reality of the fear of being ostracized should he be found out. In part, too, it is perhaps because he cannot face his strong, active feelings —they remain repressed, pushed down out of sight and out of consciousness—he can only feel shame, fear, and loneliness.

Move on now to the other instances—those where forgiveness took place within an explicitly religious framework and in which God himself is seen as its agent, though for the moment we shall focus only upon the more human face of these religious encounters. Remember *Anne*, the overworked housewife and mother who makes her weekly confession of feelings of irritation, loss of temper, and fear of her own desire for escape from a wretched marriage and longings for a bit of care to be taken of her. From her story we gather that something like this features most weeks in her confession. Nothing much changes. We are not told that she is depressed, but the picture the story conjures up for me is nevertheless rather bleak. Religious forgiveness may be keeping her going—perhaps the gentle attitude of the priest is keeping her from excesses of guilt and driving herself. We also gather that the priest does not have very much hope that *Anne* will be able to use his counsel to relax, and we do not come away from listening to that confession with much sense of a renewed and revitalized relationship, either with God or with human beings. We suspect it will be the same next week and the week after, and probably the week after that.

Robert and *Simon* are a little different. In their cases the religious acts of conversion or the prayer for forgiveness do seem to bring some change into the situation, possibly because in each case a 'crisis' existed or had been provoked. The mission address alerted *Robert* to parts of himself he was unaware of and to a certain aridness in a life hitherto found reasonably satisfactory. The light that subsequently came into and on to him was quite new. *Simon* sought out the vicar in a moment of personal crisis sparked off by the fear of impending illness or even death and the guilt of a long-standing relationship outside his marriage. Something new happened to him too. We sense that he went away a little less burdened and a little comforted by the sympathetic listening of another human being. It spurred him on to try to change something, to come out of isolation and confide in his wife—certainly about his illness and possibly even about the relationship. Though let it be said here that there can be a problem about confessional honesty on the purely human level.

Stewart feels he needs to keep his homosexuality a secret. Would it in fact be worse rather than better for him if he let it become known? In a similar vein, will *Simon* be *wise* to tell his wife about his long-standing adulterous relationship? In his need for an unburdening and the inclination of his mood towards confession it might well help *him*, but what of *her*? How is it going to make her feel, and will she be able to take it, especially at a moment when their relationship is going to need to be particularly strong as *Simon* struggles to come to terms with his illness?

In these two human scenarios there lies a dilemma that is not present in the religious act of confession, nor in the confessional-like privacy and neutrality of a counselling or psychotherapeutic relationship. The counsellor or therapist is usually not our neighbour or closely involved with our everyday life, nor does he or she normally have a vested interest in the other significant people in our lives. We presume that God can take all we throw at him anyway. In these situations unburdening and total honesty is what is needed and what usually helps. But it is a brave or naive person who assumes that this will always be so between human beings. Are there not, in fact, times when honesty can impede, rather than further, the process

of forgiveness and reconciliation? Ideally, if the religious
and psychotherapeutic situations were anything like true
prototypes of human interaction, honesty is seen to
further forgiveness, but many of us have come to ask—
often rather ruefully after an event—if this is truly so in
everyday reality.

Perhaps this is because there are, to my mind, two
kinds of honesty. There is mature honesty, and what I
call compulsive, infantile honesty. The second kind drives
itself by a need for release in the one who is being honest
or making confession. Unless such people are honest,
totally honest, they cannot feel 'good' inside. Yet the
accent is one-sided; it is 'How do *I* feel?' never 'How does
the *other person* feel?' What I am calling mature honesty
can weigh itself and its words and is not concerned for
relief at any price and at any cost to those around; it may
decide to hold itself back. Protagonists of the compulsive
kind of honesty would perhaps label this *concealment*, less
than the truth, less than the ideal. I would call it *containment*, involving perhaps a degree of ongoing discomfort
in the person doing the containing but with a concern for
the feelings and being of the listener as well as of the
talker.

This is a difficult area. I may seem to have forsaken
truth and credibility and got into doubtful shades of grey.
We may think that true forgiveness and reconciliation
depends on nothing being kept back, nothing being hidden
and perhaps this should indeed be the ideal. But the
whole point is that life on the human level is not ideal
and is normally rather mixed—mixed joy and sorrow, pain
and pleasure, hurt and hurting. In this climate honesty
may not always be the best or most compassionate policy.

From this review of some of our stories what can we
now glean about the goal of and the conditions for the
process of forgiveness on the human level?

In any 'forgiveness-needing' situation there are often
at least three unpleasant sets of feelings causing or contributing to the stress and estrangement: anger, guilt, and
isolation. They may occur in all gradations of each of
them, and in any of a number of combinations.

These feelings seek discharge—or to be made to go
away completely. In any event they seek some easing;
forgiveness, it seems, is one way to achieve this. Another
way is action, which can be constructive, as when anger

against injustice is channelled into search for reform. Action can, though, be very destructive as when it is motivated by a need for revenge, or when it is only an agitated thrashing around in the hope of exterminating the source of the awful feelings—often the other person or the relationship. Or the feelings can stay inside and become inwardly destructive; people become anxious, depressed, and effectively paralysed in their being.

Forgiveness thus *seems* to be born of *personal need*; a need to feel better inside, to become free of inner forces which threaten to poison us or tear us apart. But not all human beings appear to have this need, or sometimes it takes a long time for it to surface. *Iago* seemed devoid of it, the *Macbeths* took a long time to begin to reach it, and even then it is difficult to see in *Lady Macbeth's* sick agitated sleepwalking a true move towards the seeking of forgiveness—it is more of a compulsion motivated for the easing of torment by any means. *Pat* and *John* also have not yet reached the stage of wanting forgiveness; they are still intent on maintaining their fury and tearing their relationship apart.

The length of time it may take us, individually, to want to go from anger and hate to forgiveness varies. The possible reasons for this variation I shall explore more in the next chapter. But the fact and extent of this variation do not, I think, alter my fundamental point that the move towards forgiveness starts from an awareness of a deep *personal* need.

To this extent it 'fits' with the ideas we have teased out about sin. If sin represents the sum total of our disordered feelings and impulses that make us less than at ease with ourselves and other people, forgiveness is sought as a way to relieve this disorder. It may be sought by either party to a breakdown or disordered state—the sinner or the sinned against. It is often doubtful whether this distinction can really be maintained, for the feelings, though different, are equally uncomfortable for both. We could well say that *Matthew* was far more sinned against than sinning in that the rape of his daughter came as a bolt from the blue and as something in which he had no part and over which he had no control. By the time his fury took him over and was consuming him his needs to forgive and for forgiveness became very confused.

It is partly the conviction that forgiveness is born of

need that which always makes me sad when I read of compensation cases being pursued to extremes. I feel sad even in the cases of well-documented and totally acknowledged disasters, such as the losses of the *Herald of Free Enterprise* and the *Marchioness*, the Lockerbie bombing or even the terror in Northern Ireland. I say this diffidently as it is fatally easy to seem to be pontificating from a safe 'untouched' place, whereas I myself would probably not stand up well to the ravages and sufferings these disasters produce if I were intimately involved in them. Yet I do think that as long as we are hell-bent on getting compensation and punishment for the offenders there remains a profound isolation and estrangement in our inner selves. For the *external* aggressive energy, even hate, required to maintain and pursue a compensation cause or claim also keeps the *inner* anger and hate going *without* a chance to stop, inwardly reflect, and in the end have the possibility of coming to terms with the loss and the pain.

I do not, in writing this, want to be seeming just to reject all need for recompense, nor do I want social and other injustices to go unchecked, unconfronted, or unmodified. I continue, obstinately, to have some sense that these are best pursued by those who have, emotionally, something in themselves to spare and not by those who are temporarily completely eaten up by their feelings.

People who are unable to countenance the possibility of forgiveness may be seriously impeded in their search for some peace of mind.

In this I am not advocating a passive submission to injustice, aggression, or fate—particularly in the sense of identification with the sufferings of Christ or other religious tenets. But I think there must be an equally active *inner* way of seeking wholeness first within oneself and then being able to go out and work with the outside people and situations.

For rather the same reason, even if it looks at first to be almost a diametrically opposite situation, I tend to be equally suspicious of what I call *instant* forgiveness, peace and reconciliation, instant recovery from bereavement, instant loving of our enemies in the face of torture or disaster. If clinging on to fury and hate impedes a true inner sense of forgiveness so also, I think, does this for-giveness programme. For most, if not all, people in situa-tions that need forgiveness the anger, hate, and also often guilt are real and cannot be denied, which is exactly what the instant forgiveness programme seems to me to do.

What I am saying is that forgiveness is a *process*. It is not a once-for-all moment. It starts in a sense of *need*, often after a period of being ravaged by strong, even violent, negative feelings. These feelings and the need have both to be truly *felt* to make the process possible and fruitful.

But this is indeed only the start of something, and so far, for a process called forgiveness, it looks paradoxically selfish and self-seeking. I have written as if I saw forgive-ness—whether the bestowing of it or the receiving of it— serving primarily as the fulfilment of a personal human need. To stop here would be to miss its salient point. To my mind forgiveness is always to do with *relationship* with *another*; the 'other' may not be a close and intimate other, though it often is. The 'other' can be an unknown person or an institution or even a system or a world view. Forgiveness starts in the acknowledgement of personal need, but if it also ends there it is not really forgiveness and will be doomed to failure.

My earlier point on compulsive honesty becomes rel-evant here. The personal need may be for completely honest confession of fault, but this may take no account of the feelings of the other person. *Raskolnikov* virtually walked the globe seeking someone to whom he might confess, or a situation in which he might make confession and receive his due punishment. His agitated wanderings do not seem to me at that point to be a search for forgiveness rooted in his relationships with others, but rather a plea for release from personal torment.

It is here that we begin to need that most mysterious and often most abused of words—*love*. Love has synonyms, notably concern for another, empathy, compassion and reparation. These have the one thing, fundamentally, in common; they are all directed towards another, and to the extent which they are they militate against isolation, withdrawal, and lonely hatred. One of the best illustra-tions of the transformation of a human being through the redirection of his energy from miserly self-seeking to compassionate other-seeking is perhaps that of *Scrooge* in

Dicken's *Christmas Carol*. *Scrooge* the miser becomes *Scrooge* the philanthropist, but also changes from *Scrooge* the isolated one to *Scrooge* who can find joy and fulfilment in the company of other people.

Sally and *Carol* of our stories are feeling their way towards this transformation. They have some sense that the way forward lies in meeting and getting back into relationship. The main effect of *Simon's* encounter with *Martin* in his role of confessor is to enable *Simon* to go away and relieve his isolation by sharing some of his difficulty with his wife. *Stewart* is not ready to speak to someone else yet. His isolation is still all-pervasive. It cuts him off from family, friends, church community, and society at large. He thinks that they cannot forgive him for what he is, but I think there is the strong possibility that he cannot forgive them for their treatment of him, and so has to turn away from them.

Sustained turning away is, I think, ultimately inimical to the process of forgiveness for it cannot allow the growth of concern, understanding and love. *Separation* there may have to be for a time as indeed was the case with *Sally* and *Carol*. This sort of separation comes when we need to be able to see things straight. The other person may have come to take on too much for us; they have become the crime or the hateful feeling personified or incarnate, as it were. As long as that persists we cannot see them as themselves but only as that which is hurting us. They may also be standing for a distorted and unknown part of ourselves—the hurting or betraying or cruel part of us. Alternatively, a possible real part of them can come to represent for us the whole of them and we cannot see beyond it. When such distortions of perception as these have set in we may need a period of cooling off in order to have a chance of getting things back into perspective.

Paradoxically, the separation must not be too long because projections and distortions also flourish when there is no contact with actual reality. If we never see or meet the hated one then we can keep our picture going undisturbed by the reality of the actual person. Separation is useful, even necessary in the short-time; long-term it may add to the false tints of our picture. Only when we can again see the other person as they really are is it possible to begin to mend our relationship with them. It is when the distorted picture persists and cannot be relieved that it becomes most unlikely that forgiveness can take place.

What, though, is the *nub* of this human process we call forgiveness? We have looked at some of its preconditions; we must feel the need for it and want it, and this is true of both parties in any breakdown situation. Otherwise it cannot easily happen. I say it must be reciprocal, but in some instances it is possible for it to be a bit more one-sided.

We cannot be forgiven by another if he or she does not want to forgive us, but it is possible to forgive someone else even if they do not acknowledge it or even feel the need for it. In this case what we are doing is allowing some process to happen *within our own internal world*.[1] We are forgiving this person or thing as they exist in our mind and heart and that, though falling short of a full reconciliation between two actual people, is something rather than nothing. Similarly, if another person will not forgive us we can do something to help ourselves, though it is much harder this way. We can in fact forgive ourselves and this means taming the image of the other person inside us so that that image no longer nags at us or persecutes us. When we do it inside ourselves the hope is that our inner world becomes more benign; we are also made more free and ready to recognize potentially helping and reconciling changes in the actual external people and world around us.

So forgiveness is essentially something about changing our *inner* dispositions—the imaginary people and configurations in that organization of images we call our inner world and which I explored in the earlier chapters on sin. This inner change is necessary and fundamental, but there are other elements too. In the external world the process of forgiveness usually involves some acknowledgement of responsibility—the 'I'm sorry'—and often some reparative move or gesture. The way this process works is mysterious. Do changes in our inner world facilitate changes in our external world, or is it the other way round? I hope to shed some light on this in the next chapter. Here I want just to say that assumption of responsibility and growth in concern and reparative capacity are a feature of both inner and outer processes.

Reparation is a double-edged sword. It can so easily

become confused with placation. True reparative movements stem from a genuine concern for the other person
and a desire to make good any damage they may have
suffered and sustained at our hands. Placation is born of
a concern in us to ward off the continued wrath of the
other. Many a parent and child know intuitively the difference between the two without having to call them by
their long names. We have the familiar parental cry, 'And
don't think you can just suck up to me and expect everything to be all right—you have to be really sorry and
show that you are.' In other words, placation will not
work. Or we have the shy movement of a child back to
its parents having become temporarily estranged from
them—perhaps with some small gift or creation, perhaps
not—but the element of true concern is unmistakable.

Of course in the end no concern however genuine is
completely altruistic. As I have indicated, the process of
forgiveness stems from a personal *need* rather than the
spirit of largesse. But the extent to which this need can be
mixed with real concern for the other person makes the
difference between placation, which may in the end go
nowhere, and reparation which heralds a new beginning
and the potential for something better.

This is a very salient point. Forgiveness cannot take us
back to where we were before the breakdown happened.
In one sense if it could it would be unfortunate for that
would be the best recipe for getting in the same mess
again! It is not totally wise to 'forgive *and* forget', but
this interpretation of the aphorism needs qualification.

If to forgive *and not* forget means that the feelings of
injury and rage are still harboured, and waiting in the
wings to reassert themselves at every moment, then the
relationship is still flawed and broken. Forgiveness has to
require some sort of new start when the memories of
the past do not automatically shape the expectations and
climate of the present and future. But this is far easier
said than done. We are often, even quite involuntarily, in
the state of 'once bitten, twice shy'. It is difficult not to
live in some sort of fear that the same thing may happen
again. What, we may ask, has fundamentally changed so
as to prevent this happening? We cannot answer this
question to our assured satisfaction so we are scared to
take the risk and go back into the relationship or situation

wholeheartedly. This in itself can increase the likelihood of our fear being fulfilled. But there is a fine line between this level of distrust which can be paralysing and potentially poisonous and what I call a healthy realism about the possibilities of the new situation. Those who close their eyes and ears to what has happened and to all possibility of it ever happening again may not be able to make a 'redeemed' situation work. They are likely to walk back on all fours into the same old situation. We cannot 'unhave' the feelings we had or pretend that we did not have them or that the awful thing never happened. All these are now indelibly part of ours and the other's history.

So in a way 'forgive but do not forget' has a profound ring of truth in it. It is not possible, nor may it be wise, to forget in the sense of deny or blot out. Some memory will and must remain. But it is the way it remains or lives in us that makes the difference. It does not have to be the dark harbouring of pain and hatred that we saw, for example, in *Iago*. The essential other ingredient is something that comes into the orbit of the word *transformation*—if we want a word with religious overtones—or *integration* if we are feeling for something more psychological. These words, each in their own way, stand for what happens when the memory of the feelings that we cannot forget interacts—*in full consciousness or as full consciousness as is possible*—with a growing desire to take responsibility and the arousal of empathic concern. A 'successful' such interaction is of the essence of a deep and lasting forgiveness.

In simpler terms: when hate and love meet what happens? Does anything happen? Will one survive the other? As I hope to show in the next chapter, both religious and psychological dimensions claim that something does happen. A new amalgam, as it were, of feelings is forged. But since we cannot go back in time this new amalgam will have the quality of *experience* not *innocence*. It may necessarily include the acceptance of loss— whether the loss be the tangible loss of some aspects of a relationship or the less tangible loss of ideals of self and others—and it may properly involve a grief and *mourning* for what was and now cannot be. The love inherent in forgiveness will have to show something of the quality of compassion; it cannot be love in its first so-called innocent bloom.

The act and process of forgiveness thus to me always includes an element of quiet grief, as well as the resurgence of something we may want to call quiet joy at the restitution of contact and of relationship. It does not normally happen all at once. It has to grow and often has to be worked at very hard. *Sally* and *Carol* are probably going to find their first meeting difficult. They are likely to be wary of each other, diffident and a bit awkward. Neither of them is likely to be able to say quite what they want to all at once or even at all in a first encounter. How much they want that relationship to be restored is likely to determine how much work they put into it, and to determine the quality of their mutual forgiveness.

Pat and *John* are not at this stage. As far as we can see neither of them has been able to say the necessary 'I'm sorry'. And there is an additional difficulty for them. A baby has been lost. Something irreparable has happened. That loss cannot be made up. There may be another baby, but there cannot be that baby and they somehow will have to deal with this memory. As we have seen, an element of irreparable loss is inevitable in all breakdown-and-forgiveness situations. Things cannot be just the same as they were before. Where something of what is lost is tangible in the way that the aborted baby is, which is always so in situations involving actual damage or death, then it must be harder to deal with—both outside and inside. The loss is too real and the reminder too constant and all-pervasive for the pain to heal easily.

It is in these cases, particularly, that much of the work of forgiveness has to be done inside each person. In other situations we might be able to get by without having to do this, but here it becomes imperative. It may seem obvious that *John* of our story is going to need to look at why he did not want the baby. It may have been for superficial economic reasons, but there may also have been deeper, hidden fears in him about the personal responsibilities of becoming a father, or things 'left over' from his own experience of having a father.

Pat is more complicated. On first sight she looks the aggrieved, even innocent, victim and she could easily become stuck in this role and with her feelings toward the actual *John* sitting across the table from her with the whisky bottle in his hand. Unless she can reflect in herself and in terms of her own personal history what the loss of the baby and motherhood means to her as a woman and the child of another woman, *Pat* is not going to find it easy or perhaps even possible to sort out her feelings towards *John*. It is possible that she, too, was anxious about the baby. Perhaps even she didn't want it, for reasons deeply personal but unknown to her. There may be feelings that she has repressed and could not bear to be conscious to her. As long as she cannot look into herself *John* will remain as the convenient outside place in which to locate all feelings of anxiety, anger with her own childhood and her own mother and others. As long as he is seen to be the author of the abortion, she can believe it was *not* her. She can decide the nasty feelings are in *him*, not in *her*.

There is a real problem about forgiveness in this 'split' situation. Many instances of severe and intractable breakdown of relationship are 'split' in this way. By 'split' I mean that one set of feelings is felt to be located in one side of the breakdown and another set of feelings is located in the other.[2] It goes without saying that the 'nasty' and unrespectable feelings are by definition those which the other person has, not oneself, except in the case where one person is determined to stay as the villain of the piece who is beyond hope and beyond redemption. Then the other person is usually all-worthy and oneself is all-sinful. The process of *forgiveness* involves the bringing together and the integrating of often opposite feelings. Normally this means the bringing together of such sets of feelings within the same person. We can then become a 'bigger' person with more to spare in terms of our capacity to be concerned about the other person and our ability to offer them something.

If *Pat* and *John* do achieve forgiveness in their relationship on this basis, it will necessarily involve them each in facing parts of themselves that they are currently conveniently seeing only as in the other person. The prospect of this may be, even if they are unaware of this, just too frightening and painful to embark upon, and as long as this is so it is most unlikely that forgiveness can take place. Something will always block it. There will always be the household chore found left carelessly undone at the moment where it looked as if they might achieve a

breakthrough, or the sudden flash of irritation in the middle
of a more constructive talk that immediately ruined it and
put them back to square one. Blockages will occur if either
of them has a lot unconsciously invested in not getting
into the difficult and painful parts of themselves. If forgiveness doesn't start at home, that is within each of us,
the odds are that it may not start at all, or will in its turn
be hastily aborted.

It is not only in attempts at reconciliation between warring people that forgiveness needs to start at home. It is
equally true for other situations. In the present climate
of church and even social thinking *Stewart* is unlikely to
find *enough* acceptance of what he is either from the
church, the local community, or his family. To be sure, given
the Bishops' report on homosexuality in 1991,[3] there is
hope for some change at least for the laity of which he is
a member. The report *seems* to be saying to him that it is
acceptable for him to be homosexual and to act as if he is.
Yet the incipient double standard of that report is likely
to prevent it having the full impact that it might have on
either clergy or laity. It is an advance on previous thinking,
but it may not be seen as such. It may not be enough for
one so chronically ashamed and withdrawn as is *Stewart*.
The laity, as 'graciously permitted' to be practising homosexuals are likely to feel guilty and possibly patronized,
given that this 'permission' is set in the context of the
promulgation of the intrinsic perfection of heterosexual
love and Christian marriage. The clergy are likely to feel
hostile, both to the episcopate and to the laity since little
is being given to them and much is being demanded.

In this climate *Stewart* is unlikely to feel secure enough
to emerge from his isolation and feel a worthwhile person again. The situation is just not supportive enough,
and potentially far too unpredictable. The only person
from whom *Stewart* could find forgiveness and acceptance is the one who is, to an extent, in his own control and
that is *himself*. Yet I have to say 'to an extent' because patterns laid down in the past are making it difficult for him
to love himself. He had a childhood during which he did
not dare approach his parents with anything like the
truth. He 'knew', rightly or wrongly, that they would reject
him. He has been isolated too long, and he is currently in
a pattern of what we might call pseudo-reparation for his

presumed sinfulness in his selfless workaholic lifestyle. This is pseudo-reparation because it is not the fruit of a sense of being accepted for what he is and what he can offer from his experience. He *drives* himself, partly to punish himself and partly to keep his feelings at bay. The 'driven' pattern seems more placatory than reparative.

As with *Stewart*, so with *Sheila*. She is the pillar of the church nightly tormented by her imperfections and never able to feel the love of God, nor that of humankind. God apparently cannot forgive her and make her feel good inside. We, from outside, can discern the roots of this in her relationship with her father for whom she was never good enough. He was the stern implacable father who, though now dead, lives on, but inside her rather than outside her. If she is going to be able to feel more at peace with herself and with God her inner world is going to have to change. It seems to be peopled only with harsh, unforgiving figures. More benign images are needed for her to be able to forgive herself and integrate a love of self with her habitual self-hate. But how on earth is she going to be able to make this change or somehow let it happen? People cannot just 'decide' to make changes in their deep inner world. Prayer and God are clearly not working for her, and her inner distress must be becoming cumulative, thus making the task even harder.

It is here that we approach the essential mystery in forgiveness. What makes it possible for some people to set in motion and maintain the process by themselves and without outside help, either religious or psychological? This seems to be what *Sally* and *Carol* are trying to do; we do not know whether they will succeed, but people do. Some people cannot sustain the process by internal means alone, but they can do it partly externally and partly internally. They have a benign enough inner world for them to be able to absorb shifts in the *mores* of society, or they can take in from the religious dimension—through prayer, or the liturgy, or the ritual of the sacraments. They are able really to hear, inwardly, the proclamation of God's forgiveness and it 'works' for them. They sense, feel, or just accept that they are forgiven. Thus it is possible to go on, to make a fresh start or do whatever is needed.

We sense that *Simon* may fall into this category. He was able to receive some comfort from his encounter with the vicar in a semi-confessional milieu. We are not so sure about *Anne*. Her weekly confession is certainly helping her to keep going. It regularly restores the status quo after a week's hassle and heartache over a sick husband. We are not told enough about her to know whether she approaches the weekly ritual in a mood of trusting hope and realistic acceptance that nobody is perfect and that a bit of spring-cleaning is sometimes necessary. If she does then the experience may be healing for her even if a little bit at a time. But she may approach it more in the way of *Sheila*, with a heavy heart and no real hope that anything will ever be very different, and that it is just her confession that stops God writing her off, as it were, as a no-good person. The verdict remains open but the form of her confession as we heard it does not fill us with overmuch confidence that it is being a source of steady growth and development for her.

Others still cannot find forgiveness, in part or at all, internally, neither can they come to it through a mixture of internal reflection and external help. Something blocks the two connecting, or the only connections that are made are those which reinforce the old internal pattern. We could make a fairly safe bet that *Stewart* hears all the condemnation of homosexuality and the Aids threat that society and the church can sometimes seem to offer, but that he somehow cannot hear the support and comments on the other side that are also offered.

We see, therefore, that people are very different in the way they can or cannot modify harsh judgements in their inner world and so participate in the external process of forgiveness. We have some idea of why this variation should be. The root of it lies in our psychological make-up and history. The fuller exploration of this is for the next chapter.

But before ending this chapter I should like to spend a moment reflecting whether forgiveness is *always* potentially possible or appropriate on the human level, or whether there *are* occasions when it cannot be and should not be. Can we easily think in terms of forgiveness for the likes of Hitler and Stalin? Even more importantly, can we ask or expect that those who were their victims should be able to forgive their tormentors? Are there some evils outside the human process of forgiveness? If so, are they outside the religious dimension and divine process also? The early church thought in terms of some unforgivable sins,[4] and there is the mysterious sin against the Holy Spirit mentioned in Mark 3.29.

From this chapter we might be able to define further that sin against the Holy Spirit and think of it in terms of a resistance to transformation. Whilst black is persistently seen as white or vice versa forgiveness is not possible. In this sense I guess we all sin against the Holy Spirit when our disposition hardens and we become stuck in a way of thinking such as 'The other person is in the wrong—I am not.' As we have seen, this hard, rigid attitude makes it impossible for the forgiveness process to start, and for any new light to be allowed to shine upon the situation.

This is a sobering thought. Instead of the sin against the Holy Spirit being the ultimate that only the most wicked could possibly fall into—never ourselves—I am suggesting that many, if not most of us, are in it more than occasionally. Perhaps, in fact, it is not so terrible in itself, but it will become terrible if we can never melt that rigid attitude. For the mutual distortion of black and white may then remain forever untransformed and we shall stay living with a distorted inner world. That would be a tragedy. Obviously it does happen. But it is not for wholesale condemnation as the ultimate sin. It needs understanding so that we can see what we are up against and seek the help we need.

The earlier part of my questioning remains as to whether there are human situations objectively beyond the range of forgiveness. Are there situations that must be kept black, where to say that there can be any white in them at all would be perversion? In such circumstances is holding firm not a rigidity that should be softened, but the truth that may not be compromised?

What I say now I can say only very tentatively and with a certain fearfulness of being deeply offensive to some people. I find that I can do no other than think that only forgiveness can move certain situations forward regardless of the evil in them. And I have to include within this instances of people caught in bitterness in the aftermath of disaster or personal tragedy that happens through criminal acts, notably murder; those caught in the Jewish Holocaust or the Stalinist excesses or other oppression and torture of peoples. On one level I cannot see how the victims can know peace or the world move forward until some sort of transformation of these horrors can happen. Without this and without forgiveness retaliatory violence is likely to happen in a never-ending cycle or spiral. I offer both 'cycle' and 'spiral' as metaphors because sometimes violence may not necessarily escalate—the original act may have been the most violent and most evil—but it never gets reduced either. In other instances the spiral escalating effect is obvious.

But, on another level, I do *not* think that those of us not intimately concerned with those human situations have the right to pontificate about forgiveness, demanding that it be exercised and condemning when it is not. It is simply too much for us to ask even in the name of the ideal of Christianity. It is equally offensive for us to regard it as a failure in another person when it is not offered. Both personal and corporate history and the psychological patterns of generations are involved.

It may seem a little strange for me to be at one and the same time 'willing a profound end', but being uncertain as to whether it is possible. Yet this is exactly the place in which I am standing. I do not think that anything less than forgiveness will be healing, but I do not know that healing in all such situations is possible. I wish it were but I cannot demand it.

This chapter leaves big unanswered questions. I have tried to address the issues on the human level only—from straight inside me—without bringing in overmuch either the religious dimension or psychological theories. I wanted to do it this way to 'ground' this reflection in ordinary humanness. But we are now going to need to turn to both religious and psychological disciplines if we are to pene-trate further into the mystery of why this human process of forgiveness—and indeed also the religious process of forgiveness—sometimes works for people and sometimes does not. These disciplines of theology and psychology each in their own way can enlarge the context in which we reflect on forgiveness, and in this we hope also for an enlargement of our understanding and ultimately for more effective pastoral care.

Notes

1. See Chapter 2, Note 18.
2. 'Splitting' is one of the means of defending ourseves psychologically against unpleasant inner experience. See Chapter 3, Note 13.
3. *Issues on Human Sexuality* (Statement of the House of Bishops of the General Synod of the Church of England, December 1991).
4. Unforgivable sins were the 'capital' sins of murder, adultery and apostasy. See Chapter 2, Note 21.

FIVE

Double Vision?
or
The Religious and Psychological
Stories of Forgiveness

—————

I start this exploration with some memories of the stories of my first chapter. One is the General Confession of the Eucharist; another is the story of *Sheila*, the 'pillar' of that church. A third is *Pat* and *John*, the couple at the service who are having rows at home, and a fourth is *Simon* who came to his vicar, *Martin*, in the silence and peace of the church on Saturday evening to unburden his fear of death and his shame about some aspects of his life.

In two of these examples an interchange between God and a human being has already taken place. One instance is very general and anonymous, the other is very intimate. *Michael and Margaret Church's* small son, *Mark*, probably speaks for the entire congregation when he asks his mother in that all too penetrating whisper, 'What's negligence?' His father's mind was on football at the time. The rector's attention was also elsewhere. It was more focused on his personal inside agonies than on the role of priest and absolver that he was acting out in the service.

We can guess from *Sheila's* story that the General Confession and Absolution do not usually help her much either. They take nothing away from her nightly struggle with Thomas à Kempis, which shows her how far she falls short, in her view, of the imitation of Christ. To her way of thinking she is *always* negligent, or worse, and the ritual words of forgiveness do not seem to change that. We do not know whether she ever personalizes this in private confession to a minister. I suspect not, for a discerning priest would have sought to facilitate her

getting further help. She is, objectively, in a state of *affliction*,
rather than a state of *sin*. Without help, it goes on and on
unremittingly inside her. It seems she cannot talk to people.
God is at best deaf, and at worst God is the source of more
interior persecution.

On the other hand, *Simon, was* helped by his encounter
in the church. He went away more peaceful, and more
courageous. What 'did' it for him? The experience of being
listened to, at his pace, in the story of his deepest fears?
The act of confession and the taking by him of some sort
of responsibility for his past life? Or the sense that the
encounter opened up to him another dimension, namely
the healing presence and power of the God to whom he
had appealed?

Between *Pat* and *John* there is yet no attempt to forgive.
Neither does there seem to be any conscious desire for
forgiveness. The picture here, particularly as we see it
through *Pat's* outbursts, seems to be one of frozen, angry,
isolated misery. It is almost as if she would not be able to
hear *John's* 'sorry' anyway even if he, for his part, was
able to say it. She cannot let him in to her that far. It feels
as if she could not bear to stop her diatribe. Her hurt and
anger protects her, in a strange, bizarre and upside-down
way, from both further pain *or* comfort being inflicted or
tendered by another human being. We could say that
this couple is *not ready* for forgiveness, but it is also hard
to see how the present state of affairs can ever change so
that they will be. How can something break into their
unremitting and remorseless cycle? It is a cycle which is
likely to spiral out of control.

We have here three different scenarios. One is totally
human; one is very human but with the religious dimension overarching and penetrating it; and one is ritually
religious with little of the deep human things seeing the
light of day. It is against the backdrop of these stories
that I want to explore the religious and psychological
'stories' of forgiveness.

I ask myself first why am I combining in one chapter
the religious and psychological stories of forgiveness
when I separated the dimensions whilst exploring the
concept of sin? I think the answer can be found—at least
in part—in the chapter just passed. Forgiveness has
ordinary human currency through and through; sin has

come to have human currency through the passage of time but is essentially rooted in the religious story. So we can know, or recognize the absence of the experience of forgiveness from inside any human position and from within any discipline. Forgiveness has its own characteristics and momentum. To look at it from within one dimension only may distort it and we have, if we can, to let the various disciplines shed light on it simultaneously—daunting task though that is!

I was going to go further and say that we can experience human forgiveness at any age and at any point of our development, but as I paused to draw breath, as it were, I questioned this. I have a sense that we may be able to *experience something* of forgiveness at any age, but whether we can truly *know* it for what it is and so experience its reciprocal giving and receiving to the full I am not so sure. We may like to think that this distinction between 'experience' and 'knowing' is academic and even false. After all the word 'know' is used in the Bible for that most intimate expression of relationship between human beings, namely sexual intercourse— surely experience at its most total? Yet that is at its most fulfilling only when it takes place between consenting adults within a context of mutual, voluntary and emotional surrender. Those adjectives 'mutual', 'voluntary' and 'emotional' are all-important, for they add something to the experience of sensation and 'raise' it to the experience of knowing.

Perhaps I am on to something here. Maybe this is something that can help us see when and why forgiveness 'works' and when and why it does not. Who are the people between whom true forgiveness can take place? Can they be very unequal in status or age or development? Can they truly come to 'know' each other? Can forgiveness really be one-sided? I hinted in the last chapter it may have to be if there is no external other to forgive, or if that other is not willing. Then the one who seeks to forgive or be forgiven must work only upon the images of hurt and betrayal they have imagined and built up inside themselves. As I go on writing and let my theme expand, other questions present themselves. Is forgiveness a feeling, an act, a change of mind or heart, or what? What is the place of confession in the process? Is there a difference between the forgiveness that takes place between fellow human beings and that which happens between human beings and God?

We are now one step further on from the pure *descriptions* of the human situations at the beginning of the chapter. We are beginning to reflect on them in order to try to make sense of them. Certain questions are already beginning to emerge. But we need a frame of reference. This chapter offers us two. They are the *religious* and *psychological* 'stories'—or ways of making sense of—forgiveness. I entitled this chapter 'Double Vision' deliberately because double vision is ambiguous and can be two-edged.

We get double vision, humanly speaking, when our two eyes are not quite in tune. Instead of each eye helping to sharpen up and bring into focus a single image, two images are produced which overlap and are superimposed on each other. Yet normally the resulting image is not so distorted as to be completely unrecognizable. But the distraction of two component images saps our energy and our perception.

In this sense, the religious and psychological stories have sometimes appeared to distract from or even obstruct each other. Yet I am proposing to let them focus together on the theme of forgiveness. We could get any of three results from this process. First, they could operate as a well-synchronised pair of eyes to illuminate our theme consistently, and without distortion. Second, they could produce veritable double images—so far apart that they can hardly seem to be related in any meaningful way. Third, they could, as I think they may, produce genuine 'double vision', where some parts overlap, some are sharpened up, and other areas obscure or distort the overall shape. Outcomes one and two would be easier to use. In the first there is no conflict. In the second there is such a separation that we could attend to and explore each of the images separately and take our pick of them at the end of the process. This would only be possible if we could start from a position of thinking that 'soul' and 'psyche' are two different realities.

Yet it is the stance of *Clergy Stress*[1] and this book so far that they are not different realities. Spirituality and theology contain an implicit psychology. The study of the human mind and person is inevitably done within a larger philosophical frame of reference made up of the issues,

questions, and answers that each of us has at any point of
our lives in relation to the great 'whys and wherefores'.
We inevitably have such a frame of reference even though
it may not *consciously* impinge on us too much for most
of the time.

I am writing as someone who tries to live in and
between the religious and psychological stories in a balance
which is not fixed but very fluid over time and situations.
At one period I was 'all religious'; I may now seem to
have moved to the 'all psychological'. My current balance
is not necessarily that of my readers. This fact sets us all a
task. I must to try to acknowledge when my balance is
personal to me. I must present it in a way that facilitates
dialogue rather than demands acceptance. My readers
need to read with discernment and use my offering as a
tool to find their own balance.

I suspect that the two stories will produce a degree of
double vision and perhaps some real and distinguishable
areas of conflict. I want to take up the conflicts in the
next chapter. In this one I want to focus on that part of
the resultant image to which both stories contribute—the
overlapping areas.

The Religious Story

The forgiveness of sins is a credal statement and as such
it takes us back to a connection that we might have been
in danger of losing. Forgiveness, in the religious story, is
paired with sin—not just with the making better of a
human situation in which two people are hurting each
other. Indeed in the gospels Peter uses the word 'sin'
even when he is describing an interaction between two
human beings, 'How often shall my brother sin against
me, and I forgive him?'[2]

So forgiveness in the religious sense is trying to 'deal'
not only with human disharmony but with sin and all
the hugeness of that theme that we discovered in earlier
chapters. It is trying to deal with our relationships with
God, other people, and ourselves; but the ultimate frame
of reference is God. Sin is to do with God. In the religious
story forgiveness, too, is to do with God.

Furthermore, in 'dealing' with sin the religious dimension must deal with both original sin and sin(s). The history

of the church and religious thought shows the way in which this has been thought to have been achieved.

It is not clear that in Judaism that there *was* any way of dealing with 'evil imagination'.[3] It seems to have stayed as a fact of experience, to be lamented certainly as in the Psalms but only overcome by acts of faith. In part, the advent of the Messiah was awaited as the agent of deliverance not only from temporal ills but from apocalyptic judgement on things external and interior. The ritual of the Day of Atonement and the sacrificial rituals seem to have been more associated with cleansing and expiation from actual sins, rather than with the state of being sinful.

In Christianity the way of 'dealing' with original sin was and is baptism. The Anglican Book of Common Prayer proclaims this quite unequivocally:

> Sanctify this Water to the mystical washing away of sin . . . grant to [them] . . . the thing which *by nature* [they] cannot have . . . None can enter into the kingdom of God except he be regenerate and born anew of Water and of the Holy Ghost.[4] (my italics)

The language of the revised Alternative Service Book softens this somewhat and also emphasizes more the other element in baptism, namely acceptance into the family of Christians, but it still says:

> we who are born of earthly parents need to be born again . . . Repent and be baptized in the name of Jesus Christ for the forgiveness of sins.[5]

I have been quoting in both instances from the services for the public baptism of *infants*. These contain promises of repentance and of intention to live 'forthwith according to the will of Christ' made by godparents on behalf of the infant. There is *not*, however, the sense that if these promises are not kept that the 'grace' of baptism will be invalid. Indeed the act of baptism in an emergency, by anyone, of a seriously ill or dying infant *and* the perceived need of this supports the view that something 'external', objective, and irreversible happens in the sacrament of baptism. Baptism changes the state of the one baptized irrespective of full belief or otherwise. We see this reflected in the thinking of the early church.

They imagined that unbaptized babies who died went to an eternal limbo. They would never enjoy the fullness of heaven, but would be spared the consuming pains of hell. The inference seems inescapable: without baptism, original sin and human nature reigns.

We have here a strong proclamation that humankind cannot deal with the depths of our nature entirely from 'inside'. Repentance and change of heart and mind are certainly needed, but without the 'nudge' of baptism, as it were, nothing can get started. It is almost as if baptism works like an antibiotic. It provides a stimulus to our own immune system to kill off insidious infection and hold this position until the body's natural immunity and strength can take over and fight for itself. This strong view of baptism of course must inevitably follow from the equally strong view held by the early church, which we have already reviewed in Chapter 2, of the deadly nature of original sin and the disastrous consequences if it is not dealt with.

There are other historical developments and controversies about the nature of baptism which have showed themselves through the ages. Many focus on whether this sacrament confers the full gift of the Holy Spirit necessary to enable us to go the furthest way along our Christian journey within the church community, or whether something extra (such as the Catholic and Anglican rites of confirmation) is required when once a person comes to 'years of discretion' and is able to think, will, and answer for themselves.

But the outcome of such arguments in no way compromises what does seem to be agreed. Baptism includes as part of its essence a moral cleansing. In this, Christian baptism seems to be a derivative from the baptism of John the Baptist. Baptism was then already known as a rite of passage for the incorporation of proselytes to Judaism into the Jewish community. John the Baptist transformed it into an expression of deep repentance and forgiveness on an interior level. The fact that Jesus himself submitted to such baptism was taken as a confirming sign of this. To this central idea of baptism as the agent of cleaning and forgiveness there has been and is very little resistance.

So, baptism 'does something' to sin and the state of the person. When it is administered to infants it is believed that it does this irrespective of the response of the person being baptized. One of the things it 'does' is to confer remission and forgiveness of original sin. Baptism removes a 'taint'. The controversies in much later times about the baptism of infants versus adult believers' baptism seem to me to be expressive of attempts to probe the mysteries of such a claim. Can the 'taint' be removed without our full cooperation? Is there something more or less magical about the process? How does the need for baptism relate to the idea of humankind being *created* in the image of God and possessing a spark of the divine in us from birth?

Here, in admittedly rather 'external' terms, is laid bare the depths of the mystery of sin, with two opposing points being made. The one implies that humankind partakes of the Spirit and image of God and that we are capable of developing so as to activate progressively that Spirit within us. The other proclaims that human kind is doomed to disaster without the intervention of something outside and other than to ourselves.

If we left the theme of baptism here, with the statement of the dilemma to which it gives rise, we would miss an important point. Christian baptism was administered first in the name of Jesus Christ and later in the threefold name of the trinitarian God. The element of baptism which makes possible the forgiveness of sins is not the exact performance of a magic-like rite, but the *access* this rite is presumed to give to the saving and forgiving power of God. It is God who forgives; not the act of baptism in itself. In Christian thought the theology and practice of baptism cannot be divorced from the theology of what we may call redemption or atonement. In our present-day Eucharist the great central thanksgiving prayer recalls and represents to us the saving power of God in Christ:

> It is indeed right . . . to give you thanks and praise, holy Father, heavenly King . . . through Jesus Christ your only Son, our Lord . . . *through him you have freed us from the slavery of sin . . .*[6] (my italics)

Baptism is but the agent of this saving work of Christ. It is not the work itself. To continue our exploration we must now turn therefore to this work of God in Christ.

Christian atonement theology gathers up, builds upon, and transcends much of the thought of the Old Testament on sin and forgiveness. It is difficult to do justice to the huge amount of thought and writing in this area without letting it loom disproportionately large in this book, and as I have said before this is not meant to be a theological treatise or history as such. I shall therefore attempt to distil only those aspects that I think are vital to the development of my theme.

We have already noted that one way of looking at sin is to suggest that it is that which turns God hostile to us, that almost nullifies God the creator and God the protector. This is reflected in the history of the Old Testament when as a result of sins and misdeeds the protection of Yahweh for the Israelites was periodically withdrawn, and they fell prey to another material, social, or political disaster. In some instances the punishment would be vented on the whole people unless the individual evil-doers could be identified and cast out. Yet, alongside 'satisfactory' punishment there are other 'methods' given in the Old Testament for reversing the hostility of God and returning things, as it were, to 'normal'.

There is the way implicit in the development and codification of law, particularly laws relating to cleansing and purification. The bulk of the books of Leviticus and Numbers lay down long and complex systems for achieving those goals. The idea is that if you follow instructions, do it right and get it right God will not forsake you as a people. If you do not do things in due form, be wary. There is also the way of sacrifice. It has always been maintained that Old Testament sacrifices, even the so-called sin offerings, were expiatory in nature rather than propitiatory or placatory. This means that they should be seen as expressions of sorrow for sin rather than as attempts—after pagan traditions—to neutralize the destructive power of an angry God. But there are variants on this.

In the tale of the scapegoat[7] we have a strange mixture of themes. One goat is sacrificed to God as an expression of the offering of fidelity and obedience. There is nothing placatory here. On the other goat is laid, through the hands of the officiating priest, the burden of the peoples' sins and then it is sent out with this burden into the wilderness. Parity between God and people in this case is achieved by dividing the good from the bad and getting rid of the bad into the desert. Abraham tries hard to change

God's angry mind by suggesting that if he can find an ever-reducing number of good men in the City of Sodom this will be sufficient to keep God's wrath at bay. God can then be on the side of the preservation of the city and will not destroy it.[8]

In general the Old Testament is more concerned about the survival of the people of Israel as a race than about the eternal or temporal destiny of individuals within that race. In fact, where individuals are concerned the position often seems arbitrary. Why was Abel's offering intrinsically more pleasing to God than Cain's? Why is the morally disreputable Jacob, who won his father's favour by a trick, preferred to the apparently upright Esau? Only David seems to get his moral deserts when he is punished for sending to his death Uriah, the lawful husband of David's mistress, Bathsheba. It is difficult to escape the conclusion that much of the Old Testament sees the mind and will of Yahweh as identical to that which in human, temporal terms makes for the survival of the race and reasonably harmonious living conditions. Here indeed is one of the first indications that issues of sin and morality are not identical.

But the Old Testament has other strands yet. There is the great poetry of the exilic and post-exilic prophets who begin to use the language of personal relationship for the content of the covenant between God and his people. They try to make sense of the strangeness of a covenant relationship in which the people are allowed to suffer. Thus we have such passages as this:

> But now thus says the Lord, he who created you, O Jacob, he who formed you, O Israel: 'Fear not, for I have redeemed you; I have called you by name, you are mine. When you pass through the waters I will be with you, and through the rivers, they shall not overwhelm you . . . Because you are precious in my eyes, and honored, and I love you . . .'[9]

or

> When Israel was a child, I loved him, and out of Egypt I called my son. The more I called them, the more they went from me . . . They shall return to the land of Egypt . . . The sword shall rage against their cities . . . How can I give you up, O Ephraim! . . . My heart recoils

within me, my compassion grows warm and tender. I will not execute my fierce anger.[10]

Furthermore there are the beginnings of hints, notably in the so-called suffering servant songs of the second Isaiah, that suffering itself can be redemptive, though again more for the race than for the individual. For example:

> But he was wounded for our transgressions, he was bruised for our iniquities; upon him was the chastisement that made us whole, and with his stripes we are healed . . . by his knowledge shall the righteous one, my servant, make many to be accounted righteous; and he shall bear their iniquities.[11]

Running through these strands is the idea of the Messiah who either in time or at the end of time will intervene to reverse the fortunes of the race.

Later still we have the development of the 'wisdom literature'[12] which does seem to get nearer to affirming the personal story, worth, and destiny of *individuals*. Here it is not Israel or non-Israel, but the wise or the fools and these last two words carry connotations of deep-rooted good or evil—moral and religious. Knowledge of wisdom is not confined to the sphere of the intellect but extends to the whole of the person.

It is into this mixed heritage that Jesus and so Christianity was born. The baptism of John shows a move towards individual repentance. Forgiveness of sin *was* known about as shown in the already-mentioned question of Peter about the number of times it was possible or could be demanded, but the cycle of sin and punishment in individuals was also well-established. Unlike the Old Testament, the New Testament contains stories of individuals who are not—like the patriarchs and judges of the Old Testament—composite figures within an essentially corporate drama. Yet the corporate dimension is not lacking from the New Testament. Jesus formed a community of followers, and indeed he seems to have seen his mission as a fulfilment of the destiny of the people rather than cutting across that corporate destiny.

But another note creeps in, most notably in the writings of St Luke. Luke's Gospel introduces material on the fatherhood of God to individuals. Such is the tenor of

Jesus' saying, 'A sparrow does not fall to the ground and die except the father knows it',[13] and the revolutionary start to the Lord's Prayer with its 'our father'. The salvation and well-being of the individual person become important in their own right.

St Paul's letters are mixed. He does not forget either that he was a Jew or about the corporate nature of Christianity, but he had an individual conversion, and much of, for example, the letters to the Romans and the Corinthians are concerned with how individual people find their salvation and ultimate fulfilment in Christ.

Maybe I am reading later Western individualism too much into New Testament times. I do not know, but I do not think that the fundamental direction of what I am saying is wrong. With a rise of concern for individual salvation also comes a concern for the mystery of individual responsibility, most clearly exemplified perhaps in the baptism of John,[14] the parable of the prodigal son[15] and the fate of Judas.[16]

The baptism of John required the individual to take responsibility for his state before God. This reverses the Adam myth where responsibility is laid first at the feet of Eve and then on the serpent. The prodigal son makes full confession of his sin to his father, taking personal responsibility for changing his mind and the direction of his life—'he came to himself'. St Paul's conversion experience involves a personal encounter with Jesus whom Paul has been running away from and whose followers he was trying to destroy. Judas is a sobering example and brings us up against the great question: Is the taking of responsibility (which Judas apparently does when he goes to the priest to throw their money in their face with the cry 'I have betrayed innocent blood') enough to heal despair and the sense of damnation? For in Judas we have the unfathomable mysteries of fatalism and inevitability:

> For the Son of man goes as it is written of him, but woe to that man by whom the Son of man is betrayed! It would have been better for that man if he had not been born.[17]

Where was Judas lacking? Why did he die in despair by his own hand, when his counterpart in denial and betrayal, Peter, went on to become one of the founding fathers and the great rocks of the Christian community?

Here indeed is encapsulated the heart of the mystery of forgiveness. Perhaps we are not ready to attempt to address it directly in Christian and psychological terms. We can pause for a moment and look at it through the eyes of another great tradition—that of Greek tragedy.[18] In Judas we see a man like one of the tragic heroes, a potentially good and great man but flawed. *Macbeth* is perhaps another such. In the terms of Greek tragedy there is no stopping the fatal flaw of hubris working itself out to its climax and that climax is nearly always death. Only in the working out of judgement and death can the flaw and the conflict be stopped.

The central figure of a Greek tragedy does not benefit. He or she must inevitably play their part out to the end. It is the onlookers who can be moved to a catharsis. The expression of the emotions that Aristotle calls 'pity and terror' cleanses and eventually restores balance to the person watching the tragedy. The calm, almost prosaic, last couplets of Shakespeare's great tragedies reflect this. Perhaps the point about tragedy is that it cannot by definition include forgiveness. It cannot include anything new in the situation. Resolution is only the remorseless and unremitting inevitable conclusion of the situation.

In one sense St John's Gospel has many overtones of Greek tragedy. There are two central figures—Jesus and Judas—each of whom goes to his death. Judas dies in the true tragic way. The Jews and the disciples form the tragic chorus who comment and move the drama on, but who play a predestined part whose script cannot be altered. It would be possible to see the last cry of Jesus on the cross: 'It is accomplished' as the culmination of tragedy and yet it has come to be understood instead as the manifestation of redemption and atonement accomplished.

I have a sense that tragedy only turns into redemption or atonement through a combination of two other qualities —love and forgiveness. It may be that this combination turns out to have the name and face of compassion, but I think I go ahead of myself. Suffice it to say at this point that in the passion story of Jesus the word 'love', which is barely noticeable in the writing of the exilic prophets, becomes prominent: 'God so loved the world, that he gave his only begotten Son . . .',[19] 'Greater love has no man than this, that a man lay down his life for his friends.'[20] In the life and death of Jesus, human love and compassion—shown in his dealing with Martha, Mary, and Lazarus; with the rich young ruler; with Judas in the garden; and in many other places become paramount. In a difficult-to-perceive shift the scene becomes less external, less concerned only with right *actions*—though these remain important—but focuses more on the deep yearnings and movements of the human heart.

It is against this background that the famous injunction of Jesus that the thought is as bad as the deed[21] should perhaps be set. It has been seen as persecutory and condemnatory of people who struggle against so-called evil thoughts and desires and has been the source of much good and bad spirituality through the ages. But perhaps it is helpful to see it not as a raising of the moral stakes but as part of an internalizing process providing some redress and balance to an over-emphasis on external actions and external righteousness. The parable of the Pharisee and the publican makes the same point in a more positive and explicit way; the Pharisee speaks from his skin, as it were, the publican from his inner heart.

Into the emerging atmosphere of love come the great events of the death and resurrection of Christ. These events became the cornerstone of Christian faith and universalized the appeal and message of Jesus.

We can look at these events in many ways, and indeed they have been so looked at by successive generations. But one thing that they were seen immediately to effect was a marriage between the past and the future. The passion stories in the gospels are seen as the fulfilment of ancient prophecy. The resurrection was claimed in the Acts and in St Paul's writings as heralding a new order of being. I would want to add to this and claim that it marked a bridge or marriage between the *impersonal dimension* of the past and the *personal dimension* of the present and future.

Later theology attempted to make sense of these events to fill out the New Testament proclamation that eternal salvation had been wrought in and through Christ. There have traditionally been four strands to atonement theology[22] and they divide along what we may choose to call the objective and subjective dimensions. The objective emphasizes a heavenly drama played out, a drama not in its essence involving the man in the street; the subjective takes account of how the man in the street can relate to that drama. The objective majors on the battle between great powers and forces *apparently outside us*; the subjective allows us to appropriate that battle to our own experience.

Christ was seen as the victor in the age-old battle between good and evil. In this he needed to be armed with the power of God since nothing less could defeat the tremendous forces abroad. The dramatic accompaniments to the death of Christ in the Synoptic gospels—the darkness, the veil of the temple being rent in two and the great earthquake—reinforce the sense of a more-than-human drama being enacted. Later incarnational theology reflected on this as in Donne's poem 'Good Friday, riding westward'. God in Christ was fighting and in submitting to death he was in fact winning:

There I should see a Sunne, by rising set,
And by that setting endlesse day beget;
But that Christ on this Crosse, did rise and fall,
Sinne had eternally benighted all.[23]

This view of Christ's death of course had terrible implications. Was the creator of the universe and its sustainer dying in that moment? To avoid this required ultimately the formulation of the doctrine of the trinity. But however we understand Christ's death, we can see that a battle was being fought. It was a cosmic battle between the great opposites of light and darkness, life and death, love and hate, glory and humiliation featured in St John's Gospel. That battle is commemorated forever in the great thanksgiving of the Eucharist. There Christ is victor over the powers of darkness and sin. Another—and more human and rather more internal—way of putting this, beloved of St Paul and St Irenaeus, was the idea of *recapitulation*.[24] Christ recapitulated in himself and in his life the history and experience of humankind even to the point of death, but where humankind fails there Christ conquered and triumphed.

Christ was also seen as the victim, and this is a more primitive idea to try to understand. In crude terms we have a choice. We can see Christ as the bait[25] used to hook the devil into believing that his powers had triumphed, only to find to his horror that the same Christ was also

God and could not be beaten down. Or we understand Christ, as perfect man, was in some way taking on the deserved fate of us all by going through death to the other side and coming through. There is yet another, more placatory version: the perfect love sacrifice of Christ so to speak changed the mind of an angry and destructive God the father. Christ made satisfaction for us, or as the Book of Common Prayer puts it, 'a full, perfect, and sufficient sacrifice . . . for the sins of the whole world'.

These ideas contain shades of the suffering servant of second Isaiah: 'He was smitten for our transgressions' and of the *Agnus Dei* of the Eucharist—'O lamb of God who takest away the sins of the world'. This allusion is difficult to overlook when we remember that according to St John's Gospel Christ died as the passover lambs were being slain. At the same time the idea can be pagan in its undertones or overtones; God the father can be experienced as primitively hostile to us requiring the supreme placation, *unless* we can somehow allow placation to be transformed into creative reparation.

In more subjective terms, Christ was also seen as the supreme example which we strive to imitate. This is perhaps the easiest idea immediately to understand. It has been the basis of much spirituality before and after Thomas à Kempis' *Imitation of Christ*. Yet there are conflicts between this and the more 'objective' theories. The latter need Christ to be God or at least perfect man untainted with human sinfulness—'as we are, yet without sinning', as the letter to the Hebrews puts it.[26] This will not do for us if we are committed to follow Christ as the great example, for if he was not starting from the same position as us—the same human nature—the task of imitation will prove impossible for us. In a way this was Pelagius' and Augustine's conflict; man was capable of living according to the way of Christ in the thought of Pelagius, and in the thought of Augustine had no chance of being able to do so.

It seems necessary that Christ struggled in exactly the same way as we struggle if we are to keep alive a realistic hope of imitating the quality of his life. Yet this raises other great theological questions: if he partakes of our sinful nature in what sense can he also be God? If he is God and suffers and dies how is he to be the same God as the creator and sustainer of the universe with whose death the universe also would die?

In a strange way none of these theories of atonement absolutely require the resurrection of Christ. The work is accomplished in Christ's life and death as St John's Gospel proclaims in the final cry from the cross: 'It is finished.'[27] Yet death itself, that last bastion of sin and affliction, would not be vanquished without the resurrection. The possibility of eternal separation from God would remain. The fourth great theme of atonement theology which sees Christ as the giver of new life does, it seems, require the resurrection if the historical Christ is to be made available eternally and without limitation to those who come after him, and if new life is to be a present and future reality and not simply the recalling of a memory.

There is a maze of difficulties here and many early and modern theologians have tried to find a way through from the Council of Chalcedon onwards. In AD 451 the Chalcedonian fathers needed to posit Christ as having two natures— human and divine, neither swallowing up the other, but not separated either.[28] This sounds artificial and mechanical to our ears, and later theologians have tried seeing Christ as the human face of God[29] or as the representative[30] of God and man. Not all of God is in Christ but in God there is nothing that is not Christ-like.[31] Process theology[32] draws upon the principle of evolution in the natural world and posits development in God himself. Because of the advent of Christ there is a new development in the life of God; namely that he is able to suffer.

To some of us, both old and new debates seem foreign and arid as if they were an intellectual game in which we cannot easily join. We realize that we cannot observe God —or anyone else for that matter—from the outside; we are subjectively involved. In the existential philosophy spanning the last two centuries and the existential theology of this one we can perhaps see ways to bridge this divide between inner and outer, between theology and experience. Yet we are then faced with the ultimate problem of the nature of the reality with which we are engaged.

There is also a sense in which atonement theology is hard to internalize and make meaningful because it has been couched in terms that are *too rational and too conscious*. Redemption is certainly something with which the intellect has to struggle, but as we saw from *Sheila's* story (when her feelings would not come into line with her affirmation of faith) sometimes the intellect is defeated. *Sheila's* rational mind told her she was doing well and was forgiven; her feelings and other parts of her deeper self apparently 'refused to believe' in this forgiveness and she continued to struggle nightly in considerable suffering.

Anne, the Catholic penitent, struggled against the odds of a harsh external life. We note that *Gerald*, the priest, had some doubts as to whether *Anne* would be able to take his counsel to relax a little and not demand so much of herself. It is as if he 'knew' that something deeper inside her was not going to able to take in his words or hear with her whole being what he was saying and be able to benefit from it. The idea that in Christ she is 'justified', that she is allowed to be as she is, seems to trickle off her like water off a duck's back. But neither she nor *Gerald* know what holds her back. It is something that is not really *conscious* to her.

We may see some note being taken of our *unconscious selves* in the gospels—or do we? 'Father, forgive them; for they know not what they do.'[33] Thus Jesus prays for those who crucify him. Yet it is not clear whether their unknowingness is that they are doing their duty and not realizing that they are crucifying the Messiah. In this they are making the same judgement as nearly all the people round them. Alternatively, their unknowingness could refer to their more deeply personal selves of which this outward scene is but a symbol. Are they in fact trying to destroy the good, the love with which they are presented, and do not know this? We see something of the same in the mystery of Judas. The gospels portray him as almost foreordained to betray Jesus—in exterior historical terms rather as if he was a pawn in a great extravagant game. Yet perhaps this sense of foreordination belongs to his own deep self? Because of processes deep inside him is he 'bound' to go the way he does and make bad that which he thought was good without being able either to help himself or let other people help him?

Atonement theology, as presented in books on doctrine or the accounts of historic councils can seem one-dimensional. It is hard to know how to help it to resonate with the more fluid and dynamic levels of our being. The poetry

and music of the liturgy sometimes makes the deep truths
enshrined in it more accessible to us by affecting an area
of our being which is not under our rational and conscious control. It is presumably something like this which
gives rise to the intense conversion experience. The
proclamation that Christ died for humankind is presented
in such a way that it makes contact with the lost, vulnerable,
and unlovable part of the listener. It tunes in with feelings
that matter supremely to us and so comes alive. In relation
to the experience of conversion we may well ask whether
that 'tuning in' is to love, guilt, or fear. In a Catholic holy
week celebration we ask the same question—'Is it a tuning
in to love, guilt, or fear?' The same questions are there in
the requiem Mass—what feelings do the *Dies Irae*, the
Agnus Dei, and the *Pie Jesu* actually tune into?

We are now beginning to ask what sort of links atonement
theology can make with the human side of forgiveness
that was delineated in the last chapter. One of the links
seems to be that of *responsibility*. On the human level
forgiveness must involve the taking of responsibility. The
problem with *Pat* and *John* is that they are not ready,
humanly speaking, to do this. The sin of Adam lay partly
in the fact that he did not take responsibility. Christ, on
the other hand, is portrayed throughout his life and
death as one who supremely took responsibility—for himself and for the world. He is seen as always being his own
person, who was free and not a pawn in the game. Christ
chose his own path of obedience to the will of God as he
understood it. So mature imitation of Christ must also
involve this coming to be our own person. The giving
and receiving of forgiveness will only 'work' if it stems
from a position of personal responsibility, and if it stems
from love and not from fear. But when we start looking
more at atonement theology from this standpoint we are
inevitably beginning to explore the psychological aspects
of forgiveness.

The Psychological Story of Forgiveness

In exploring the psychological story of forgiveness we come
up, immediately, against a difficulty. 'Forgiveness' is a
word not much used in technical psychological language.
More common words are: 'concern', 'guilt', 'reparation',

and 'love'. We may also find that the word 'separation' is important.

Psychological thinking, like theological thinking, has not been monolithic or one-dimensional, and there has been much controversy as to how psychological development is thought to come about. Inevitably at this point I am choosing to use some peoples' thought rather than others, because it seems most fruitful for this particular exploration. But it is important to realize that there may be other ways of looking at the theme.

According to thinkers such as Melanie Klein[34] and Donald Winnicott[35]—who both based their theories on a degree of observation of actual infants and growing children—a milestone is reached in our psychological development when we become capable of *concern* for another person. Normally of course the person with whom this first develops is our mother. It is difficult to say at what age this happens since thinkers disagree, and it is unlikely to be the same for all of us, but we are probably safe to think of it as happening sometime within the first year of life.

I include a caveat here which applies to all that follows. We are inevitably having to use 'grown-up' words like 'concern' to describe something that belongs to our pre-grown up stage. It is important to be aware of this and realize that not all of what we ascribe to the grown-up word can be characteristic of that earlier stage. In fact Winnicott uses the words 'ruth' and 'pre-ruth'[36] instead of 'concern'. These words are probably not to be found in any English dictionary and this may be helpful since it highlights the point that we are not meaning what we would usually mean by using certain words. Nevertheless, some form of grown-up stringing of letters together is the only way we have to communicate, provided its limitations are also acknowledged and accepted.

Before we are able to experience 'ruth' or concern, there is not really enough of us as a person to think of mother as separate from us. And it is virtually impossible to have concern and care for her under those circumstances. Before this point the satisfactorily mothered infant tends to use his or her mother a little like a 'thing', and yet not completely so for there is a primitive form of relationship. The relationship centres on holding, attention, and the meeting of essential bodily needs. Mother

does disappoint during this period—if food does not arrive
when the infant is hungry, or if the mother's mood varies
from rapt attention to her baby to inevitable preoccupation with other things. When that happens—as indeed it
must in any relationship between mother and infant—we
are likely to react with a sense of frustration, fear, and
rage.

The rage inside is both too uncomfortable and too
frightening since it may seem to us that it has power to
tear us apart or blow us away into nothing. To resolve
this, it is as if a psychological sleight of hand happens
inside us. We put the horrid, 'bad' feelings away from us
and experience them as coming from mother. She, not
me, is the threatening one. Yet mother is not like this all
the time; sometimes she is good and satisfying. It might
seem to us as if we had two mothers, one 'good' and one
'bad'. In fact this sense of 'two' mothers actually helps
us to manage, as it is possible to 'forget' the bad mother
when the good one is there. But it also makes it impossible
to have any real concern about her. When she is good we
do not need to. Things are going along swimmingly and
we do not need to realize the difference between us and
her. When mother is bad it can feel as if she is persecuting
us. She is making our life unbearable. Who could have
concern for such a persecutor? The most we are likely to
manage is a sense of dis-ease which may have something
in common with the feelings of guilt in later life. When
this experience passes—as it does for most infants—it is
not processed by us for we have not the mental equipment to do so. Perhaps it is as if a heavy sigh of relief is
emitted and we go on as before . . . until the next time.
We could see it as a struggle between a sort of love and a
sort of hate, but the two do not get joined up. At any
given time, mother is either 'good', or 'bad'.

If development goes well enough, in that mother is
secure enough to enable the bad times not to be too long
or too threatening, then we can, so to speak, move on.
We begin to 'see' that her presumed 'love' and' hate' and
our experienced 'love' and 'hate' *belong to both of us*. We
love her and we hate her, and she is the same thing, person,
and reality that we do this to. At this point *concern* arises.
Because we can keep more of us inside ourselves we realize
that something I have called 'hate' belongs to us and that

it could be 'damaging' to the other. We also know 'love', though that, too, is probably too mature a word to use in this context. Maybe we should talk of 'wanting', 'needing', or 'moving towards'. Melanie Klein herself used the terms 'envy' and 'gratitude'[37] for these damaging and contented sensations in ourselves, but again even if these words express something of the presumed sensations it should be emphasized first that the adult words will not really do, and second that we are making *presumptions* about what goes on inside any infant of this age since when this period passes for each of us we shall never have easy and sure access to it again.

At this point of our development it seems that we realize a rudimentary sort of responsibility for what we can do to mother by way of damaging her. It has to be rudimentary for we have no way of testing its reality. We can grossly overestimate our power to do damage. But if we have the beginnings of a sense of responsibility— that we might call guilt—we also have the beginnings of a desire to 'repair' the damage, to reconstitute the relation- ship. If that relationship was too fraught in its earlier stages —that is if the vicissitudes of sensations were very rough —then this next stage may be rather too hard for us to manage. We can come to feel that having owned our anger and hate as part of ourselves we are in danger of being overwhelmed by them and that we have the power to kill off everything good in sight. We have not the sense that our good (love) feelings are stronger than our hate feelings.

In order to survive this new onslaught arising from inside us we sometimes have to *deny* all those feelings. It becomes as if they do not exist for us, and yet they do. It is when this pretence has needed to be excessive that they 'live on' inside us directed against ourselves for where else is there to direct them? Battered by this unknown inner onslaught we are in danger of becoming depressed.

Furthermore, at this stage with the differentiation of sensations and feelings there is also the rise of a sense of the *separateness* of us and the other person. If there is separateness then there is also vulnerability to *loss*. If there is loss there can be renewed feelings of anger and rage which again have to be held inside because there is now no other to help take some of the burden, and so the possibility of becoming depressed increases.

However, if these experiences of loss and rage are not too extreme, we find that we and mother do manage to survive them. We come to learn that good and bad feelings can coexist and that our good feelings (and hers) are stronger than the destructive ones. This I feel lays the basis for what in later life we recognize as the capacity for forgiveness. It is also the basis for a capacity for the sort of guilt which is not merely a threat but which alerts us to the necessity for us to take responsibility for ourselves and to want to repair relationships. They are felt to be worth repairing and we feel ourselves to be capable of doing it.

In the psychological world it has been hypothesized—and hypothesis it has to be since it is not easily open to independent observation or 'proof'—that this point of human development, named in the psychological discipline as the reaching of the *depressive position*,[38] is *the* stepping-stone to mature development of the personality. It is the stage at which we first come to 'know' that our 'bad' is containable in our 'good' and that reparation and creativity as well as mere survival are possible.

It is my thesis that although the actual word 'forgiveness' is not used in the psychological literature, the depressive position is the point in human development from which the capacity to forgive and to be forgiven springs. The development of the capacity to forgive depends on us having acquired some sense of separate existence in our own right and some collected experience that bad things and bad experiences can be integrated into our whole being. In religious terminology, they can be *redeemed*. Before this stage I do not think that forgiveness is really possible. There may be a sense of what we may call 'deliverance' brought about by the return of care and a reasonable state within us. This deliverance or relief will have, by definition, to come from *outside* us. After the depressive position has become established we can become able to contribute—albeit rather primitively—to our own recovery.

But it is by no means certain that we shall easily pass through these stages or indeed reach the depressive position at all. And if we do, loss or breakdown of a relationship in later life can put us back in the struggle, as it were, so that we have virtually to relive the process. If we never reached the stage of knowing and having to take some responsibility for our own feelings or sensing that we and other people are whole, rather complex 'things' it is true that for much of the time what are called the afflictions of sin and guilt may not bother us very much. But that does not mean that we are therefore healthy. For in this state we may not be able to see other people as people at all, or we may be put back in the position of having a very split existence—we love or we hate but it is hard to do both at the same time. This, I think, was the psychological position of *Iago*, *Lady Macbeth* and the *hawk*.

Alternatively, we may have reached that position all right but not have been able to come out on the other side. We may have become overwhelmed by it. The realization that we can do damage may have been too much for us and may have stayed within us as an abiding memory. It is likely that mother was not robust enough to give us confidence in the mutuality of our loving and hating processes. For in that early stage we need another to be accepting of us whether we are 'good' or 'bad'. If there is not that other we may grow up forever frightened of, most probably, the aggressive part of ourselves and racked by guilt for the evil we have done or 'know' ourselves to be capable of doing. At this stage of development the reality of what in the religious world is called sin may come to mean almost too much, so that we cannot get away from it.

In adult life we often experience memories of many stages in our development. The original passage from one stage to another is not clear-cut and complete for most of us. Bits will remain left over and can be differentially 'triggered' by experiences later in life. But in all probability the memory of one stage will tend to predominate in us later on, so that when the 'chips are down' we have a characteristic way of responding according to the intensity of the threat to our emotional equilibrium and well-being. The *fears* we tend to experience may also vary; if we 'go' automatically to the very early primitive stage of our development we may fear ceasing to exist—or just being annihilated; if we 'go' to a later stage the fear may well be of separation of a kind that can be death-like. Death, as the outcome, is common to both positions but the quality of that death may be different.

I want to end this chapter with the claim that this sort of psychological thinking can shed light on atonement theology as I described it earlier. The 'double vision' has been set out and the task is now the focusing of the single image. And at this point I shall concentrate on those areas which *can* be sharpened up, not those where the twofold look seems to make for confusion rather than clarity.

I need to ask that we shall be allowed to cast God in the 'role' of mother or care-giver and ourselves in the role of infant or child. Of course this is not the whole of our relationship with God—witness Adam being cast in Genesis as co-worker with God[39]—and it is important that it is *not* seen as the whole of the story, but it can be a useful *part* of it.

In this scenario the 'objective' ideas of redemption and atonement can be seen as related analogically to that bit of our experience when mother seems to die on us— when she does not seem to afford us protection from the forces inside and outside us. The controversy as to whether God is angry and needs placating or whether Christ should be seen as making satisfaction for the debts we owe and the punishment we deserve can be seen as parallel to our doubts and confusion at various stages of our development. In the earlier stage when mother is seen as alternately good and bad, the doubt as to the mood of God towards us is indeed relevant. Given this part of our human experience it is not surprising that we have a tendency to split God in the act of redemption or atonement; but if God stays split there will be no real reconciliation, just a placation of anger with submission. As on the human level anger and love have to be brought together so that the mother who is experienced as good and bad is also known to be the same mother, so we need to come to know that the God who was in Christ reconciling the world to himself is one God in whom love and wrath are balanced, and, as we believe, wrath is contained in love. But as in actual human development it takes us a long time to experience and know this.

So in some respects the objective theories of atonement seem to me to be describing the vicissitudes in our relationship with God. They counter the fears of non-being and annihilation that we realize we cannot deal with only from inside ourselves. They may be necessary if the offering of redemption is to be universal, for not every human being has progressed to the stage where the fears can be managed inside. Those theories of atonement can provide a shield, or container, or holding power, and the assurance of survival within which we can rest and gather ourselves for our own part in the fray. In a sense they 'deal' with that aspect of original sin—the relics of our most primitive inner worlds— that we know little about consciously and which we cannot make 'good' just by conscious willing that we should.

This way of thinking makes provision for all of us whether we unfortunately tend to live life on that rather primitive undeveloped level or whether we only make occasional unwonted excursions into that realm. It may be that many conversion experiences reach down to that level, despite the affirmation of individual responsibility that is often made as a part of them. The experience of conversion is intense and often the accompanying sense of deliverance and freedom are also intense. It is these extremes of intensity that indicates that the experience may be reaching down to that part of our being where it is difficult for us to have control.

But I think those experiences of being saved can be incomplete, in so far as they do not represent the full depressive position where we have the capacity for unforced concern, appropriate guilt, and the germs of mature personal responsibility. They can seem not to allow for the *free* operation of love. For this we need the idea of Christ as our example and in a strange way also that of Christ as the giver of life. Christ as the example of concern for all humankind invites us over the threshold from primitive magic to more truly authentic personal existence. As the saviour he is the agent of deliverance, but as man he shows us additionally the part we have to play in our own redemption. In his life and death are shown the depth of love and concern, and in the ongoing relationship with him and the new life that is offered we are allowed to feel our separateness from him and his standard in a true depressive guilt that can transcend itself and become creative.

This was what did not happen to *Sheila* when she could never get beyond her sense of failure and her fear of being cast out by God. Her guilt persecuted her. It seems to stem from an earlier level of her development and could not be used to repair her damaged self and her relationship with God and the outside human world. So too with *Lady Macbeth*; her guilt, when finally it came, was sterile. It led only to death—not to renewed creation.

In a strange way it is not guilt—whether it be mature and appropriate or infantile and persecuting—that is important. Addresses given in holy week often focus on guilt in the face of a divine love and goodness which is being crucified by sinful humans. But if they start and end with guilt then I think they miss the point. For psychologically guilt is not an end in itself but is rather an indicator to the relative strengths of love and hate. The greater the guilt the greater the possibility that our hate is strong and that we have not acknowledged it. It is hate not guilt that we have to battle with; it is hate not guilt that has to be contained by love. Love is the latecomer in development forged out of the conflict between our primitive levels of attachment and wanting and hate. We may call it the capacity for love or we may call is the capacity for compassion or forgiveness and I .think we would be tapping into the one reality.

> It is very difficult to *explain* this but I am positing that the event of the death of Christ can stand as an external symbol of the universal, internal, depressive position of our human development—the place where love and hate can interact to their fullest and that interaction can be creative.

I am therefore suggesting a strong *correlation* between the Christian experience and theology of redemption and the psychological story of human development, particularly that part of it which involves concern, responsibility, love, and forgiveness. Where I stop is at the great question of whether the two stories are *correlates* only, in the sense that the theological story represents the external clothing of deep psychological truths, and that it works *because and only in so far as it does this.* Even as such it would be supremely valuable as a way for us to focus and dramatize our inner conflicts. But many would say that this falls far short of full-blown Christian theology, for on this reading any event that could represent adequately the conflict between love and hate would do as well. There would be nothing unique to it and it is a long way from the sense of a unique event 'which changed the shape of things entire'.

At this point I can do no more than say that it seems to me that in many ways a particular religious story and a particular psychological story validate each other. Yet they are both in a sense born of faith and neither of them is amenable to verification by purely rational and scientific enquiry. The conflict as to whether we can and should say more than this about the relationship between them remains, and must be taken up, along with other potential conflict issues, in the next chapter.

Notes

1. Mary Anne Coate, *Clergy Stress* (SPCK 1989), pp. 5–7.
2. Matthew 18.21–22 (RSV).
3. See Chapter 2, Note 17.
4. Book of Common Prayer 1662, Public Baptism of Infants.
5. *The Alternative Service Book 1980*, Public Baptism of Infants, p. 244.
6. ASB, pp. 130.
7. Leviticus 16.15–22.
8. Genesis 18.22–33.
9. Isaiah 43.1–2, 4 (RSV).
10. Hosea 11.1, 2, 5, 6, 8–9 (RSV).
11. Isaiah 53.5, 11 (RSV).
12. See, for example, Proverbs 1.1-7, 10; and the Wisdom of Solomon, in the Apocrypha.
13. Matthew 10.29 (author's paraphrase).
14. Matthew 3.1–6.
15. Luke 15.11–24.
16. Matthew 27.3–10.
17. Mark 14.21 (RSV).
18. For a discussion of the same theme, see F. W. Dillistone, *The Christian Understanding of Atonement* (Nisbet 1968), chapter 4.
19. John 3.16 (AV).
20. John 15.13 (RSV).
21. Matthew 5.28.

22. Atonement theology is explicated in, for example, J. N. D. Kelly, *Early Christian Doctrines* (A. and C. Black 1958), chapters 7 and 14; G. Aulen, *Christus Victor* (SPCK 1931); H. E. W. Turner, *The Patristic Doctrine of Redemption* (Mowbray 1952); St Anselm, *Cur Deus Homo,* see J. M. Rigg, *S. Anselm* (London 1896), and Dillistone, *Atonement.*

23. John Donne, 'Good Friday, 1613. Riding Westward', in John Hayward (ed.), *John Donne: A Selection of His Poetry,* Penguin Poets (Penguin 1950), p. 174.

24. See Romans 5.18-19; 1 Corinthians 15.21; St Irenaeus, *Against All Heresies,* 3.18.

25. See Gregory of Nyassa, *Oratio Catechetica,* 21-26. The idea persisted through the writings of the church fathers, though it was repudiated by some in its crude form.

26. Hebrews 4.15 (RSV).

27. John 19.30 (RSV).

28. 'The Definition of Chalcedon' 451, cited in H. Bettenson, *Documents of the Christian Church* (OUP 1963), pp. 51-2.

29. See J. A. T. Robinson, *The Human Face of God* (SCM 1973).

30. See D. Solle, *Christ the Representative* (SCM 1967).

31. See A. M. Ramsey, *God, Christ and the World* (SCM 1969).

32. See, for example, J. B. Cobb and D. R. Griffin, *Process Theology: An Introductory Exposition* (Westminster Press 1976), or N. Pittenger, *The Lure of Divine Love: Human Experience and Christian Faith in a Process Perspective* (Pilgrim Press 1979).

33. Luke 23.34 (RSV).

34. See H. Segal, *Klein* (Fontana 1979), pp. 78-90; R. D. Hinshelwood, *A Dictionary of Kleinian Thought* (Free Association Books 1991), pp. 138-55; 342-3.

35. D. W. Winnicott, *The Development of the Capacity for Concern* (1963) in D. W. Winnicott, *The Maturational Processes and the Facilitating Environment* (Karnac Books and the Institute of Psychoanalysis 1990), pp. 73-82. (First published Hogarth Press 1965.)

36. D. W. Winnicott, *The Depressive Position in Normal Development* (1954) in *Through Paediatrics to Psychoanalysis* (Hogarth Press 1975), pp. 262-77, especially pp. 265-6.

37. M. Klein, *Envy and Gratitude, and other works* (Virago Press 1988). See also Hinshelwood, *Dictionary,* pp. 167-78, 313; see also Segal, *Klein,* chapter 11.

38. The 'depressive position' is a hypothesized stage of childhood development, during which the child becomes able to relate with love *and* hate to the same *whole* 'object' (person), and in this way develops a capacity for concern and reparative activity. See works by M. Klein and D. W. Winnicott, and Chapter 5, Notes 34-6.

39. Genesis 1.26; 2.15.

SIX

The Tower of Babel
or
Conflict Irresolvable?

―――――

In the last chapters we have looked at two different languages for the expression of ideas about sin and forgiveness. Chapters 2 and 3 explored sin, and Chapters 4 and 5 explored forgiveness. The languages were those of theology and psychology. I was not and am not exploring them for the sake of intellectual curiosity alone, though I cannot deny that they are fascinating, but more urgently to see if we can shed some light on the far from intellectual question of why some people are more troubled by a sense of 'sin' than others, and why forgiveness 'works' for some people and not others.

In many ways I was pleased with the outcome so far since it seems to show that the psychological story as I know it and have experienced it is a helpful undergirding to the theological story. I found it useful to relate the idea of 'original sin' to our primitive inner worlds and the theme of redemption and atonement to the hypothesized 'depressive position' of human development. The language of sin and atonement began to resonate with my psychological understanding.

I say this because I have at different times in my life been deeply involved in the disciplines of theology, psychology, and psychotherapy, with the latter being the most recent. But it has not been a linear progression. I found it both compelling and satisfying to find that Christian atonement theology made sense psychologically, but at the same time it was not complete sense. New questions were raised. These were uncomfortable questions that would not go away. I used my 'double vision' in the

127

last chapter and found there to be some overlap and some non-overlap in the images formed, and it is with the areas of non-overlap that I want to be primarily concerned in this current chapter.

In using both languages upon the same theme is there a danger of myself and others constructing a 'Tower of Babel' when we think we are communicating between the languages but may in fact be getting further apart. Instead of getting to a closer approximation to the truth of things are we going to arrive merely at a confusion of tongues? I think we might do just that if we go for 'fuzzy' truth, if I rest on my discovery that in some respects the theological and psychological stories do mesh with each other. We need rather to be honest and clear about the points where they are in conflict. This is not necessarily in order to resolve the conflict, for this may not be possible, but to know more clearly where we are. If we do not do that then we will be in danger of trying to *reduce one language to the other.*

Probably it is impossible to stop something of this 'reduction' happening inside ourselves. Wherever we are on our personal journey one language is likely to be for us primary bedrock and the other interpreted in terms of it —whether we realize this or not. We have only to consider various developments in theology during this century. Liberation theology[1] sprang from the passionate hatred of oppression rampant in the socio-political environment rather than from abstract theological considerations. Feminist theology was, it seems to me, born of the experience of women, first as women and secondly as theologians. It is difficult not to draw the conclusion that in both these movements theology has been reinterpreted in terms of overwhelmingly compelling human and social experience. Indeed human passion was needed for there to be enough impetus to challenge the long-standing biblical injunctions such as 'the powers that be are ordained of God'[2]—and the various texts on the submission of women.[3]

This is the richness of the religious heritage. It is sufficiently multichrome and multidimensional for parts of it to be differentially emphasized in different times. So truth can be explored and hopefully enlarged. But the process reminds me of that of a camel getting up; it doesn't get up equally and evenly on all four legs at the same time—one leg straightens a bit, then another and so on, so that at some points in the process the camel looks hopelessly and bizarrely lopsided. So our present passion is our best energizer in our search for truth and yet also perhaps a potential source of distortion just because it is our passion and we have given it both rational and non-rational commitment.

It seemed to me that the psychological story was a possible partner for theology in the areas of sin and forgiveness. For sin and forgiveness seem so obviously about what goes on inside and between people. But in making that choice I have already set a direction. A socio-logist might have preferred to look at sin in terms of *social*, rather than personal alienation; *social* rather than personal control. I do not think the social and personal are mutually exclusive but I have indicated an emphasis. Furthermore, I have drawn upon a particular part of psychological thought, namely that which derives from the psycho-analytic tradition. I gave my reasons for so doing in Chapter 3 when I argued that other forms of psychological thought neither connected with nor dealt with the root of the problem. But people who speak these other languages more fluently than I might well want to contest this.

There therefore emerges immediately the point I hinted at in the last chapter. Psychoanalytical beliefs are every much a matter of faith as theological beliefs, in that they cannot absolutely be proved. *Some* direct 'evidence' is available, mainly from the analyses of young children; other evidence is far more remote and indirect being the attempt to *reconstruct* the story of infancy and childhood from work with adults. None of us can see our inner world. None of us can recall exactly the experiences of infancy. The experience is filtered for us and made acces-sible only through layers of intermediate personal history and re-evaluation. Even so-called cathartic memories of childhood are difficult to sustain as being an accurate account of the actual experience. The issue of the inci-dence of child sexual abuse shows this. Did abuse actually happen or was it fantasy? In the last chapter I claimed that a child's development and a person's maturity partly depend on how he or she resolves very early conflicts between love and hate and that mother is the most important other person in this drama, but I do not actually

know this. I continue to think it likely enough which was
why I was encouraged when I found that this sort of
thinking meshed in with atonement theology, which I
presumed had taken the form it has for good religious
and theological reasons.

We may call this good reason revelation. It is the way it
is and the way it has somehow been shown to us. But that
begs a very great question—how *does* revelation come to
us? We can of course cite the book of Exodus and say it
comes from heaven written on tablets of stone.[4] There is a
sense of permanence and immutability about this sort of
symbol. We can move away from this slightly and say
revelation comes through the tradition enshrined in the
collective wisdom of more than two thousand years of
history and religious experience put into words. The
word 'revelation' suggests that something is made clear
to us that we did not know before. I am reminded of Ian
Ramsey's concept of 'cosmic disclosure'.[5] There undoub-
tedly come leaps of consciousness, of awareness—the
ah-ha moments when everything seems clear. Those
moments can happen in prayer, or in a religious conversion
experience. They can happen more slowly and gradually
in the everyday life of the communities of faith. They can
happen in moments of insight in psychotherapy or during
the long, more imperceptible process of change that therapeutic work more usually involves. They can happen to
individuals or they can happen and be distilled through the
reveries, meditations, hard thinking, and life of *groups* of
people. The thing these moments have in common is that
we see something that we did not see so clearly or at all
before. Something is revealed to us that we could not
necessarily have predicted, far less guaranteed.

Thus far, there is no inevitable conflict between the
contexts, religious or psychological, in which such revelation can take place. But the difficult questions are: Whence
comes this revelation? How can we evaluate and come to
trust it? How do we decide we cannot? Even in religious
circles questions about revelation have been a problem
down the ages. That which to one person or group has
seemed the authentic and undisputed voice of God has
been to others very much more the voice of human frailty,
or—to people of a particular way of thinking—the voice of
the devil.

There are many examples of this throughout the history of Christianity and other religions and I shall pick out one or two to illustrate the point. In relation to the inclusion of Gentiles into the Christian church we have Philip, Paul, and others—'Yes'; Peter with many more reservations until his own moment of enlightenment.[6] It remained a matter for considerable bitter controversy in the early Christian community, which was resolved only by the patient slog of argument and counter-argument. Earlier than this, back at the very birth of Christianity, the question was: Was this the work of God or the ultimate betrayal of the truth of Judaism? So many people did not know and the resulting persecutions tell their own story. There was no quick and easy agreement on the mind of God. In that event and indeed often since the 'Gamaliel'[7] solution finally prevailed. This is basically to say: 'Let's wait and see what happens to it.' In other words, consent to the human process wrapped in a faith that proclaims that God will finally claim and work for his own victory even when the nature of this is unknown to us.

Look, too, at the Inquisition. For us today this is a monstrous and barbaric institution whose machinations can in no way be justified by the gospel. Yet to the people of the time they apparently could. *We* might want to look at the interaction between the Spanish psyche and certain of the gospel texts; the Inquisitors apparently felt no such need. The 'truth' was outstandingly clear— revealed in all its glory and buttressed by more of the same 'truth'.

In our own time the two main areas of such polemic debate seem to be the issues of women's ordination and the nature of human sexuality. These two areas have generated more heat, warfare, uncharity, and near-hatred among Christians than any others. To some people these issues represent the painful process of the enlightenment of the church to a wider experience and grasp of its own vision. The further will of God is being revealed. To others this 'evolution' is going against tradition and the immutable heart of revelation. The priesthood cannot be anything but male and any sexual activity other than heterosexual behaviour within marriage has the nature of sin.

No less difficult are issues that seem to be even more fundamental to the heart of the faith. I am thinking of

the debates on the transcendence of God first given
expression by John Robinson in *Honest to God*,[8] and the
later controversies surrounding David Jenkins's thoughts
on the resurrection and the virgin birth,[9] and latterly on
the nature of hell and the Christmas stories.[10] Such issues
in my opinion illumine the heart of the question I am
addressing—'Whence comes revelation?'

To all of us who profess Christianity, or indeed any form
of religious faith, I suppose that the *ultimate* answer is
not in doubt. Revelation comes from God. But this does not
resolve the issue, for we cannot agree *how* the revelation
of God is mediated to us. Is it indisputably recognizable
as the truth of God? How do we apprehend it?

Herein lies the heart of the conflict between much
theological thinking and psychological thought. Religious
thought, even when acknowledging the immanence of
God *inside* us, indicates that revelation 'comes to us'. This
would I think be true even for that dimension of religious
thought that believes that 'grace works through nature'
—we still have to enquire about the nature of 'grace'.
Psychological thought has not needed such a concept;
the discernment of truth comes about through human
endeavour. Such endeavour can include the phenomena
of insight, and intuition; both of these do allow for
moments of disclosure. Another view would see the
discernment of truth as rooted in the gradual struggle
between truth and counter-truth, *within* individuals certainly but also *between* individuals, groups, societies, and
communities of faith.

The point where this dilemma is most immediately
relevant to this study of sin and forgiveness is that of the
central point of atonement theology. It has reverberations
through to the credal proclamation of the forgiveness of
sins. We proclaim faith in the 'Lamb of God who takes
away the sin of the world', and yet some of us are confronted with the question of *how* this happens. Is it
something that happens 'objectively' and outside us, or
are we talking rather about a change in our emotional
and mental state—a change in our *inner* world? Or both?

To one group of people the death of Christ two
thousand years ago changed the face of history, and
changed objectively the relationship between God and
humankind. A consequence of this is the belief that only

by participating in that event can we come to experience the salvation and forgiveness that it purports to offer. We of ourselves can add nothing to it nor take anything away from it. Other people cannot 'take' this 'objective' stance. They—we, for I confess I come into this number—have to attempt to engage with it in other ways. One way that helped me for many years was to see those events as like a cross-section cut through a tree. Cutting the tree at a particular point allows us to see the circles inside it— representing the nature of the God of love and forgiveness —that have *always* run up and down the tree. In this sense there is no *new* thing but a new and definitive *illustration of what has always been there*. This sort of thinking inevitably modifies the uniqueness of the event to some extent, though it is still possible to say that no event, before or since, has made the position so clear to us. But the question is: Does thinking like this fall betrayingly short of the gospel?

Furthermore, religious language talks of 'taking away'; wiping away sin as if it had not been—or at the very least removing it. Psychotherapeutic thought thinks in terms of integration rather than removal; the depressive position signals a resolution of the conflict between love and hate not by denying the hate and anger or pushing it away from our consciousness, but through coming to the emotional realization that both can exist and that love can be the stronger.

In fact this way of psychological thinking is not so far from the Christian story of redemption, understood in a particular way. Sebastian Moore, in *the Crucified is no Stranger*,[11] and drawing heavily, I think, upon Jungian concepts and terminology, talks of the necessity of letting anger rip at the crucified and risking the death of our own ego in the process—in some sense risking our own crucifixion—in order to allow a truer self to be born. This is true to much Christian experience and writing on rebirth and forgiveness *except* for Moore's insight that it is through the experience of the acknowledgement of our anger, not its repression or suppression, that our truest and fullest self can be born. When this cannot happen we cannot take responsibility for our own being and stay stuck in guilt or fear.

Moore delineates two sorts of guilt: the guilt of being

unloved, which he calls neurotic guilt; and the guilt of
being unlovable which he calls real guilt. This seems not
unlike the two sorts of guilt I also have been talking about
—though I think mine are more intense and potentially
disabling than his. These are persecutory guilt, whose
origin lies way back in the mists of primitive confusion
and distortion when we could not own our own hate and
anger and had to experience it coming at us from outside
us; and depressive guilt which comes with the rise of
concern and our emerging ability to take responsibility for
our total being with all its facets, loving and aggressive.

It is my thesis that only depressive guilt can be relieved
by the religious process of confession and forgiveness.
Persecutory guilt cannot, because it does not stem from
our whole integrated being but from a self that cannot
yet integrate into a whole or take real responsibility for
its actions and feelings. We are ruled by 'other gods'.

Indeed we have gods inside us from our earliest years.
Our inner world has large benign figures or large menacing
figures, and there are also the fantasized representations
of ourselves as omnipotently good or omnipotently bad.
Much has been written in psychological circles about the
innateness or otherwise of these internal representations.
Are they universally with us at birth or are they fashioned
through our actual experience of the first 'big' people in
our lives? They are more than humanly big, for because
of our real helplessness as infants the actual people have
the character and power of God in relation to us. They *do*
have the power to fashion for us 'the world entire'.

I am seeming to say that our first experience of God
comes from our first experience of human beings. I could
go on and say that this may be such a terrible experience
that we may want to deny it ever having happened; or we
may be unable to deny it and that harsh, persecuting God
remains and grows inside us. Alternatively, we can have
a benign God *inside* us formed by the real predominance
of good and loving experiences over hateful annihilating
ones, or we can somehow fashion a good God inside us
by denying and putting away from us all our non-good
experiences. None of us of involved in dynamic psychology can deny the power of these internal images. They
can operate with all the absoluteness we come to associate
with the God mediated to us through religious thought
and practice.

We can go on and say that often these internal gods are so fixed that we cannot change our internal world by ourselves. We require an intervention, and the question must be about what sort of intervention will 'work'.

One such intervention is life. Our self evolves in interaction with our environment, and if the gods and countergods of our inner world are not too deeply entrenched then there is a possibility for modification through the meeting of that inner world with human or social experiences that can contradict it. It is possible for us to reevaluate our inside selves—for better or worse. For many of us something of this is possible, and the more sinister of our inner figures conveniently remain unconscious to us for much of our life and do not cause us much trouble because they are well defended against.

I think, however, that it is a mistake to assume that because there are no indicators of a less-than-benign inner world that it is not there in our deep unconscious. The behaviour of a whole nation during the Nazi persecution or during the Inquisition shows that under certain circumstances there can be a resonating between people of deep unconscious material so that defences are lowered and the unthinkable becomes first thinkable and then doable and finally done. This frightening possibility cannot be discounted, for it has happened. But for many of us much of the time this very inaccessible inner material remains that way either because it is too well shut away or because it is to an extent neutralized by a more conscious layer of less damaging material through which we function for most of the time.

But if life triggers the deep layer, either by extreme stress or by certain life events, the intolerable can happen; the secret part is forcibly opened up. When this happens to a person in an uncontrolled and dysfunctional way we tend to want to say that that person is going mad. He or she is then fighting for the survival of their personal being. They use ways such as hallucinations, furies, and other bizarre actions which most of us do not need to use for our being is not subjected to such a violent attack.

The intervention of life can therefore be a double-edged weapon. It can help contain and mature our inner being. It can help us to function at a level removed from the usually secret primitive layer in all of us, *or* it can expose us to that very layer. Which it does is not, of course, directly under our control, neither do we come to the later stages of life with equal defences against this frightening inside. We may be rigidly trying to keep it at bay and yet at the same time be fragile because of the threat of the breakdown of those all-too-necessary defences, or we may have enough good inside us built up from actual good experience to act as a good enough container for our primitive layer to last us all our lives. People who live in different kinds of inner world do not easily understand the language of another because the levels of consciousness and defence are such that one person's experience is genuinely not another's and so is not recognizable.

Another form of intervention is that of developed *religious faith and practice*. The effect of this can also be either benign or malignant. Which of these it is will depend on the raw material, the inner world it encounters and whether we have encountered—or chosen to encounter by reason of the very nature of our internal self—a form of religious faith and practice that will help heal and mature our inner world, lock it up further or rip it apart. The inner gods are powerful, and the impact of an equally powerful external religion can have a devastating effect upon the ensuing interaction.

We do not have to go far to read stories of people who have been broken by contact with extreme religious cults that have posed an intolerable threat to their already fragile identity through their alignment with powerful and malignant inner gods already enthroned in the person. And indeed less extreme systems of religious belief or practice can reinforce unhelpful and life-denying personal traits and psychological dysfunction and damage. But we have also countless attestations of people for whom religious faith and practice—either through a conversion experience or in a more gradual living out and deepening of faith—have allowed an alliance of the God of love with a flickering inner world of love and goodness so that this flickering has become a steady flame. The difference between these sorts of people and their experiences often seems to lie in what happens to *sin and the negative*. Is sin subsequently accepted, tolerated and worked with or is it forever eschewed as the most dangerous threat to salvation and a person's sense of well-being?

The more catholic ritual of repeated confession and absolution—whether general or particular—is intended to assist this gradual inner healing and integrating process towards a growth in compassion that knows and does not have to forget or deny the darker side of the personality. But in the process the external God interacts with the inner gods and there is a dialogue between them which works better for some people than for others. Why it does so is for the next chapter to tease out in more detail. Here it is sufficient to note that the effect of religious practice, like that of life, can be double-edged.

Third, there is the re-intervention of that which was mainly responsible for the original climate of our inner world—namely human intervention. This of course is by no means absent from a religious framework. Judaism and Christianity, particularly, see human fellowship, human interaction, and human loving as part of—not extraneous to—living in relationship with God. Sin is conceived of as operating between us and our fellow human beings as well as between us and God. There is implicit and often explicit recognition that God and humanity are not *completely* distinct from each other, even though the distinction is also made.

In the world of psychotherapy the agent of healing or otherwise—and the 'otherwise' must be allowed, for psychotherapy is not automatically and infallibly a healing process; it can go wrong—is unmistakably human. The aim of psychotherapy is not, however, to substitute one god for another, however helpfully benign the substitute; it is not to let the omnipotent power of suggestion of a therapist take the place of an omnipotent inner world. This is a fragile course at best just because there is no real change; our inner world remains vulnerable to the rise of other gods—both human and non-human. Psychotherapy aims to reduce omnipotence: both the omnipotent power of early memories and early inner representations and to an extent our dependence on the certainties and absolutes of life.

At its best, psychotherapy helps us to become less threatened by both our inner world and external events in so far as they resonate with this. Therefore we need less rigid defences against the impingement of experience, both inner and outer. Psychotherapy aims to strengthen the 'I' that is at the heart of our being—not as in some religious practice to deny that very self—and to give us more effective ways of organizing the mass of feelings, memories, and thoughts that make up that 'I'. It aims to help us to know that we can survive even if much of our earlier experience has conspired to tell us that we cannot. But the change that comes through psychotherapy comes essentially from *inside*. The external other person cannot do it *for* us; not that is if the change is to be lasting and fruitful for our further independent development. To be sure, one of psychotherapy's main ingredients often lies in repeating and externalizing with a therapist some of the conflicts and memories that have made up our inner world and re-experiencing some of the dependencies and frustrations that have gone into it. This is often done in relation to the very person of the therapist with whom we are working. But we do this not for its own sake but so that we can have another chance of mastering parts of our inner world; this time under more favourable conditions.

The therapy of the kind I am describing does not, though, seek to substitute a good present experience for a bad past experience. In this it can be very unlike the religious conversion experience or even the day-to-day life of a community of faith preaching love, joy, peace, and forgiveness. In analytic psychotherapy the original bad experiences need, optimally, to be confronted, and gone through, and re-evaluated, not papered over with 'better' experience.

I am, though, thinking of psychodynamic therapy deriving from the psychoanalytic tradition.[12] There are many other therapies that do focus on the positive. Such therapies emphasize positive relationships—therapeutic and other—and positive thinking, and I do not want to be seeming just to decry them. But I am not sure that they reach the heart of the problem. I fear they may rest in the end on a denial of the darker aspects of human nature. This denial may be sufficient, and after all we do not want to take a hammer to crack a hazel nut, but it also may not and the last state of the person can become worse than the first. Furthermore, I do not think such denial does justice either to the totality of psychological experience and thought, or, more surprisingly perhaps, to Christian and other religious thought, which in their talk of sin and allied subjects, do appear to seek to 'know what is in man'.

There is, however, one important caveat that I shall
need to return to later, and it is this. Is the psychological
way of confronting and reliving frustration and badness
too hard for many of us? In some cases is it beyond both
our motivation, our means, and possibly the strength
and capacity of our inner being? It presupposes the existence of some part of ourself that can somehow manage not
to get overwhelmed by the more unruly and disturbed
parts of ourself as they emerge into the light of day. The
psychotherapeutic world has, in more recent years, found
ways of working with people whose inner gods are very
unfavourable or whose inner heart of being that is not
currently possessed by malignant gods is very small, but it
is a painful, time-consuming, and at times risky enterprise. We may ask: Can it serve the more universal needs
of humanity as well as that religious practice which at its
best builds and strengthens rather than confronts and
dissects?

We all have to answer this question for ourselves, and
to find the way of healing that is best for us that we can
embark on with conscious integrity. This of course may
change over years and within a lifetime.

But in all this I realize I am posing and sharpening up
the great conflict question. I have, I can see, tended to use
religious and psychological means of healing as alternative kinds and levels of intervention. I have indicated
that our ideas of God are as they are because they are
derived from our early experiences of human development. I have gone further to claim that atonement theology
rings true not because it is revelation but because it is in
accord with the principles and process of that same early
development. In a word I may well have seemed to
reduce God and religion to a matter of psychology, and to
have reduced the great mystery of immanence and transcendence in God to the dialogue between our inner and
outer gods. I may to many readers have seemed to have
been in the business of explaining *away* and devaluing
religion and its objectivity.

In one way I cannot deny the charge. As I indicated
earlier in this chapter, we are, at varying points in our
lives, likely to accord one level or understanding of
experience a primary sense of bedrock and reduce all
others to it. So at present I may be seeming to reduce

religion to psychology, and assessing religious thought and practice by the criterion of whether or not it is satisfactorily explainable in psychological terms. There are those who will be doing and have done the reverse. Of these perhaps the 'tour de force' synthesis of Frank Lake in *Clinical Theology*[13] is the best known recent example. Reading Frank Lake I think it is clear that his bedrock is his evangelical Christian faith into which his psychological thinking had to fit—not the other way round. It is, in fact, very hard not make one sort of reduction or the other, unless we are forever on the fence and without any convictions, biases, or even passions which will in turn make us rather less than human.

I do not actually think that I have devalued the religious quest or religious truth. But what I have written depends for its credibility on the theology that humankind is made in the image of God, and that therefore an understanding of humankind may open the way to an understanding, albeit a partial one, of God. It does not preclude God or the religious quest and community, though it leaves more agnostic than is probably comfortable for many people within the community of faith the questions of how God is experienced and known.

My psychological thinking allows for the primacy of love and compassion. Indeed it validates and confirms that primacy. It allows for ultimate striving towards a certain sort of life in which love ultimately is paramount, and it allows for the primacy of relationship—rather than possession of another or withdrawal—in which we can give ourselves and be given to. It allows me to continue to think and feel that the Christian story approximates closely to that unknown reality inside me and outside me which I have bet my life on discovering and experiencing. I do not think the fullness of that reality can be found in me alone or in any single human relationship. It is the dim and partial apprehension of that reality that determines my set towards existence; whether it shall be self-seeking or a wondering at the ultimate mystery of life; whether it shall manage to embrace all the reality that life offers and confronts me with or seek to cut some of it off and deny it. It allows for the ultimate hope that 'we shall know, even as we have been known'.[14]

All that has not changed. The difference is that I am

much less clear as to the exact conditions and meaning of human wholeness than I was twenty years ago. But in so much as I do not see myself as omnipotent, nor would I hope to end my life self-seeking and self-interested beyond a certain healthy point, I claim not to have deserted my religious roots.

But perhaps the most important point is not my individual position, but the affirmation that my personal position is not the only possible result of trying to probe the psychological underpinnings of religious faith. It may have been inevitable for me, but not so for other people. For some this sort of exercise may be anathema to their faith; for others it may be facilitating. Let it be emphasized that the enterprise itself is a matter of faith, not certainty, and therefore its results have provisionality built into them. It is offered as one way to look at the realities that seem to face us, and as an exploration in which I have needed to be honest, partly because only that can allow the necessary space for others to be themselves too.

There *are* conflicts between the 'credo' I have here outlined and 'orthodox' Christian faith. The main one remains the nature of revelation. I have suggested that revelation is the product of forces outside and inside us and that therefore revelation can change and can evolve. I would not care to say definitely that process theology, which talks of evolution and change in God,[15] is a necessary additional outcome of this sort of thinking. I think it is *one* outcome, certainly; another is to maintain a belief in the *eternal* nature of God and say that it is *we* who are taking generations to unravel this and that there are hiccups and discontinuities in the process. The question must be not whether we have as yet got it quite right, since it seems most likely that we have not, but whether our unravelling is going in the right direction. Has that which we worship as God 'always'—even if *we* have not always known this—somehow included (though the language here is difficult since necessarily I speak analogically) that which we can come to know as the best, most integrated and highest in human nature? Has God 'always' been redemptive in that in some mysterious way the existence of love and hate, and the triumph of the former over the latter, has always been there in Him? Or do we return to a more dualistic idea that posits hate as somehow arising and operating in man, not in God, and so redemption is a 'new' enterprise?

I cannot answer these questions with any certainty and I think no one really can. I feel sad when Christian and other religious thought forecloses them. I do not think the dialogue with psychological thought can answer them definitively either, but I think it may illumine the journey.

I would want to say, though, that 'pure' psychological thought is not usually the other partner in the dialogue for it is as difficult for psychological thought to be pure as it is for theological thought to be pure. Rather, human experience, *however* we try to conceptualize it, is the bedrock. So for another way in, I would like at this point to return to Andrew Elphinstone and his *Freedom, Suffering and Love*,[16] to look at another person's engagement with what are, in many ways, the same questions even though his vantage point is different.

As I understand it, Elphinstone completed his book shortly before he died, and he was aware that he was dying. He was thinking and writing, therefore, under a great shadow. But the presence of such a shadow can concentrate our heart and mind to focus on the essentials, and the non-essentials slip away. So it is likely to be worth listening to the story of a man writing under such a shadow. He is no reductionist, in the sense that perhaps I have laid myself open to being by reducing theological ideas to psychology, but he takes pain and suffering as his bedrock. It is inconceivable that he was not building to a considerable extent on his own experience. For on what else could he or any of us build?

For Elphinstone it is the evolutionary process of humankind that is central, and in this, most definitively, the universal experience of *pain*;[17] pain which is physically, emotionally, morally, and spiritually neutral. This originally neutral pain is then somehow assailed by and possessed by 'evil', and he does posit the existence of an evil force within the encompassment of God but sufficiently far away from him in the huge mystery of freedom 'because freedom is large enough and God's plan is sure enough to contain opposition not only in the mean little rebellions of man's imagination but in the more powerful and sinister realms of the spirit'.[18] He also talks of how we may 'see God and ourselves bearing the scars and showing the marks of the pains of that long evolutionary pilgrimage which gives to God his creation and to the creation, by grace, its divinity'.[19]

Elphinstone thus can start where I find it difficult to start—with belief in the independent being of God and the being of evil. Pain and evil belong to the ancient world; love is the newcomer and the intruder.[20] In all this he is very much talking of a process of struggle in which God and the creation both participate.

I would be able to paraphrase him by saying that in the smaller human realm we could conceive of the mutual struggle with neutral pain, natural aggression, and aggression turned sour that occurs between every mother and her infant. *He* goes on to say that it is the meeting of pain with love that denotes forgiveness. *I* am tempted to draw parallels between this and the rise of concern and desire for reparation that I hypothesized take place in human development.[21]

Elphinstone has the same question, however, that I have:

> Traditionally in Christianity human suffering has been painted as a mystery in some way allied to the whole problem of evil. Equally the suffering of Christ has been regarded as a mysterious, unfathomable act of divine love by which the wrong at the roots of the human situation has been reversed; and by which a limitless source of grace and forgiveness has been supplied to carry that reversal into action . . . Yet the hardest problem of all—for theological thinkers and (the) ordinary thinking person—was to see how the suffering of Christ really did undo the consequences of human-kind's enmeshment in evil, and really did open the way to forgiveness for even the most wicked . . .
>
> Perhaps it is reasonable to expect that these things should be hidden in the depths of mystery . . . On the other hand, perhaps it is not altogether right to leave things like that; . . .[22]

He, like me, is unwilling not to probe as far as he can. He gives his own answer, I think, in his assertion of the struggle of Christ not to be deflected from confronting pain in all its painfulness:

Christ went relentlessly and indeflectably to the strong-
hold from which the power of evil exerted pressure to
make man dance to his tune. There in a very great moral
and spiritual battle, he showed it to be possible, in the
summoning of every source of will, obedience and
love, to emerge undeterred by these pressures. He made
himself master in the hitherto demonic department of
pain, drawing it back into the creative resource so that
the whole structure of human personality could be
freed from bondage to evolutionary forces and given
the ability to grasp the life which transcends evolution
. . . It is not until we have penetrated into the meaning
of forgiveness that we can see the deepest point of this
disarming of the devil and the most complete point at
which pain is lifted to creative power. In forgiveness
the love which encounters pain is made supreme, and
the pain thus encountered by love is drawn finally out
of the control of evil.[23]

What I think Elphinstone does not answer is how the
benefit of this struggle going on in Christ transmits itself
to the rest of us. Other atonement theorists have said that
it is because Christ is not *just man struggling* but because
he is also God. Therefore the God in us or the us in God—
however we like to phrase it—shares in and benefits from
the struggle. This still leaves the question 'how?' which
has been answered in terms of human belief, faith,
commitment, and the grace and gift of the sacraments of
baptism and the Eucharist.

I have an admittedly halting scenario of my own which
may penetrate a little more into this mystery, and I offer
it now hesitantly. Yet in so far as my offering it to my
readers is also an offering to myself, I find even as I am
writing that I am moving forward a little from my agnostic
place of even a few pages ago.

I think it is possible that the Christian themes of
atonement and redemption can be seen as mirroring the
struggle of all our human development, and in this sense
can be universal. They can articulate for us that which
perhaps we do not all need to know individually and psychologically, though some of us will and indeed will need
to for our human health and perhaps salvation.

The development of human beings is a struggle from
primitive pain—even the pain of physical birth—through

confrontation with the inevitable 'hiccups', some greater some small in the relationship between us and earliest care-givers, most likely our mothers, in which the infant equivalent of anger, rage, frustration, meaninglessness, and despair have to be survived. Love comes in early from the side of the mother if all goes well. Love here mean at least her profound attachment and commitment to the infant she has co-created. To the infant, love comes later as primitive needs are tamed and there is the growth of reciprocity and separateness. Perhaps it is not too fanciful to see in the Genesis story and then in the gospel proclamation symbolic equivalents of the human process of gradual differentiation. That which grew within a sea of waters and fluids becomes a separate being, capable first of expressing primitive need and then a form of love deriving from concern, the beginnings of responsibility, and the desire for the well-being of another. That some of this is wrought through suffering even in the best of mother–infant relationships is inevitable since no baby escapes some distress. For some this suffering can be intense and too great.

If all goes well enough it may be that the human story and the redemptive story correspond enough so that both are validated and each can be fed by the other. The religious redemptive story is then available to us for the healing of our human scars. It heals, I think, because it authentically mirrors *that which we have already experienced* and know somehow and dimly, yet surely, to be the truth. In this may lie the uniqueness of the Christian position—at least for Westerners, for I would not to make over-quick and presumptive claims beyond our own civilization. The story tunes in to that which we already intuitively know. It carries on the process of our human maturing and gives it a universality that goes beyond our particular story.

In this interpretation there is for me—as for Elphinstone —no 'Fall', only an onward struggle. It is not a magical struggle that will automatically come out right, any more than the story and process of human development automatically 'works' for any mother and child. Many of us spend our professional lives working with people for whom it was manifestly not so. Some of these people may be helped by the Christian proclamation alone or by trying to live according to the tenets of the Jewish faith; for these the religious dimension complements and assists the struggle that is already going on. But sometimes the religious dimension builds on sand and represents too rapid a turning away from that which *was* the reality for a person to that which he or she *would have liked* to have been the reality for them. There can be too rapid a forswearing of anger, pain, doubt, and the whole negative dimension in favour of love, joy, peace, and fellowship. If this is so then sometimes conversion, or Jewish or Christian living, or forgiveness, or the sacramental life 'works' only for a time and comes to have an 'external' flavour which is superimposed on the human without understanding or without any internal blending of the religious and human levels. The correlation of the stories was there but the real meeting between them was not able to be.

For others the stories cannot resonate with each other at all. Religion does not 'work'; forgiveness, human or religious, does not 'work' for there is no basis in experience. Sometimes we make valiant efforts to make it work as we saw that *Sheila* did in her life of unremitting struggle to live according to Thomas à Kempis. For these people the struggle may have to be lived out again with another human being in psychotherapy.

What I have said in these last few paragraphs is still, I guess, quite a long way from traditional Christian ideas on redemption, atonement, and forgiveness. Readers will have to decide whether it still devalues or makes void the idea and sense of God, or whether our relationship with God corresponds to the deepest and most universal process in human life and history. I cannot prejudge the issues for others and so will have to let the case rest here. I have not resolved the conflict nor penetrated the mystery. I am not starting from the same interior place as Elphinstone, neither do I agree with him at some points, but nevertheless his writing was a great help to me in exploring my own level.

Can I give the forces that go between humans—those of love and hate—a 'life of their own' which is perhaps what is required to reaffirm the *transcendence* of God? I do not know, but to those who can reaffirm this transcendent reality but who are still bothered by the great 'how?' question of redemption and forgiveness, it is possible that something of what I have said may serve as some small illumination.

Elphinstone makes more than I can of the sense that love is revolutionary, and that it is a newcomer to the scene. He cites a confusion between salvation and evolution and says that this does violence to the necessary grapple of love with evil.[24] I think he is both right and wrong in psychological terms. Love is more revolutionary for the infant than for the mother. The watershed for us in our human development is when we can feel concern and real guilt and begin to take responsibility for our contribution to the state of things. Even then it is not responsibility as we know it as adults. It is more the recognition that many different feelings *do* belong to us and do not have to be split away from us and made somehow no part of us. I am talking as if this was achieved once for all at a definite point of our development, but of course it is not. We have the lifelong task of extending our self-awareness and our internal freedom. But it is perhaps nevertheless true that it is attachment that is natural; the distinctiveness of love has to emerge. There is an element of revolution in the process in that the fullness of love is not easily predictable from the experience of primitive and natural attachment.

For a mother, love for her baby is evolutionary in so far as she comes to motherhood with some idea of what love is. Of course her love has much of the primitive mixed up in it because pregnancy and giving birth is a primitive process. In some ways a mother is attached to her baby in as primitive a fashion as the infant is attached to her. But there is something different in that the mother builds on what she already knows of love. The worst difficulties between mothers and children arise when the mother has not got enough good experience of loving inside her to experience motherhood and its loving demands as evolutionary. When the step to motherhood is too revolutionary then all may go wrong. But in human motherhood love is not naturally the newcomer, and in so far as it is it may in fact never get born at all.

There is a final area I want to explore, one also taken up by Elphinstone in his last chapter on 'the vindication of God's honour'. The ancient redemption and atonement scenario allows us to play many roles within it. Perhaps we are the Christ struggling to become our own person and confront the pain of separation that is an escapable part of this task. Perhaps we are the disciples caught in a sense of guilt and responsibility. Perhaps we are the persecutors experiencing the strength of our aggression and hate. We are reminded of the picture of the crucifixion by Blake, where God the father upholds the cross of Christ and contains and supports the drama that is being played out, in the same way that a mother contains and supports the developmental struggles of her infant.

The drama of this image may perhaps show us why the satisfaction or angry God theory of the atonement can be frightening to us. It drives the wedge between the Father and the Son, that could correspond to a dreaded wedge between mother and infant. Without her support we cannot do our essential part of the work of development. If that happens parts of us—the bits we cannot contain within us, our rage or hating or sense of excited aliveness perhaps—will have to die without the hope of resurrection, sometimes for a near or complete human lifetime unless someone else can make it possible for us to restart that inner work

This is why Elphinstone's last pages are so important to me. They always were from the time I first read the book, but I could not then see why. I think I can now. In those final pages he attempts to deal with that strand in the tradition of which he says:

> One of the hardest things to accept in the traditional theory and outlook of Atonement doctrine has been its insistence on placing man so wholly 'in the doghouse' about all that has gone wrong in the world. God gave man free will—that has always been admitted—and yet in acting part in freedom, part in ignorance and impetuosity, part in stupidity, part in malice and outright sin, part in sheer muddle and doubt, man has had to lay all guilt and blame on himself and grovel over his own wickedness. Hence some of the difficulties attached to deciding exactly what Christ was doing in order to put man right with God and restore him to God's favour. Hence also the ordinary man's problem when he asks why, if God has given freedom and so permitted things to get into a mess, need man bear the whole blame for making the mess? It is a perfectly valid question.[25]

Without compromising his own theological position of the reality of sin and the possible alienation of people from God and themselves he goes to on to say of Christ's life and death:

> Dare we discern anything so outrageous as the idea that here God is making an atonement towards man for all that his desired creation costs man in the making: that he was making love's amends to all those who feel, and have felt, that they cannot forgive God for all the pains which life has foisted, unwanted, upon them? It is certainly true that man, struggling to perceive the justice which his God-like nature demands cannot forgive God for the fate which freedom's caprice has brought his way . . . Perhaps God in his love stands, not only as the bestower of forgiveness, but as the Father who, for the sake of the created whose glory is his desire, even stoops to invite the forgiveness he cannot deserve in order to make it one degree easier for man to be drawn into the orbit of love.[26]

God must give as well as take, and acknowledge responsibility even if, within a free creation, the state of affairs could not be helped. So too must our human care-givers give, in order to make possible in us the act of forgiveness that all of us will have to make if we are to become free of the scars that their inevitable imperfections will have left on us. Herein lies the mystery of reciprocity at the heart of human development and ultimately of adult human and human–divine forgiveness. If there have been no human models—of actions no less importantly than of words—how can we become free to make the act of forgiveness ourselves?

The mother who does not treat her child only as an extension of herself, who can allow the child growth into separate freedom, who can allow the aggression and the forgiveness, who can accept that in some ways she is the inflicter of pain as well as the giver of nurturance and goodness, conveys—even pre-verbally—something redemptive to the child. The religious mystery of redemption comes to ring true *because we have already known it.* But it is difficult for the human story to have a different ending—to be over-ridden by the divine story—when the initial human story was not good enough. The mystery of redemption affects all of us in our 'normality'; it is more

150   *Sin, Guilt, and Forgiveness*

difficult for us to take it in and truly benefit from it when our experience of its human counterpart has gone beyond the parameters of the 'normal'.

What then can we conclude? Can the languages of psychology and theology blend and mix? Or is there in the end only a Tower of Babel? This chapter has attempted to probe the conflicts between the languages. The ultimate basis for faith that there *will* be some blending is my contention that we have each of us already participated in the redemption story in our earliest human life. Human development is and has to be a redemptive process if we are to achieve adulthood.

These last two chapters may have seemed rather theoretical and divorced from the practical human stories we meet in our own lives or those I was attempting to capture and describe in Chapter 1. I see these chapters as necessary as I could not take further the exploration of why forgiveness sometimes 'works' and why sometimes it does not without them. But I now need to return to the more specific and 'down to earth' issues of how we manage when we confess or listen to confession, forgive or are forgiven.

Notes

1. See C. Geffre and G. Guttierez, *Theology of Liberation* (Concilium 1974).
2. Romans 13.1 (AV).
3. For example, 1 Timothy 2.11; Titus 2.4–5.
4. Exodus 24.12.
5. See I. T. Ramsey, *Models for Divine Activity* (SCM 1973), especially chapters 1 and 5.
6. Acts 10.9–48.
7. See Acts 5.38–9.
8. J. A. T. Robinson, *Honest to God* (SCM 1963).
9. David Jenkins, when Bishop-designate of Durham, 1984.
10. David Jenkins, Christmas 1993.
11. Sebastian Moore, *The Crucified is No Stranger* (DLT 1977).
12. 'Psychodynamic therapy' draws upon psychoanalytic theory to understand a person and their interactions in terms of their childhood development and unconscious as well as conscious processes. These become manifest in the relationship that develops between therapist and client, in which the client is likely to 'transfer' on to the therapist feelings

and memories which originally belonged to other relationships, predominantly—but not exclusively—with parents.

13. F. Lake, *Clinical Theology: A Theological and Psychological Basis to Clinical Pastoral Care* (DLT 1966).
14. 1 Corinthians 13.12 (author's paraphrase).
15. See Chapter 5, Note 32.
16. Andrew Elphinstone, *Freedom, Suffering and Love* (SCM 1976).
17. Elphinstone, *Freedom,* chapters 10–12.
18. Elphinstone, *Freedom,* p. 100.
19. Elphinstone, *Freedom,* p. 104.
20. Elphinstone, *Freedom,* pp. 95–9 and chapter 13.
21. Elphinstone, *Freedom,* pp. 109–10, 122 and see Chapters 4 and 5 of this book.
22. Elphinstone, *Freedom,* p. 118.
23. Elphinstone, *Freedom,* p. 122.
24. Elphinstone, *Freedom,* chapter 13, and especially p. 130.
25. Elphinstone, *Freedom,* p. 146.
26. Elphinstone, *Freedom,* p. 147.

SEVEN

'Go in Peace'
or
Forgiveness, Healing, and
Deliverance

———

I am thinking of two instances within the liturgy when the phrase 'go in peace' is used. One is at the dismissal at the end of the Eucharist where the proclamation is: 'Go in peace, to love and serve the Lord'[1] and the other is at the end of the rite for private confession where the version is 'The Lord has freed you from your sins'.[2]

The Eucharist or great thanksgiving stands as a remembrance and re-enactment of the redemptive work of Christ, 'through whom we are freed from the slavery of sin'.[3] As such it includes—as do all public services—prayers of penitence and confession and the proclamation of absolution. Sin, it seems, is always with us, even though we are delivered from its enslaving and death-dealing consequences. The service reiterates the truth of our human condition that we cannot live up to the ideal of living without sin. Confession and forgiveness are, as it were, routine parts of our relationship with God. It is clear that the prerequisite of forgiveness is confession—as we saw in Chapter 4 when we were exploring the purely human face of forgiveness. Forgiveness needs the acknowledgement that something is astray and the beginnings of taking responsibility for this.

The phrase 'go in peace' at the end of rite of confession has a more personal, authoritative note for the hearer. But the message is the same; the assurance of the freedom to go on again in renewed trust and love.

Yet why is it that this assurance does not reach some people, even in its most personalized form? For it does not;

152

some people cannot seem to know inside themselves a sense of freedom and forgiveness. I hope that the preceding chapters may have given us the beginnings of ideas as to how and why this should be so, but in order to try to understand it more fully I would like to look again at some of the human stories of my first chapter in more detail. Those stories gave us four instances of confession and forgiveness in its more or less explicit form, and two instances when something like the process might have been called for.

First, we have the general confession in the parish Eucharist which we participated in through the medium of the *Church* family. Basically the act of confession passed them by—only *Mark* wondered what 'negligence' was. *Michael Church* was busy seeing football patterns in the reflections of the sunlight. *Margaret Church* apparently made no connection between the confession and her own rueful thought that there is no peace in the world despite her prayers and the prayers of others. Would they have missed the confession if it hadn't been there? Most probably not, so in some way it was not at all speaking to their condition, though nevertheless they and all the congregation joined meekly in with it. Perhaps it is very hard for the general confession to speak to us unless we are already very attuned to its contents. In times of corporate disaster or danger, senses may be heightened and the words and the sense get through. But in normal times the general confession does not consciously penetrate into our individual inner worlds, and it is probably hard for us to own it as in some way belonging to us.

That is not to say that it does not penetrate at all. I argued in *Clergy Stress* that some of the impact of any liturgy takes place beneath our level of conscious apprehension and awareness of it.[4] If it did not then the liturgy would, I think, feel less than complete though without people being able to identify easily the source of this incompleteness. Perhaps it is just because something 'goes in' that we are not aware of, that we cannot easily reflect upon it and it may *seem* as if nothing has got through to us.

The general confession often does not 'work' because it is too impersonal and does not resonate with us; we have no individual part to play in it. It may be different when the group that has come together for worship is a smaller, self-contained group. In, for example, a religious community many of the group's members are intimately known to each other, and there is some subliminal sense of the corporate state of the whole. It may also be different when the worshipping group is built round a common *cause*— for example, world peace, world poverty, Aids, Christian unity—and all the elements of the service, including the confession, reflect that cause. The theme is already there, passionately alive to the individuals involved, and it concentrates their minds and hearts at all parts of the service. Or it may be easier for the general confession to be meaningful for all worshippers at specific times of the liturgical year. Lent, Advent, and Holy Week are the most likely. At these times the whole liturgy is penitential, and our inner being can be more open to that theme whether or not we bring to it anything special of our own. A *general* confession needs something else to make an individual person's involvement and engagement with it *particular*.

Forgiveness, confession, compassion, absolution; these are great words, but the realities they reflect can only really be taken in and absorbed by people when they have a personal human face.

This is not universally true. There have been other symbols of the wrath and forgiveness of God often taken from nature; the storm, the thunder, the earthquake, and the calm sea. Yet it is noticeable that in the meeting of Elijah with his God in the wilderness, the Lord was for him not to be found in the earthquake, wind, or fire, but in a still small voice.[5] Great natural symbols can clearly rouse something in us. They can move us at levels that we cannot easily articulate, but perhaps only when the communication is humanized do we have a chance to take in, reflect, and understand so as to grow. Human beings need other human beings and human communication in order to become more maturely human. Even Romulus and Remus, kept alive in the legend by the wolves around Rome, had each other for company.

I have, therefore, come to think that one of the conditions for confession and forgiveness to 'work'—that is bring relief and growth in love and awareness—is that the interchange shall be *personal*. By 'personal' I do not mean that only our highest, most maturely personal selves are involved; some of the ritual clearly resonates at a more unconscious level than that. It is more that it must involve a personal element. Where the impersonal reigns, increased fear, rather than increased love, is likely to be the result.

We have already looked at stories where personal confession actually takes place. *Robert*, the university student, makes a confession—along with several hundred other people at a mass rally—which gives him a conversion experience. The bubble of his 'satisfactory' life gets pricked and he feels he is being told through the rally that his eternal being is in danger unless he submits to the Lord Jesus. He also *seems* to be getting the message that a renewed sense of sin is the condition of love.

Conversion experiences through the ages, from St Paul and St Augustine on, have clearly been able to start someone off on a life of dedicated and joyous belief and service. Indeed great joy is often one of their hallmarks, together with a very sure sense of forgiveness and of being loved by God that can sometimes be so elusive. It is important to say this before I go on to explore one or two points that have always troubled me about such experiences.

It seems to me that there can be a danger in 'conversion' in that it has the potential to push us back into the most primitive level of our human experience. In particular, if it is built up to in a certain way in the context of 'hell-fire and damnation' preaching it can require us to split[6] ourselves apart in a strange way. All the bad is in us and all the good is in God. Without God we are rotten, nearly damned, and can do nothing for ourselves. Therefore salvation consists in letting God's love drive out our sin and badness. This seems a long way from the mature position in which love and hate are both present in us, but we have come to trust that our love is stronger than our hate.[7] In this sort of conversion experience we learn, certainly, that the love of the *Almighty* is stronger than our badness, *provided* that we admit that we are all bad, and that this love coming from *outside* us will somehow take away all our badness.

Since, as we have seen, our inner worlds cannot just be eradicated or changed in an instant, there can come to be considerable psychological strain and even danger through a 'conversion' of this kind, just because it depends on this splitting apart of good and bad instead of letting them come together and become, as far as is possible, integrated and contained within a growing sense of self.

This sort of converted self cannot grow of itself—it can only grow in submission to the Lord, so it is difficult for it not to remain fragile. It can come to remind us of a mother–child relationship in which the child is said to be really bad and the mother is really good and the child has no authentic goodness inside. So the child grows only with a *borrowed* self that depends for its very existence on the goodness of someone outside. If good appears inside the child it will be perceived as pride or arrogance; if bad reappears then two things can happen. Either it has to be driven away with repeated submissions to the will of the Almighty, or—if this does not seem to be working—it has to be ascribed to the works of the devil. When this last happens *both good and evil* are put outside the self and it is difficult to see what can be left of our personal being; possibly nothing.

Under what sort of religious and psychological circumstances could conversion have this negative outcome? Clearly I am doing far less than justice to an experience that has helped many if I seem to be saying that it is an *inevitable* outcome. It is not. I think it is something about whether we turn to God predominately in response to a sense of *love and trust* or a sense of *fear*. Psychologically this may well depend on the depths of the inner world that we bring to that experience—much of which may be still unknown to us.

It is hard for us to recognize and respond to the love of God (or human love for that matter) if we have never known human love and if our inner world is most at home with criticism, punishment, or fear. Conversion brings often immediate relief. It is like the bad feelings being taken away when mother returns after an absence; badness is replaced by bliss—*until the next time*. Conversion has the potential for providing a container, or breathing space, or shield of love and holding within which development can take place, and in the most favourable of situations this happens. But what unfortunately it can sometimes alternatively do is to induce a rigidity and an all-encompassing fear of returning to the previous state because that state, and the pain inherent in it, has not been confronted or mastered. That sort of conversion experience perhaps stops us suffering from what we are, but it often breeds rigidity in us which makes us only associate with like-minded people, unable to tolerate the fact that some other people have different experiences and find different ways to God, and also unable to bear the feeling of the absence of God. Should we seem to lose God we have two choices only; either we have betrayed him and can only be restored by a repeat of the conversion submission, or we elect to lose God altogether and so lose faith. The equilibrium is too fragile and we have not been helped to bear and tolerate our real selves, but only to get rid of ourselves.

Conversion can also act as a *deliverance* when people would find the full consciousness of the nature of their being and of the being of God too anxiety-provoking and even persecuting. If it is serving this function then perhaps it relieves actual or imminent persecutory guilt. But I do not think that it necessarily helps us to take responsibility for the person we are and to grow as people.

We often talk of conversion as 'seeing the light', but the problem comes if we see the light only in God and concurrently see our own darkness by that light *but have to turn away from it*, scoop it out of ourselves and lay it on Jesus. This may certainly be deliverance, but I am not sure that it is *forgiveness*. I am not sure that it heals our wounds and scars, and it seems a far cry from the theme of judgement in St John's Gospel which as I see it was intended to light up dark crannies so that they could be cleansed rather than exterminated.[8]

If, alternatively, our inner world is more benign, and we have known—dimly or a lot—what love is, then a proclamation of the saving love of God is likely to resonate *with what is already there*, draw us to imitate it, and deepen our self-giving. An acknowledgment of our own unworthiness may well form part of this response, but this will be *contained* in our desire to love more, not forced out of us by fear.

On the *religious level*, perhaps it boils down to whether or not we can believe, and indeed whether or not it is presented to us as such, that the love of God is already present in us, through the indwelling of the Spirit—that spirit that 'moved upon the face of the waters'[9] and breathed into our nostrils the breath of life.[10] In other words, perhaps it depends on our view and theology of creation—are we or are we not made in God's image? I am reminded here of one of the hymns to the Holy Spirit that I think exemplifies this drawing and converting power of love:

O Thou who camest from above
The pure celestial fire to impart,
Kindle a fire of sacred love
On the mean altar of my heart.

There let it for thy glory burn
With inextinguishable blaze,
And trembling to its source return
In humble prayer, and fervent praise.

Jesus, confirm my heart's desire
To work, and speak, and think for thee;
Still let me guard the holy fire,
And still stir up thy gift in me.

Ready for all thy perfect will,
My acts of faith and love repeat,
Till death thy endless mercies seal,
And make my sacrifice complete.[11]

In this hymn the power and love of God and our appropriate creaturely response seem set in almost perfect balance.

But in any experience of heightened awareness and desire for dedication I think that a lot must depend on what happens after the initial moment—whatever has given rise to that moment and however it was induced. If it is no more than a moment of heightened awareness, which becomes the sole way in which we can relate to God in a sort of stalemate where any emergence of our personal being will be bad apart from the repeated invoking of the conversion experience, I do not think a self can grow. Some fundamentalists would not mind this for they would say that we have no self of our own anyway—only the one we find in Jesus. I vividly remember from an evangelical Sunday school the reminder that the cross was the 'I' crossed out! It is one thing to choose to discipline and even deny a self that we already firmly have—as did Francis of Assisi. It is quite another to develop a false self that can only exist in precarious equilibrium between a sense of sin and the almighty and overwhelming power of the Saviour.

But if the moment of heightened awareness can be a prelude to a greater awareness of personal responsibility in which the love of the Lord is used as an adjunct to strengthen our own love then a mature self can grow. It can be a moment of clarity in which love is seen to be worth having and possessing both inside and out, and it is seen that only increased love—not increased fear—can counter the darkness we also find in ourselves.

We now come to two people who make personal and explicit confession in church; *Anne* who does so regularly, and *Simon* who approaches a priest when he is in crisis. It is not quite clear what happens to *Anne* as she makes her regular confession, but what does seem to filter through is that the priest's regular counsel makes little real impact on her. We gather she comes back week after week accusing herself of much the same things. The priest urges her to relax, gives her light penances, but does not seem to have a great sense that anything will change.

In one sense we could suggest that *Anne's* confession safeguards her equilibrium in a very difficult domestic situation, and this is not to be despised. Furthermore, in letting another human being in on her thoughts, fears, and perceived failures she is perhaps helped to modify and keep in check the thread of self-punishment and harshness to herself that we guess is inside. If she con-fessed to God alone it might be too impersonal for this to happen unless her God is somehow more benign and gentle than her own inner voice, her superego.[12] The priest may not make much inroad—he does not seem to be able to help her to re-evaluate herself and her situation, to give thanks to herself for the times when she manages her frustrations well—but he is perhaps helping her to tolerate her anger and even giving her the impression that it is to be expected and is not *so* dreadful. In this he probably functions as a helpful intermediary or filter of a merciful God to counter the effect of *Anne's* habitual internal god that we suspect may well be harsher than God's human representative.

But we can well imagine that the same dialogue, or something very similar, may go on for ever and ever, and become part of the framework rather than an agent for change and growth. That may be an over-harsh judgement; perhaps over the years the message of mercy, toleration, and self-understanding and acceptance may get through, but it is a long slow business. We wonder too whether the very ritual—weekly as a pre-condition for receiving communion—is itself stopping *Anne* take real responsibility for herself in her situation. We cannot tell but at the least it seems that the process is reinforcing *Anne's* struggle to gain the sense that her anger and frustration can be contained by love and understanding; the problem is that it is at present *another's* love and understanding, not *her own*. Her occasional bouts of anger are kept in check not by love but by *guilt*.

Anne's guilt is not excessively persecuting; it is much more like depressive guilt in that it relates to things *in* her and not *outside* her and is perhaps steadying her and protecting her from having to know the extent of her hostility, for it can be 'dealt' with once a week. This may be enough for her, but she cannot use and be the whole of her person—it is difficult for her to grow.

As shown in *Anne*, confession and forgiveness can give support and keep an equilibrium. Yet the dynamic of forgiveness can also bring about change because it can confront and bring together some of the warring factions in our inner worlds. But to see this we have to turn to *Simon*, the business executive.

Simon's situation exemplifies the potential and possibilities in confession and forgiveness. He is not used to coming to a priest to confess, but has been driven here by his inner state. His inner world is near to exploding on him and his most conscious need is a need to talk, and share.

Perhaps anyone might have filled the bill—a close friend or a colleague—but *Simon* chooses not to go that way. He chooses to come to someone he does not know very well, but whom he recognizes as possessing a role and perhaps symbolizing a level of reality for which he feels the need even if he has not worked it out to himself very clearly. He senses in himself that his turmoil is not just to do with his fear of his illness and his vulnerability in the face of it. This sense of vulnerability might make him less likely to go to his friends—with them he has to keep up a face. We do not necessarily have to look very deeply to see why he might prefer a relative stranger. But he goes beyond this and actually chooses the vicar and the church, and when he has talked about the facts he makes a connection between his illness and his sense of not having been a very good father and husband which lead on to his halting confession of his long affair. He does not seem directly to be attributing to his illness the quality of punishment; it is rather that the possibility of death is making him reflect on his whole being, not just his body.

After the informal confession two things happen. *Martin*, the priest, senses that he is being asked to reassure *Simon* that his 'bad' bits have not put him outside the love of God. The absolution is not formal, but the prayer offered is for forgiveness that God will accept *Simon* both with his illness and his falling short. The result in human terms is that *Simon* rapidly becomes less isolated. He wants to go home and talk to his wife about his illness. We guess that he may ponder during the coming months over whether or not to tell his wife about his infidelity. To do so might bring them together or drive them apart in what might be the last period they have together if the doctor's worst diagnosis should prove correct. But we have the strong sense that forgiveness has increased rather than decreased *Simon's* capacity for personal responsibility. Perhaps, more than he consciously knew, he came to the church looking for somebody or something to hold and contain both his great and understandable fears about death—for life and death are after all part of religion's business—*and* for somewhere where he could bring his whole self, take stock of it, and take responsibility for it. We have the sense that he may well go back to the vicar, and if indeed he becomes really ill the vicar may become much more involved. He may want to make confession again, but if he does it will *not be the same confession*, for he will have moved on, and it will be because there is a *new* area opened up for growth.

This, as with *Anne's* story earlier, is an extrapolation. Neither story may go the way I have outlined. *Anne* could confound us by growing rapidly in love, compassion, and self-understanding. *Simon* may get stuck in bitterness or self-recrimination and be unable to move forward. Yet something in the *tone* of these two encounters makes me feel that the first impressions are not wrong. *Anne* and *Simon* seem different sorts of people, and my hunch is that they have different inner landscapes. *Anne's* is more tortured and tortuous with jagged rock nearly hidden behind smooth rounded hillocks. Can things be rearranged so that the landscape can be seen in its entirety, or not? *Simon's* landscape, I would guess, is already more flexible; there are both rocks and hillocks, but they are as they are, some in the foreground and some in the background. There are potential dark caverns, one marked 'fear and death', others with no name; but their entrances are not overgrown with shrubs and bushes—we would be unlikely to fall into one by mistake, though we might not have time or inclination to explore them all. There is also some blue sea with tranquil dune grass and birds. It is an outdoor scene with some light and some dark. The clouds are gathering but so far the basic shape of the landscape has not changed. Translating, we could guess that confession 'worked' for *Simon* because he was already able and willing to let light in, to face reality and to take responsibility.

We turn now to two people who do not make, as far as we know, any use of private confession. One is *Stewart*, the isolated homosexual man who wants to get away from his inner turmoil, but who is in no state to use the church's ministrations to sinners. He already feels persecuted by his sense that the church thinks of him as, at best, a second-class citizen, and, at worst, a perverted sinner. In fact, both these attitudes towards homosexuality *are* met with in the communities of faith at the present time. *Stewart's* feelings are not without a reality base, but he distorts them in that he has come to feel that 'everybody' thinks that way. He feels persecuted so much that it drives him into deeper isolation and mistrust, and probably deep inside him, into rage at the injustice. In so far as the Christian community cannot tell him he is all right and worthy of respect, he is going to have to find a way to say this to himself in order to raise his self-esteem. Only then might he be able to examine and acknowledge any contribution he has made and is making to his own isolation and discomfort.

We suspect *Stewart* pushes away overtures of friendship

and relationship, but that is understandable. He is not at present in an emotional place inside himself from which he can do anything else. Neither does he have good memories inside himself to draw upon; he has only those of the parents he could not trust with the truth. The considerable fear that he may have HIV does nothing to relieve the sense of badness and persecution. He finds it hard to forgive himself for the injury and irreversible damage he may already have done himself through the various ways he has sought in the past to relieve his loneliness and isolation.

Stewart does not need confession at this moment, though he might think he does. Perhaps he does not need therapy either, except in so far as he has become unable to come out of himself and relate. Maybe what he needs most of all, if he can accept them is support, acceptance, and friendship. If he could talk to someone as a first step it could be invaluable, for only then would we really learn whether his resistance to being accepted, to hearing something other than the reactions of his parents, is so great that he may also need therapy so as to become freer of those now internal parental and authority figures.

Second there is *Sheila* who, as far as we know, practises totally private confession at least nightly—and probably more often. We are not told whether she confides her sense of unworthiness and inner turmoil to anyone else— we suspect not. She seems to be in quite a state and some help is needed beyond the much-thumbed Thomas à Kempis, but without knowing her better it is difficult to know just what. If she talked to the Rector, either informally or more formally, he would almost certainly want to say to her that her nightly agonies of confession of presumed peccadilloes were unnecessary and that God is not as hard on her as she seems to want to be on herself. He might also be able to pick up on her loneliness since her mother died and wonder whether she is being thrown back too much on an inner world which has never been very friendly or self-accepting. Or he might not—depending on the level of his self-awareness and training.

We can perhaps see how *Sheila* has fashioned her God in the shape of her harsh exacting father for whom she could never do things well enough, could never please, and from whom she could find no affection or love. The

God who prescribes behaviour and is seen as the source of ideals and prohibitions is vulnerable to this sort of projection. We can see it; the question is, can *Sheila*? *Could* the minister point it out to her and firmly make the point that further confession is likely only to exacerbate—rather than relieve—her need to placate her sense of guilt?

If *Sheila* could hear that message she would already be on the road to emotional and spiritual health. If she cannot then perhaps it means that she is too caught up inside within an inner mood that has the image of stern father all over it, and even one of a mother who could not protect or save her. Perhaps her mother was never there at the crucial moments of the past—and she is dead now. She remains ineffective or even standing in memory as a further model of cowering submission to a harsh man. It could be more complicated still if *Sheila's* father had not seemed so stern and demanding to anyone but *Sheila*. We might then wonder whether the trouble was something in that actual relationship or whether *Sheila* had arranged her inner furniture from even earlier experience so as always to have this atmosphere. If either of these scenarios hold then almost certainly reassurance or challenge of her religious system would not reach her, and an unravelling of her false and harsh convictions through therapy might well be necessary. The state she has got into suggests this.

In our literary examples we have two further instances of 'confession' not working—*Raskolnikov* and *Lady Macbeth* but they are poles apart in their make-up. *Raskolnikov* is in a mixed inner place; in part his guilt and his compulsive need for confession are only too reality-based. He *has* committed a murder and his need for relief from his internal torment through confession is manifest to the extent that he has to give himself up. But his guilt and fear—as shown in his dream of the grey mare and his earlier efforts to resist his crime—do not *all* stem from the present. He, too, seems to have been persecuted by his past and so his efforts to take responsibility in the present have something of the surreal about them, even though on one level they seem only too justified by the event. His trial and punishment may expunge his guilt for both or they may not; if the original is not expunged then the compulsion to repeat his crime could continue.

Confession of the obvious may not be enough, even where there is sincere repentance as there does seem to be in his case. The inner world has not really changed even though the inner set of mind seems to have.

To make a real difference confession and forgiveness must often touch our inner world at a point beneath the level of consciousness. It may be something of the genius of the liturgy and the ritual for private confession that their symbols are such as reach our inner worlds. Some of the most archaic and stubborn parts of our being are connected with powerful religious images. Those external images, if they are benign—the reassuring words of the liturgy, the understanding of the priest, the invocation of the mother of God—can somehow filter down through our being to the level where the more frightening images live and make change possible. A harsh father-in-God or a harsh external image of God the father can, though, do the reverse, and render our inner world more entrenched and malevolent, less open to the liberating power of forgiveness.

Last, we look again at *Lady Macbeth*. What are her dream-like outpourings? They look like confession. They look like a plea to someone, somewhere for some sort of forgiveness. The doctor quails before her—she needs a priest. Yet a priest could not reach her, nor she him, simply because she is sleepwalking and there can be no real personal contact with her in this state. Neither can sleep, as claimed in an earlier line of the play 'knit up the ravelled sleeve of care'.[13] For her it is the means of displaying and describing her torment, not that of relieving it. Neither therapy nor confession can help her, for she has put herself into a state in which she is inaccessible to both.

In fact *Lady Macbeth* herself acknowledges her own impermeability to help in her subsequent suicide. Could anything have helped her? Can healing, confession, therapy, or forgiveness operate when there is no conscious cooperation of any kind? We do not know, but communities of faith have believed that something can happen in the offering of absolution or the last rites even to unconscious persons. Yet that offering is but half—the one side only—of what is normally required in forgiveness, either by God or humankind; the other is the act of confession which *Lady Macbeth* could not make. In some ways she had no chance, yet we are given no sense that her innermost being really wanted a chance. Her innermost being was in torment, but in no state to own herself or her acts, and so she died.

Judas Iscariot remains an eternal mystery here. He did make a conscious and responsible confession to the high priests—'I have betrayed . . . innocent blood'[14]—he threw back the money, but received no relief. Perhaps in essence he was condemned to suicidal despair because his inner world—still destructive—directed him to the wrong place to make his confession. He went to confess to people who were not interested in him or his fate; to them he was simply an agent they had needed and used. *Peter*, on the other hand, chose to put himself into the hands of the Lord he had wronged and denied—'the Lord turned and looked at Peter. And Peter . . . went out and wept bitterly'.[15] He experienced the healing power of felt grief. The tragedy of Judas is perhaps not so much his crime, but that in his remorse and turmoil he did not know to whom to turn.

It seems to me from these stories that in exploring confession and forgiveness we are considering at least three different levels of activity. The first is what I call confession and forgiveness proper. The main point I want to make is that this is a much more mature activity than has sometimes been recognized.

There are instances in literature when priests have refused to hear confessions because the person is not ready for it. One such comes in Susan Howatch's[16] sixfold work of life in the Church of England over sixty years. There is some sense in *Glittering Images* and *Glamorous Powers* of people going to confession because they felt they ought to, and almost as an insurance policy against their nature and their desires. But in *Glittering Images*[17] there is a long dialogue between *John Darrow*, a monk, and a young priest who is in a personal mess. Most of the dialogue is confessional in nature, and at one point the young priest, *Charles*, wants to cut the whole thing short and make a formal confession so that he can return to communion. But *Darrow* refuses to hear it at that point, saying that it would not be complete as *Charles* has not yet fully understood or acknowledged the complexity of his actions and feelings. The confession comes at the end when much more is known and much more genuine responsibility can be taken.

Confession and forgiveness form a process that requires the taking of personal responsibility in the knowledge—as far as possible—of what has gone wrong and what has gone into the situation. Its aim is not just to be a way to bring relief, though it often does, but to enable pain, anger, and hurt to be faced, encircled in love, and a new beginning made. It involves the facing of guilt and being able to discern that to which the guilt really and maturely belongs.

Confession and forgiveness operate on the level of depressive guilt. They are a way for the person not to deny their darker side, but to realize that with God, at any rate, they can be contained and integrated into our being in love. The process is not a tribunal for which appropriate punishment should be meted out, for the real penance is in the true and mature acknowledgment of sin, which is painful enough of itself.

When the sacrament has to be repeated weekly and has become part of the routine of the Christian life, as in much of the Roman Catholic Church, it is difficult for every such act to reach this maturity. If this is not realized then the whole can become less than a mature exchange.

Of course, within a human relationship forgiveness cannot be guaranteed in the same way as it is in the religious sphere, for the other person or persons are not God and may not be able to tolerate and accept the concern and reparation that are offered in the act of seeking forgiveness. That is a risk in human terms that we have to take, and it is perhaps a mark of more mature humanity that it knows this and can tolerate the thought and sometimes the reality of being rejected.

Confession is, in this way, intended to lead to growth in understanding and love. The danger is that it degenerates into a placation with or without felt anguish as a precursor of this. This is, perhaps, the danger with the more routine use of the sacrament, and possibly also with the use of the general confession in large gatherings. 'Placate, have an insurance, in case the other person or God might get angry.' Confession truly needs to be willingly undertaken. It is not surprising that confessions in other spheres, such as under the duress of police interrogation, sometimes turn out to be false. The more primitive our motives for making a confession, such as when we are ruled by threat or fear, the more likely this is to be the case.

It may seem here as if I am making value judgements on different kinds of confession, and suggesting that it is something—along with forgiveness—that we do well or badly and something in which we ought to be able to change and mature.

I think there is *some* truth in this. In psychotherapy it often takes time to learn how to be a patient or client in order to make best use of the process. But the judgement is pragmatic rather than value laden, much more an acceptance of what is possible. On the human level, if we look at instances when our efforts at forgiveness and being forgiven have not worked out, it may well have been because neither party was mature enough, that too much of fear and the need for placation was still in the process. Yet, on the religious level, it would be a travesty of grace and the sacraments to demand, as it were, standards for the ability to make confession and receive forgiveness. I am suggesting something rather different. I offer a partial *explanation* of why religious confession and forgiveness sometimes seem to bring no relief and no real change— namely, when confession does not come from the mature part of ourselves. That is hardly our fault, and it may not be something that can be easily changed for all the reasons that we have been exploring in these pages, but a good spiritual director who detects something of this may be able, nevertheless, to help.

None of us can be mature all the time in our approach to God and each other; some of us will find it hard to be so for some or even any of the time.

So I move to my *second* level of confessional activity. In this the acts of confession and absolution have to go on under less than mature circumstances, and they have a character closer to a healing process rather than a growth process, though I do not want to be seeming to set these two terms in antithesis to each other. The nuances are delicate and one process shades off into another; overall in any exchange one may be predominant.

I am reminded of the distinction that Winnicott[18] made when he asserted that classical psychoanalysis could only be used by people who had reached a certain level of psychological development; only then could interpretations make sense and be tolerable. Other people required 'management' which he describes as a holding— not without exploring—but providing a containing within which a strengthening of the person and a reliving of earlier fears and stages can take place. I think there is an analogy to this in the religious dimension. Some people need to make confession—in the sense that they need to share their deepest fears and inadequacies with another person and before God—for quite a long time during which they will feel relief but in which some of the elements of the mature process, especially the capacity for personal responsibility, concern, reparation, and increase in love, will not be able to come to their full fruition. If this is not understood and the process is not held and guided by the priest, people may go through the ritual, get no help from it, and even repeat and repeat it in a sort of compulsion, but never freely move or grow. This was *Sheila's* dilemma and she was not being held by anyone, person or God.

For people like this confession is not quite appropriate, but absolution may be. They are truly not able to be fully responsible for the sin or sins they acknowledge but they need a sense from God of his acceptance of their afflicted state. For these people counselling or psychotherapy is indicated, though not necessarily instead of the religious activity, or the sacraments of healing can well be added to the confessional framework. We cannot and should not deprive people of recourse to religious sacraments and dimensions, but if they are not to degenerate into a sort of magic, then further help is needed for them to understand with their being how they are approaching God. They need something certainly, but it is not in one sense forgiveness, for the things that are troubling them they are not as yet in a personal and emotional position to avoid.

In this we are back at the distinction between *original sin* and *sin(s)*. Confession is really for sin(s). Original sin, that is the total of our tendencies and inadequacies that we are only more or less aware of and can do little to change immediately, but which may then result in actions and words we may well then call sin(s), needs not so much formal confession but counsel and healing within a confessional attitude. Theology suggests that original sin is 'dealt' with in the great sacraments of

baptism and the Eucharist, but humanly speaking—
because of the nature of our individual inner worlds—we
do not seem always able to internalize them. The outward
and visible sign and the inward and spiritual grace are
not commensurate.

It seems to me that what the great sacraments are
proclaiming is something more about the attitude of the
forgiver than the forgiven. God is forever exercising an
attitude of loving-kindness (grace) and love towards his
creation, fighting on our side, and—in the great Eucharistic
thanksgiving—proclaiming victory. The extent to which individual human beings can tune into this heart and activity
of God, take advantage of it, and realize the potential of
the great promise seems to differ.

Baptism and the Eucharist remain as the great proclamations of God's attitude—the parent who creates his children
in love and does not give up on them. But for some of us
baptism and the Eucharist alone do not seem sufficient for
our inner healing. They are the earnest and the promise
of it, but our capacity to be drawn into them may be limited
by our human experience, and we need some human help
before we can participate more fully.

Many of us rub along with confession—general or private
—for much of the time. Then life reveals to us a particular
area where the disorder of original sin, or as I would like to
put it in psychological terms, our scarred inner world gets
exposed and needs help. Some of us live in that area of our
being for much more of the time and need more constant
and sustained healing. In these cases it is not that forgiveness is unimportant, but it has more of the quality of
holding, toleration, and love—toleration and acceptance
of the hurt that another's immaturity has laid upon us
without laying on them the whole burden of conscious
consent to and desire for the infliction of the hurt.

We see something of this in the words from the cross:
'Father, forgive them; for they know not what they do.'[19]
When on a deep level we are not aware of what we do we
cannot take full responsibility; we cannot confess to more
than we know, and it cannot be required of us. Indeed
many a child has been forced into an intolerable place by
parents and others by being forced to confess to 'wrongs'
they had no idea they had committed. Despite the parental
'you should have known better' they had no means

whereby to know better. Understanding rather than blame is needed. We *and* God are asked sometimes to exercise forgiveness without requiring confession. Only conscious sin can really be confessed—this is almost a truism—but unconscious hurt and sin can and often must be forgiven if a relationship is not to break down. Yet the person on whom the unconscious hurt is inflicted *is* still hurt and it is hard always to be forgiving and not to retaliate. Sometimes we are capable of this; sometimes we are not, so human relationships not infrequently do break down.

It is not completely clear either in the Jewish Scriptures or in the New Testament—witness the story of Ananias and Sapphira[20]—that God is non-retaliatory. There is quite a lot of evidence for the opposite. Yet the highest point of the prophetic messages[21] and the Christian proclamation from the cross seem to be saying that God, in his highest essence, *is* just this: non-retaliatory, forgiving love. So when we make him out as less than this we are projecting ideas on to him from our human and parental experience?

This does not preclude all idea of the wrath of God. God's anger must surely exist, but I would want to trust that God is somehow beyond and through the depressive position[22] of human beings; that God's wrath is contained by his love and does not spill over into mindless vengeance. Some may say that here I am fashioning God in, *my* desired psychological image, and that charge must to an extent be true. But it is what I have taken in from my psychological and psychotherapeutic experience and I cannot think that God as we have believed in him is less than the highest and best in humanity.

This has been a digression, but I was making a case for a level of confessional activity that needs something of Winnicott's management approach in addition to and sometimes instead of absolution. This may take the form of the sacraments of healing, pastoral or spiritual counselling, or it may take the form of psychotherapy.

The third area of confessional activity is that of deliverance. I see this differing from confession in the following way: a person who wants forgiveness is prepared to confront their pain, hurt, and anger. The one who wants deliverance hopes and tries to drive all these things away. Yet the problem of deliverance—though not I think a problem in forgiveness—is that of the parable of the

devils who are cast out of a person.[25] The person is swept
and garnished, but *empty* and so is vulnerable to the
entrance of yet more devils. Forgiveness carries the hope
of permanence for in the process of forgiveness the person is not emptied out, but something is added. There is
confrontation with the pain and the sin, and the person
can be more of a person afterwards than before. Deliverance, because it is out of our control, leaves a person
potentially empty and vulnerable, which is why the rite
of exorcism is usually conducted within a setting of a pro-
fession of faith, healing, and necessary follow-up. Even
so, does it help a person to grow against the threat of future
attacks? I have to say that I do not know. If the images of
God and Christ and goodness are firmly implanted, will
the inner 'soil' be rich enough to sustain those images'
survival and growth, or is there some danger of their
withering and dying? Spiritually and religiously we are
put in touch with the power of God, but psychologically
we can remain very limited.

So, deliverance could tend to make us experience, even
more than we may do already, God—and other people—as
powerful 'others' who have all the good (or all the bad)
and all the power. We have no natural good inside us and
our bad is so bad that it cannot be tolerated and we have
to be delivered from it. Such is the longing of someone
suffering from what I call persecutory guilt—the only
relief is seen as the *taking away* of the torment and the
tormentor.

The only time that deliverance *language* seems really
justified is in a context—which I have to admit I find difficult—in which people feel that their torment, badness, or
evil is to be ascribed to the invasion of their person by a
malignant force or the devil. I have great difficulty with
this and note with relief that diocesan exorcists take great
pains to exclude, if they can, all psychological factors
before permitting a ministry of exorcism and deliverance.
I have to allow for people to feel that there are times
when nothing less than the invasion of a malignant
force can be causing the torment—allow it both because it
is a sincerely held view and because it still belongs in the
mainstream of church life. Perhaps others have, in their
turn, to allow me my scepticism. I would need to be con-
vinced that it was not psychosis nor the overflow of an

uncontained primitive level of functioning at work.

This malignant possibility apart, I would usually and normally be hoping that even within a 'deliverance ministry' bad, guilt, sin—call it what we will—could be integrated within a person by the process of helping them strengthen their sense of self. Confession and absolution have their place in this if they serve this end of strengthening the person. So also does prayer for the calming of anxiety and fear. But how far integration can be achieved by the religious and sacramental acts alone I am not sure. What is likely to help is the combination of these with the solid support and integration of the afflicted person within the Christian community, so that the whole can become more personal rather than less personal, less of a magical deliverance from evil and more of a containing for a person of what they are finding difficult to contain for and within themselves.

It must be clear from the foregoing that the level from which and on which we make confession will inevitably depend on the state of development of our inner world. The more primitive and dark our inner world the less likely we are to be able to use and benefit from it in its formal form, and the more likely we are to need also some form of counselling or therapy. Even the general confession presupposes that we have reached a stage of development in which we can find it meaningful, and many of us have not, at least not all the time. But the *confessional attitude* of sharing and acknowledging and the sense of a God who can withstand our onslaughts and our backslidings is often secure enough for us to grow slowly and gradually into love and maturity.

I am hoping that this chapter will have helped us to see a little more of why sometimes forgiveness 'works' and why it does not. It seems to me to depend on whether it is, in fact, forgiveness or rather healing, therapy, or deliverance that are needed and being sought. Yet how can we tell? How can a minister or priest to whom we go tell? Can we undertake more than one of them at the same time? There are no easy and foolproof answers to this, but I want to take time in the next chapter to explore these issues a little more in the interests of a more effective exercise of pastoral care.

Notes

1. *Alternative Service Book 1980,* Holy Communion Rite A, p. 145.
2. Rite of Penance (Mayhew-McCrinnon 1976), Section 49, p. 44.
3. ASB, First and Second Eucharistic prayers.
4. Mary Anne Coate, *Clergy Stress* (SPCK 1989), pp. 136–7 and especially pp. 177–9.
5. 1 Kings 19.12.
6. See Chapter 3, Notes 13 and 22.
7. Psychologically, the 'depressive position'. See Chapter 5, Note 38.
8. See John 3.16–22 and 12.46–7.
9. Genesis 1.2.
10. Genesis 2.7.
11. *English Hymnal* (Geoffrey Chapman, OUP, Mowbrays 1933), number 343.
12. See Chapter 3, Note 9.
13. William Shakespeare, *The Tragedy of Macbeth,* Act II, Scene 2.
14. Matthew 27.14 (AV).
15. Luke 22.61–2.
16. S. Howatch, *Glittering Images, Glamorous Powers, Ultimate Prizes, Scandalous Risks, Mystical Paths,* and *Absolute Truths* (to come) (Collins 1988–).
17. S. Howatch, *Glittering Images* (Fontana/Collins 1988), p. 241.
18. See D. W. Winnicott, *Metapsychological and Clinical Aspects of Regression within the Psycho-analytical Set-up* (1954) in *Through Paediatrics to Psychoanalysis* (Hogarth Press 1975), pp. 278–9.
19. Luke 23.34 (RSV).
20. Acts 5.1–11.
21. For example, Hosea 11.8–9, Jeremiah 3.11–12.
22. See Chapter 5, Note 38.
23. Matthew 12.43–5.

EIGHT

'Now We See in a Glass Darkly' or For Those Who Make and Hear Confessions

I have two personal memories of sin and confession that I would like to use here because I think they could help-fully 'earth' some of what the last chapter teased out in a more conceptual form.

The first I share with many people, particularly perhaps those of my own generation. When I was confirmed into the Anglican Church I was given, as we all were, a book of devotions for use before participating in the service of Holy Communion. It seemed to presume that one went to Communion on Sundays and therefore suggested a time of preparation on Saturday nights. I used this book on and off for some time, but what struck me was the emphasis it seemed to put on sin and confession of sin. There was even a rather frightening bit in it which was echoed in the words of one of the exhortations of the 1662 Communion service that suggested that if you went to communion in a state of unrepented sin then you kindled God's wrath against you and ate and drank to your own damnation![1]

I don't think that exhortation was ever actually *used* in the Communion services I went to. Neither was its parallel in the same Book of Common Prayer which seems to exhort almost the opposite, namely not to refrain from coming to Communion but to come in penitence and with a heartfelt desire for amendment.[2]

I sort of got the message but it didn't really mean much, because I could not really relate it to my inside self. It matched up a bit with the displays of bad temper that I always seemed to be getting into in those days. I could

175

see those might need forgiveness—whatever quite that word
meant—but I had no real idea how, nor had I any idea of
why I should be subject to losing my temper and provoking
the wrath of others around me. I said something to God
about it, but nothing much changed, but neither did it
bother me very much either. I didn't naturally think of
God as being that harsh and the words didn't resonate
fearfully.

Suppose, though, I had been *Sheila*. Reading and
pondering those exhortations on my own would have
been very unhelpful to me. We gather she uses Thomas à
Kempis, not necessarily the Book of Common Prayer, but
the effect on her was quite devastating. It increased her
sense of unworthiness and renewed in her not peace or
trust in a merciful God, but a sense of torment. We guess
that *Sheila* always felt in danger of being condemned and
near damned by God.

Perhaps here we have the two extremes. In my adolescence the words and the theme meant very little to me;
they meant far too much to *Sheila*, but neither of us
understood the true nature and meaning of sin. I could not
hang the external theme on anything inside me to make
it real; *Sheila* could not get outside herself enough not to
hear the theme in a very one-sided way.

It was the same with the worshippers at the Eucharist
I described earlier. The *Church* family understood very
little of the confession—it was not relevant to them. For
Matthew, the Rector, the confession and absolution were
difficult that morning. They reminded him of his own
state of anger and fury at the episode of his daughter,
and made him question what he was doing daring to
pronounce forgiveness to others.

There is a large question emerging for us:

How do we grow into being able to have a mature
sense of sin and forgiveness?

My second memory is of much later on when I had
become used to the practice of private confession and
absolution. I remember feeling depressed, then going to
confession and confessing this, only to be told that this
was no sin and that what was really needed was not
•absolution as such but the chance to talk about it, and
that it was a pity to have to go to confession in order to

get that sort of understanding and help. I was lucky in that the priest to whom I went was discerning of my inner state at that time; he sensed that though something was wrong in my relationship with myself, other people, and indeed God, it was not something I understood enough, was necessarily culpable for, or could really confess. Something needed healing and in this an ongoing assurance of the love and mercy of God had its place but it was a long way from what I called in the last chapter confession and forgiveness proper. It came much more into what I called the second level of confessional activity —the need to acknowledge and explore my deeper self with the help of another person.

The questions that arise from this sort of memory and occasion are:

How do priests and confessors—as well as the person themselves—know what is needed? Indeed what quite is needed? Is it healing, spiritual counselling, psychotherapy, or more than one of these?

There are no easy and foolproof answers to either of these sets of questions, and I can now but indicate possibilities that readers may care to take further for themselves.

First:
How Can a Mature Sense of Sin and Forgiveness Grow in Us?

It is unfortunately easier to see first what may *not* help a mature sense of sin and forgiveness to grow. Two candidates for this are a degree of unthinking obligation and an over-mechanistic emphasis on external formality and ritual without a corresponding increase in inner understanding. The key words here are 'unthinking' and 'over-mechanistic', for there is nothing wrong with obligation and ritual as such.

The liturgies and rituals of the various churches have always contained the element of acknowledgment of sin and absolution by the priest. As we have seen, though, there can be a danger of this becoming so formal and external as to go past virtually without making impact; we tend to see it as 'part of the service—that's all'. In more strongly Protestant and Reformed churches this danger is somewhat obviated by their emphasis on confession as an essential element of an individual's relationship with God to whom we are ultimately and individually responsible, but the element of corporateness and the sharing of the acknowledgment of sin with another human being who is a representative both of God and the human race is often missing from those traditions. This is what *is* afforded in the practice of private confession. In my opinion this is most helpful when it is voluntary and undertaken because a person feels the need for it as a stage in growth and commitment. *Simon* felt a need and sought out his vicar in his distress at his illness.

The danger of exalting the practice of private confession to a mandatory level seems to me to be that it can come to be undertaken not for its own sake but because it is *seen* as desirable and in some sense as the cure for all ills. I am thinking of that period in the development of Anglo-Catholicism when to go to confession was seen virtually as a test of belonging to a particular section of the club—that part which valued very highly identity with the Roman Church. It also may have promised more than could be delivered.

In some churches there is the requirement of confession before communion or before the great festivals. I would be unwise to comment adversely on the discipline of a community of faith which is not my own and of which I may therefore lack adequate understanding. The ongoing insight that the requirement enshrines is that a relationship that is marred by blocked-up channels and resentments—be it with God or human beings—does not permit the mutual interchange of love to the same degree as one that is not suffering in this way. Guilt and shame, particularly, can then make it impossible for people even to *approach* each other—as it did Adam and Eve in the garden when they felt constrained to hide from Yahweh.[5] Falsity in relationships, or pretending that all is well when it is not does not augur well for relationship, either between human beings or between human beings and God. For these reasons I can see benefit in the guidelines to regular and even recommended confession.

But I have to admit that I am unhappy about the sense of *absoluteness* in the requirement, that to approach God and communion not being in a state of grace or without

confession risks damnation rather than healing. It must
depend on the degree of consciousness involved. To
approach God in communion with a consciousness and
intention of going against him is a distortion of things
and a muddling-up of white and black. In an extreme
form, love and hate, good and bad, can become perverted
and mistaken for each other and I guess that such a state
of being can become permanent. It leaves us in a psychological position of which the concept of the sin against
the Holy Spirit is the theological equivalent. In so far as
we are intent on calling good bad and bad good, we are
very distorted within ourselves. We are unlikely to be able
to recognize ourselves, other people, or God as we and they
really are. All our relationships are in danger of becoming
obscure and destructive rather than life-enhancing.

All this is, however, *descriptive*—a sense of what could
and may happen, because it is the way things are and can
be. It is a long way from the *prescriptive* comment 'unless
you do this it will happen'. It is meant not as a dire warn-
ing but a quieter statement that if we approach God in a
particular state of not wanting to be with him and hating
some of the aspects of our relationship with him, then
the resulting encounter may leave us stressed and in a
bad way because there is little or no congruence between
our actions and our heart. There may therefore be times
when we will benefit from—and even need—confession as
a part of our approach to God in communion or prayer,
but this is not the same as saying 'always'.

The danger of a very ritualistic process of confession is
that it can become almost 'automatic'—*confession without
understanding*. That does not permit people easily to grow.
We need to ask: What do people go to confession for? One
clear answer is 'for forgiveness of sins', or 'absolution'.
Furthermore, it is the forgiveness of *God*, not humankind,
that is sought. This has always been so and is reflected in
the proclamation that the forgiveness offered is independent
of the worthiness or unworthiness of the human being
who pronounces it on behalf of God. Yet this emphasis
can undermine the quality of the *confessional exchange*,
leading at some stages in history to its degeneration into
a formal exercise that people underwent relying on its
formal efficacy, but without hope or expectation of getting
much enlightenment or help from it. That was quite

satisfactory, for the aim was towards wiping the slate clean and settling the score rather than the promotion of a dynamic process of spiritual and emotional growth and the deepening of relationship between God and a person. I am putting this rather crudely, and some may think in an extreme and distorted way, but I make the point sharply to reveal what I see as an underlying tendency.

We could see this happening in the case of *Anne* who makes her weekly confession and receives absolution with great regularity and faithfulness. I asked in an earlier chapter and I ask again now: 'does she grow?' The slow process of growth *may* be going on inside her, but it might be useful if the formal act of confession could sometimes be supplemented by a more extended chance to talk the situation through. Confession and absolution are doing their work, but without further spiritual counselling are they doing enough? Is *Anne* aware of what exactly she is taking responsibility for as she confesses? Or is she reacting from a learned sense that certain sorts of behaviour, like anger, or fleeting thoughts of another relationship are wrong, or from the need to keep her inner world functioning on the level of guilt and not that of the powerful feelings that may underlie that guilt? I should emphasize here that when I talk of *spiritual counselling* I do not want to confuse this with formal psychotherapy or therapeutic counselling which have different parameters.

Indeed asking for advice or spiritual counsel has always been a part of the confessional process but its importance has been differentially emphasized at different times and by different traditions. Nowadays it may even be true that many have come to regard confession as a part of spiritual direction rather than the other way round. The shift from a formal requirement of corporate and personal discipline to a healing, educative process is there. Yet, alternatively, there are others who choose to use the act of confession and receiving forgiveness more as a form of self-discipline and less as a source of help. Absolution and counsel are both important, and part of the growing process for any individual is learning what is the optimum balance of the two, for *them*, at any point of their lives.

So, in the worlds where private confession is practised, we can rightly find all sorts of patterns: people who consult a director regularly, but only formalize this in confession occasionally; people who find it best to talk first and make a confession at the end in distinction to the older practice in which spiritual counsel normally followed the confessional act; and people who keep up a steady, thought-out discipline of confession which is supplemented by occasional spiritual counselling. It is for each individual person to work out with a minister the best pattern for their particular needs or stage of development.

How then do we grow to develop a mature and healthy sense of sin and an appropriate consciousness of when this spills over into sins(s); that is into actions and feelings that could be hurtful and harmful to us and to others? For to be without a sense of sin at all would not be healthy, for we do fall short of our own ideals and 'the glory of God'. Within a religious frame of reference to think otherwise would be to take the power of God to ourselves and ultimately to ossify and stop growing. I think we grow in two ways of which one is through the specific exercise—in whatever form and tradition we know and experience them—of confessional activities. But they will have no meaning in a vacuum. The other, more gradual and imper-ceptible, way of growth is through the continuing life of the community of which we are a part. If that community is trying to grow in love, in awareness, and in service, then individuals within it can also grow. And it is my belief that it is within an orbit of love, not fear, that we can come also to know, acknowledge, and work through the things in us that prevent love, freedom, and growth. Increased love and compassion can, paradoxically, increase our sense of 'sin', but the price of that should not then be increased fear, anguish, or depression. If it is, then something is not working out right.

We come then to our second set of questions:
How Do We Know When Things are not Working out Right and How Do We Deal with Them?

If we look back at *Sheila* we can see that very often it is difficult for the person in the middle of this situation to know that something is badly amiss or how it has gone amiss. In some ways we are likely to be dependent on an outsider. In the religious, confessional context we are considering, this may well be the priest or minister.

This puts a heavy burden on ministers, and indeed has

implications for the training of ministers in pastoral care in both the religious and more psychological areas.

On the religious level there can be difficulties. If a minister *really* believes that a depressed or anxious mood signals a lack of trust in God and partakes of the nature of sin, what are they going to do if and when they encounter depression and anxiety of a quality that absolution, prayer, or exhortations to trust and love cannot shift? Are they going to be able to recognize that another sort of help may be called for?

There will be those ministers who cannot. There are communities of faith in which psychological help of any kind is regarded as dangerous to and undermining of faith. But people holding this view will probably not have persevered with this book this far anyway! For those who have, the following guidelines may be of help.

There are people for whom the religious proclamations and rituals serve only to increase their distress. God may become harsher and more persecuting and it may be seen that the person cannot trust human beings easily either. Talk of the trust and love of God may increase depression and anxiety, as the person comes to feel sinful and more condemned at not being able to experience it. Or they may be people who are unable to reach out in any sort of relationship with the Christian community. The inner world of all these people may be such that they cannot use the religious life and the religious community unless that disordered world of theirs is more specifically and directly addressed.

There is, however, a caveat here. There may be some people who can get enough by staying on the fringes of the community and being 'let be'. They could not take anything more intimate, and exhortations to join in or participate are likely to precipitate a withdrawal. If this is understood, the community of faith may be able to hold such a person who would not perhaps easily be able to benefit from more intense help—either religious or psychological. After a long period of time of being accepted as they are they may, of their own accord, be able to move closer and find some relationship. This sort of person cannot be rushed.

This could, in fact, be the case with *Anne*. We wondered earlier if she can grow through her rather impersonal practice of confession, and suggested opportunities for talking outside the ritual, but this could be a mistake. She and her priest *may* be being intuitively wise—we do not know what possibilities there are or are not for change in her external situation or internal disposition. She and the priest may be doing enough to contain the difficult situation to make it bearable *for her* from day to day.

But if we are not dealing with a person like this, and usually we will be able to discern this by the *intensity* of a person's distress—for the person who needs to be left alone does not usually present with distress of an intensity that reaches out to others—what can be offered?

I think that what is needed is something that partakes of what I called the second level of confessional activity—namely the chance to share our deeper thoughts and feelings, whatever they be, with another person. This could be in confession, provided the minister can accept that it is likely to be the sharing that is important and that he may get told things that are not to him sin(s), but much more of the nature of *affliction*. They may not be sins but the person will need to express them often as such as part of a sense of alienation from God, an inability to feel joyous and alive. Strictly speaking, absolution is not required, but prayer may well be.

The alternatives are more extended opportunities for spiritual counsel, or psychotherapy, or possibly both. In one sense all psychotherapy has an element of confession within it, as nearly always people come to talk about their innermost shameful secrets, their presumed inadequacies, and their relationship muddles. Some would want to say that only the psychotherapist or only the priest is needed. This may be so and for some people it could be very confusing talking to more than one person at the same time and could also give opportunities—both conscious and unconscious—for the two being set in opposition to each other or even played off one against the other.

But if a person's religion is important to them it may also be very important for them to relate psychological insights to their religious faith. They may not feel able to embark upon a psychological journey unless they feel the religious dimension is also being held and addressed. Because the role of the priest and the psychotherapist are different, I tend to think that it is often preferable for there to be two conversations going on rather than for the psychotherapy to be embracing and addressing explicitly the religious as well as the emotional dimension. It can happen, for example, that after gaining insight in psychotherapy a person may wish and feel the need to make confession to God through a priest, and may feel more able to do so maturely. It would, I think, be confusing if that priest was the same person as the psychotherapist.

I am aware that some people will disagree profoundly with this and feel that for people with religious faith a religious psychotherapist or counsellor is the ideal because of the degree of understanding and acceptance of the religious dimension afforded by them. But what is thought to be understanding can become an avoidance of the heart of the emotional problem. Furthermore, psychotherapy normally involves the therapist facilitating the person to explore their own inner world and attempting not to bring too much of their own to it, particularly in the realms of advice, or suggestion, or reciprocal disclosure. By contrast, in spiritual direction all these *may* be appropriate. What is needed in psychotherapy with people of strong religious faith is a *respect* by the therapist for that dimension and faith. Questioning and challenge may come and be appropriate especially if it seems that the religious position is being used as an unhelpful psychological defence, but this has to be in due time and with, I believe, the consent, of both parties to that part of the process.

There are other reasons why I feel it is not possible to be parish priest/confessor and counsellor/psychotherapist to the same person. First, the boundaries of the confessional and the consulting room are different, which is why pastors trained and skilled in counselling nevertheless make a distinction between the activities of pastoral *care* and pastoral *counselling*. Pastoral care—even when it uses counselling insights—is normally exercised with the minister having to be in several roles at once to the parishioner and vice versa. These overlaps cannot be avoided. They have to be managed, and this may limit the emotional depth and intensity of pastoral care encounters. Counselling and psychotherapy take place in a situation in which the client or patient knows they do not have to meet the counsellor or therapist in any other role or in any other situation.

Second, confession and counselling have different purposes and the underlying experience of authority in each
is different. The act of confession includes the element of
submission to a value system and to the judgement—albeit
merciful, as we hope and believe—of God. Judgement and
the assurance of absolution are mediated through the
priest who, as God's representative, exercises the authority
bestowed at ordination. Counsellors and psychotherapists
do, of course, have personal value systems and the power
inherent in the therapeutic relationship should not be
underestimated, but the task of the therapist is not to
exercise authority, but to promote an inner authority and
assurance in the person who comes for help. For a minister
to be both confessor and counsellor to the same person
can create, therefore, a confusion and conflict at an
unconscious and often difficult-to-resolve level.

I am arguing that the *roles* of confessor and therapist
need to be differentiated, but there are phenomena which
are common to the two *activities*. Most importantly—and
pastoral carers and confessors ignore this at their peril—
there are projections and transferences[4] in pastoral care
as well as in psychotherapy and counselling. In fact, one
of the most potentially powerful transferences is likely to
be made to ministers. They are likely to be seen as quasi-
parental and quasi-divine omnipotent figures, not least in
the confessional. The conscious exercise of authority in
the confessional can trigger a far stronger and potentially
more regressive unconscious transference.

This can work for good or ill. A priest in the confessional
addressed in parental terminology can model a good-
enough parent: non-judgemental, non-retaliatory, so that
a person's inner world can be healingly touched by the
sacrament. Yet this very model can spill out unhelpfully
into all other contacts. The minister may be experienced
as a *real parent* and the resulting dependency can be
tremendous as every parish priest knows to his cost. This
is more likely to happen when people are living in the
'needing management' rather than 'needing forgiveness'
realm. They are often the sort of people whose actual
parenting and family were deficient or deprived. They
sometimes seek unconsciously to remedy this in later
life, by seeing all sorts of people in parental terms. Their
inner world makes it less easy for them to move between

roles and to distinguish between actual and 'as if' parental
figures and images. God and ministers are particularly
likely to evoke parental images. It can be difficult for such
people to relate to their minister as adults. The intimacy of
the confessional exchange can make for a overwhelming
degree of dependency and attachment. Confession and
absolution cannot be denied, for to be so available is part
of the promise that is made at ordination. But ministers
themselves need more awareness for they have sometimes to be able to handle very difficult situations. This
may be worse if they touch a part of the minister's own
unresolved past.

This brings me to the last area I want to explore in this
chapter, which is the effect on the priest or minister of
being the agent of absolution and hearing confessions.
For though they are, in these functions, being asked to
represent God to his people, they have to do it as human
beings, with human frailties and with parts of themselves
that they have not fully or at all worked out. The priest
who hears confessions is 'allowed' to be unworthy; it
does not affect their ministry, but sometimes ministers
are more than unworthy. Ministers may be in a mess, or
not very self-aware.

Consider again for a moment *Matthew*, the rector,
playing out his part as the celebrant and absolver of sin
at the Sunday morning Eucharist. We have already suggested that the words of confession and absolution may
have passed many of the congregation by, but I guess not
Matthew himself. I have not, of course, been in this position, but I suspect that if you actually have to say the
words of absolution then it is more difficult for these to
become completely mechanical for they remain great and
astounding words on the lips of mortal beings even in the
more muted form of the general absolution— 'Almighty
God . . . have mercy upon you, pardon and deliver you
from all your sins.'[5]

Familiarity over time must breed a certain contempt,
but it must be doubtful as to whether the most tired and
jaded of priests can become so impervious to their role
and its awesome elements not to ask themselves— at least
from time to time—'What am I doing? What is happening
in my declaiming these great words? What am I being for
the people as a whole and for any one person in particular?'

The position of being the absolver of sin must be at one and the same time that of great potential power and great humility, though this burden is lightened in the private confessional rite when the *representative* and in a sense non-personal aspect is expressed in the priest's asking the prayers of his penitent and acknowledging that he, too, is a sinner. But there are times, maybe, when the weight of the office has almost to be disowned, as perhaps was true for *Matthew*, the rector, that Sunday morning when the burden of his sense of his personal unworthiness to forgive anyone else anything lay heavy upon him. At such times it may be a relief to be just the channel and the representative of God. At other times the temptation to feel as God cannot be absent when all the liturgy is seemingly conspiring to emphasize it.

For *Matthew*, on that morning, the familiar words reminded him of his own miserable state inside himself. The act and role of absolver may be very hard on priests, for unless they are very defended against their own inner selves and being it is difficult not to let the role resonate—for good or ill—with what is going on inside, in the same way that counsellors and psychotherapists have to struggle to stay objective when what is being presented to them rings too many personal bells. Yet the training of counsellors and therapists often focuses on just this area, whilst many priests come to the ministry of confession relatively unprepared for its impact upon them.

What exactly, psychologically speaking, is any priest being asked to do and be in his role of absolver? The two words that come to mind are 'container' and 'focus'. The priest is a container in that the acts of confession and absolution involving the distant and transcendent Almighty being mediated through another human being helps the worshippers bring the thing called sin within the human orbit, so that the relationship with God of which forgiveness is a part can stay incarnate, manageable, and humanly meaningful. The priest also acts as a lens through which the sense of divine forgiveness can be focused, acquire a shape, and be taken in.[6]

But ministers approach their part in the liturgy and sacraments with their own inner world, which may be no more resolved than the congregation's. The more shaky a minister's inner world the more likely it is that the work of the confessional will expose him to its chinks and cracks. *Matthew* got a jolt in the General Confession that Sunday morning—not surprisingly perhaps because his inner situation had become rather extreme. What we hear in confession may be what our own inner being cannot bear or does not want to hear.

We may even wonder about the weekly dialogue between *Anne* and her confessor which we have already thought may have become a little stuck. We gather that the occasion is that of formal confession only—they do not talk in any extended way either in or out of the confessional proper. We may just query whether she and the priest are not talking so as to *avoid* something: she difficult feelings and he the fear that if he asked more he might get out of his depth or into realms that he as a celibate priest does not know and is fascinated or repelled by. We cannot know, but it is a possibility.

If ministers get into deep water in this area they can cover it by not really listening to what is being said in confession or by not trying to understand it. They cannot afford to understand—it would be too disturbing. Or alternatively they can save themselves by becoming judgemental.

There is another pitfall yet. Never more than in this role of confessor is there a temptation to take on the omnipotence of God, though this may be at a very unconscious level since concurrently hearing confessions consciously engenders humility in the priest. Yet it is hard for the humility to go all through to the deepest being, for the role is essentially one of power and will resonate on any unresolved area of our being which touches on this dimension.

One of the times when the priest's handling of this dimension becomes crucial is in ministry to very emotionally disturbed people, particularly the ministry of deliverance on the rare occasions where this is justified. It is here that ministers, in or out of a sacramental, liturgical, or confessional role, need to be *more* rather than *less* ordinary. They need less rather than more to take on the character of omnipotence belonging truly to the God they represent. When someone is very disturbed, good and evil have often already become polarized and split apart, and for this sort of person the omnipotence of God can be displaced on to the priest or taken to themselves in a deluded way. In these circumstances the encounter needs to be more humanly containing and less magical, so that integration has a chance to happen. Ministers who wittingly or unwittingly accept the magic omnipotent role thrust upon them can make it harder for the afflicted person to regain a hold on ordinary and adult reality. This is not to say that priests in this situation abrogate the rightful authority of their representative office, but that authority needs to be exercised in a human, and not quasi-magical way.

By its very nature there is no way for ministers easily to have any form of supervision for their confessional work. The seal of the confessional is absolute. and more so even than the confidentiality of counselling and psychotherapy. Yet there must surely be found some way for people who do a great deal of this work to get some support and insight into it and into how they are being affected by it—for their own sakes and that of those to whom they minister. Perhaps one way forward would be for ministers to share, not what people say to them, but what happens to them as they listen, to monitor where the sore points are, where they switch off and become rather automatic rather than really give attention to the human plight and their penitent. They need to notice also what sort of things make them want to be harsh and even condemning, to want to hear more from an excited curiosity and fascination. If too many difficult patterns emerge, then it may be that as ministers they themselves are in need of support, and the chance to sort out their own inner being.

These last chapters have been very individually orientated. They have been concerned with trying to explore sin and sin(s) at what I see to be their most fundamental level, focused sharply on what goes on in the dark internal recesses of each of us.

They have, however, been written from a particular viewpoint and may have seemed to focus overmuch on early human experience as the determinant of our sense of sin and our capacity to give and receive forgiveness. This has been because in one deep sense I felt I could do no other. I am, however, aware that it constitutes a slant and bias that readers will have, indeed, to evaluate.

But there is another face to sin—a more developed and

later face—the face it shows to the outside world and the *commonalities* that people share in relation to their understanding and evaluation of thoughts and actions. It is when the individual life is seen in a communal context that we begin to talk of *morality*, and this book could not be complete if I did not try, in a final chapter, to make some links between what I have written and the outside, more organized, more structured world.

Notes

1. Book of Common Prayer 1662, Communion, First exhortation at time of giving notice of Holy Communion.
2. Book of Common Prayer 1662, Communion, Second exhortation at time of giving notice of Holy Communion.
3. Genesis 3.8-10.
4. 'Projection' is a form of defence involving not recognizing something in ourselves but seeing it only in another person. 'Transference' is the displacement on to people in the present of feelings and memories that originally belonged to people in the past, predominantly—though not exclusively—parents, See C. Rycroft, *A Critical Dictionary of Psychoanalysis* (Penguin 1972), pp. 125-6 and 168-9. For some illustrations see Mary Anne Coate, *Clergy Stress* (SPCK 1989), pp. 63-4 and (for pastoral care) pp. 182-6.
5. *The Alternative Service Book 1980* (SPCK), Prayer of Absolution at Holy Communion, Morning and Evening Prayer.
6. See also Coate, *Clergy Stress*, chapter 9, especially pp. 182-3.

NINE

Sin and the Outside World

Much of what I have written so far has been about what goes on *inside* us. Of course it shows and seeps through to our outside life. Indeed we can say that our inner world determines a lot of how we experience and act in the outer world. I could, though, say that whilst I have dealt with sin in a very internal way, the specification of sin in sin(s) begins to make contact with the outer world of other people. Forgiveness spans the two. One essential part of the experience of forgiveness is that of mending our relationships with other people, but the other is how we come or do not come to forgive ourselves. In this way the gap between inner and outer worlds is bridged.

When people laughingly said to me that they would contribute to the book because they all had experience of sin, I think they were not necessarily speaking from or even tuning in to that deep part of all of us—for which I have tended to reserve the word sin, without an 's'—but to that more observable, more adult, more organized and accessible part. I *think* they were thinking of the overlap between sin and sin(s), sin and morality, and sin and crime.

There has been, both in Christianity and other religious thought, some considerable debate on the relationship between sin and *morality*. The hub of the issue can be put like this:

Does Theology Somehow Define and Determine Morality? If Something Is Morally Right Must It Automatically Stem from Something Religiously and Theologically Right?

We can take the issue even further: if something is a crime is it automatically morally and theologically wrong?

Perhaps it is in Judaism that the *mores* of society and religious thought have always come most closely together.

Indeed the books of the Old Testament make it quite clear that the laws which govern human behaviour follow and flow from the overarching law of the will of God or Yahweh: 'Thus saith the Lord your God . . . Thou shalt . . . Thou shalt not . . .'[1] The particularly homogeneous relationship between the acts of Yahweh in Jewish history and the material well-being or otherwise of the Jewish people makes this sort of quotation inevitable. Within Christianity there is certainly *a* strand of this, as seen in Romans—'the powers that be are ordained of God'.[2] It suggests a smooth flow from the inner life of Christianity to organized outer life in the world. However, the double quotation from Jesus: 'Render therefore to Caesar the things that are Caesar's, and to God the things that are God's'[3] suggests that the relationship is not that simple.

Nowadays, the split between the things of Caesar and the things of God is more obvious, and perhaps nowhere clearer that in this century's developments in attitudes to sexuality, marriage, and the family. At an earlier point the *mores* or customs of society and those of the Christian community would have been identical; the former would have followed from the latter. Now they are quite far apart in these areas. Remarriage with a previous partner still living is not seen by society as immoral or imperfect, but it cannot be solemnized in church in at least some of the Christian traditions. Homosexuality is sometimes tolerated better outside the communities of faith than within them. The practice of cohabitation before marriage is widespread and receives the blessing of society even to the extent of a change in our taxation laws. This last has not received an equivalent formal blessing from the churches for it poses a challenge to traditional Christian teaching. It is giving rise to uncomfortable questions and a degree of distress. People's hearts and faith can well pull them in different directions. This can be especially hard for parents when their children feel the need to follow their inclinations—and indeed an honestly-held belief in the nature of partnership and commitment—to adopt a lifestyle that is becoming so general among the younger generation as to be virtually the norm.

The issue is not simple. Those who do not depend on religious precepts to decide moral questions do not feel that by this they are forsaking the path of 'goodness'. An apparently contradictory position is taken by others who proclaim that 'goodness' is the prerogative of a religious and even Christian view on life and that therefore moral goodness flows from religious life. Yet in certain instances the reverse seems to be true. Faithfulness to the current official Roman Catholic teaching on birth control may result, in certain areas of the world, in overpopulation, dire hardship, and poverty. We have to ask the question: 'Is this morally defensible?'

These contradictions are capable of resolution only if it is realized that 'goodness' is not the same order of word or even idea as either 'morality' or 'religion'. Goodness is a more fundamental, more-difficult-to-catch-hold-of-and-describe idea than morality. We may recognize it when we meet it, but it defies precise definition. For those able to affirm a religious view of life it is a reflection of the essential nature of God and of mankind, in so far as the creation partakes of the nature of the creator. This *belief* in goodness as stemming from God then underpins attempts at second order theological and religious thinking; namely thinking and communicating about the relationship between this sort of God and the world as we actually live in it and as society is organized. From such thinking emerge moral values and moral customs, but 'goodness' has not been the only contributor to such thinking. Other contributors have been issues of survival, equality, peace, justice, demand, resource and religious precept. The 'high' moral ground is claimed whenever one or more of these latter issues is elevated to the stature of goodness and so given an 'absolute' value, at least for a time.

On this sort of analysis it is not at all clear that the relationship between religious and moral thought is linear in one direction—*from* theology and religious thought *to* morality and the customs of society. History suggests, rather, that they have sometimes split quite a long way from each other; at best they have been in dialogue, sometimes to the modification of both. Furthermore, in a multi-faith culture such as we have today it is even more difficult to sustain the view that general *mores* for a whole community follow from religious thought, simply because the religious thought is itself pluriform.

Back in Chapter 1 I gave a vignette from life in a Moslem

family. It featured the restricted social position of women and girls within Islamic culture and the conflict that this can cause in a family actually living in a multi-racial context. Certain customs that indeed follow from some religious traditions do not follow from others. Society, in laying down moral codes, can take into consideration religious sensibilities only in a general rather than a particular way. For example, we may be able to specify that religious education should be available to children in schools, but it is far harder to specify which sort of religious education.

Even more fraught has been the issue of Sunday trading. Contributing to the conflict has been, on the one hand, the not-essentially-religious recognition that we all need some rest from work. We could, of course, claim that even this basic principle of *rest* has its roots in ancient religious tradition, but we cannot easily gainsay that it may equally be felt to stem from purely social principles and even the current state of development of the European community! On the other hand, we have the religious principle that the hallowing of a particular day safeguards the sense of the creation not being self-sufficient, but essentially a *worshipping* creation. This has resulted in the making special of Sunday as the day commemorating the resurrection in the Christian tradition and of Saturday as the day of the Sabbath rest in the Jewish tradition. History and establishment, and now perhaps economics, have proved the deciding factors in deciding which shall prevail in this country.

It is hard, therefore, to sustain the idea that religious thought will *directly* determine a society's morality. Furthermore, religious and other interests are not necessarily identical, though for some of the time they may coincide; religious and non-religious thought often serve to provide reasons for actions whose determinants may actually be rather complex and difficult to tease out.

The story of the children leaving all their rubbish on the playing-field and then being castigated by the old lady for ruining God's creation illustrates this well. Environmentalists and religious people might both condemn this behaviour, but for different reasons and from a different bedrock. Environmentalists see it as desecrating the planet and ruining it for other people. Religious people see it primarily as desecrating the creation of God, which secondarily renders the planet less pleasant for other people. For one set of people this behaviour is antisocial, and if repeated on a large scale becomes dangerous to the survival of the race. For others it is a sin because the creatures despoil the activity of the creator.

To consider another sort of experience: are the white lies that are often told to prevent somebody being unnecessarily hurt—'I saw no point in telling her she looked awful. Why make someone feel bad about themselves?' acceptable because they are sometimes uttered out of love, or 'sinful' because they are less than the truth?

It seems that the individual has to sort out such issues; the repercussions of either decision are not likely to reverberate far beyond the particular relationship involved. But what of instances where society and the law are involved?

We are forced also to look at the relationship between sin and *crime*. Consider someone who falters for a moment at the wheel of a car, because they are distracted by some inner worry, and who causes an accident for which they are criminally liable. Is this also a sin? Is it the sin of thoughtlessness, carelessness, or insensitivity to others? With something like this it is attractive and yet over-simple to hold that it is both a crime and a sin. We can easily come to say that it is both criminal and sinful to drive in a state that is dangerous to other people. What operates here is the injunction: 'Thou shalt not drive out of control. It is an offence against love and care.' And so in a way it is, but there still must be the world of difference between a person who does this with conscious carelessness or recklessness and someone who perhaps does not even know that they are distracted and worried, or for whom the roots of the careless destructive act lie deep in their unconscious.

The issue of the relationship between crime and sin can also become more consciously complicated and conflicted. We need to consider such issues as conscientious objection, non-payment of the poll tax as a political protest against what was seen as an unfair and anti-social tax, and disregard of institutional rules of confidentiality when this is sincerely felt to be in the public interest. All these have been categorized as crime, but for many of the people who perpetrated these crimes it would, for them, have been immoral and, for those professing belief in God, sinful to act otherwise. Something they felt to be a higher value than the law and order of society was driving them.

The smooth progression between sin and morality and criminality is thus hard to sustain even on the individual level. In many ways it is a very complex issue, and when translated to the world stage it becomes even more complex.

'The powers that be are ordained of God.' So runs Romans 13.1. Yet this was not self-evident even in the two and a half centuries which followed its writing, during which the Roman state persecuted the infant church; unless we find ourselves able to say—in my opinion perversely—that suffering and martyrdom were the divinely ordered method for the strengthening and growth of the Christian community. With the conversion of Constantine the quotation became loosely true again, and more so in the days of the Holy Roman Empire, and later during the period of the sway of the 'Divine Right of Kings'. The relationship between Church and State reached its zenith, or rather perhaps its nadir, in their unholy alliance during the Inquisition. The vestiges of the relationship remain in this century in the concept of the established church and in the Anglican bishops' statutory seats in the British House of Lords. There is still some startled surprise amongst church and non-church people alike when the Church of England rises up and publicly criticizes the state, for it is seen by some as not quite playing fair. There is also still a sense that God is ranged on the side of law and order and is devoted to the enforcement of both.

Far more difficult is the concept of a 'just war' or the *jihad* of Islamic fundamentalism. As I understand it these two phenomena are not quite the same. A 'just war' seems to be trying to make the best of a bad job. War is not encouraged but seen to be permitted so that what is seen as a greater evil shall not happen. It is not unlike the defence of self-preservation for murder, though many have argued that the attitude of nations in war has gone far beyond this into the realm of a crude nationalism and self-seeking. A *jihad*, or holy war, like the crusades of old, is argued as following directly from the tenets of Islam. It is commanded rather than permitted. But in both cases the moral principle 'thou shalt not kill' takes second place, and of course in some fundamentalist sects it takes a very much more lowly place. Human life is less sacred than the holy cause.

We have also seen rebellion and subversion prescribed as a *necessary* revolt against oppression. The liberation theology of the seventies and eighties and the church's struggle against apartheid in South Africa both claimed that injustice and oppression are greater human evils than rebellion. To fight them violent rebellion was not only permitted but prescribed by some people as a necessary expression of the gospel.

The pacifists' bottom line is 'thou shalt not kill'—even one's enemies—though let it be said here that sometimes the peace movement has seemed to be very angry and violent in its own turn. Such a position may stem from religious conviction as in Gandhi, Luther King, or the Quakers, but it may equally be rooted in a human conviction unbuttressed by religious faith.

It seems clear to me that an equation of righteousness and morality, sin and immorality is not self-evident or simple. The thing that people will suffer, fight, or die for varies; it may be purity of the race or religion, it may be the fight against oppression. It may be a commitment to love and peace, or it may be a commitment to the survival of the race or the planet. These rock bottom lines can come from human values or they can be claimed from the gospel or the Scriptures. The problem of morality is that several elements can be seen to have fed into its developed form. One of these, certainly, is the religious story. Another is the biological story. A third is the sociological story or even the environmental story. Yet another must surely be the psychological story.

One thing these bottom lines have in common, though, is a concern that goes beyond purely individual issues. Indeed, some harsh forms of morality, or state law and order, go much further than this and negate the individual and their rights. For morality, laws and definitions of criminality tend to depend on *averages*. What laws are necessary to allow most people to live in peace and fulfilment? This may mean that individual needs, abilities, and troubles that are not average may be ignored or even discriminated against.

Sin, too, has a public face. Why else should there have been the complex ritual of public penance in the early

life of the church?[4] Causing a scandal, or being a stumbling-
block are still grounds on which clergy can be defrocked.
Indeed it is just this insistence on perceived public and
communal good over against the needs of the individual
that lays such high expectations on, for example, the clergy
to maintain a moral standard that is sometimes beyond
their powers. Public confession of sin and failings has
been characteristic of many religious sects, and of such
human institutions as Alcoholics Anonymous. The aim of
public confession in groups like AA is to increase support
and solidarity; in religious groups it can sometimes be
the prelude to exclusion. Religious communities have
often embodied this public accountability among their
members in the ritual known as the 'Chapter of Faults' when
members acknowledge publicly to each other breaches of
their rule. The fact that these ritualistic, 'shopping list'
occasions have now mostly been discarded in favour of a
more fundamental review of life and commitment reflects
an oscillation in us between an emphasis on public,
semi-objective accountability and a valuing of personal
commitment and the sense of mutual responsibility.

From the days when we first learned concern for
another we have come to realize that we cannot live for
ourselves alone. As we develop through childhood we
come also to realize—sometimes painfully—the power of
authority, and indeed the fear of authority. It is now
necessary to explore more fully that part of our human
development that comes to contribute to how we view
and relate to *public morality and living as part of a human
community.*

We come to the later stages of our development with
an internal world already shaped by our earlier childhood experience. And nowhere is this more true than in
respect of what we may choose to call our 'superego'[5]—
that part of our inner world which has internalized parent
and other figures often in terms of their 'shoulds' and
'should nots'. Only part of this is rational and conscious;
part, as we have seen in earlier pages, is unconscious and
primitive. This gives rise sometimes to conflict between
what we set forth as our value system and the instincts
and impulses that can flow underneath in dissociation
from those values. So a person with a harsh 'superego'
may well grow up with a fear of authoritarian values, per-

sons, and systems and yet also with a tendency to submit to these or even identify with them. Such people may gravitate to groups in society—of which it has to be said that the communities of faith are often one example—where these tendencies are valued and reinforced. In so far as their internal world reflects an uneasy and unstable balance between conscious prohibitions and injunctions and underlying impulses then the latter may come to be defended against by an even harsher attitude to those same tendencies when manifested in others—for example a harsh attitude to moral lapses or criminality.

We can also identify the diametrically opposite problem in people with too fluid or even non-existent a superego who have not enough defence against the unruly, primitive depths of their inner world which know no structure and no law. Such people collide with 'civilized' society, the law, or their nearest and dearest sometimes in catastrophic ways, often giving rise to the irresolvable question: 'Are they ill, mad, or bad?' Is the failure of a person to internalize society's norms and a sense of values a punishable offence or a cause for concern and therapeutic help? In the last analysis we have to lay on people a charge to take personal responsibility for what they are and do, whilst knowing that of some people we are, in fact, asking that which is internally impossible. Yet it is impossible *not* to lay this charge if society is to live in some sort of peace and security.

But it is not as simple as this because society is unconsciously motivated by more than the need to live in peace and security. It seems to have its own sort of corporate 'superego' which is sometimes relatively tolerant and benign and sometimes punitive and vengeful. This corporate internal sense of concern and values is fluid, and therefore the dividing line between uprightness/health and criminality/sickness may vary both over time and over communities and states. We tend to call this superego 'public opinion', but, like our own personal superego, more than opinion seems to go into its formation. It has archaic and primitive facets—relics of the law of the jungle —and when these interact at an unconscious level with external factors, like economic deprivation, or an experience of violence or catastrophe, strange things can happen. Those who react with frustration and rage can do so more than usual, and violence escalates. Others show their violence more in their cries for blood and punishment.

Nowhere do we see this more clearly exemplified than in the vicissitudes of attitudes and work towards the reform of the prison system of this country. A few years ago, the emphasis was on how to make that system more humane, more therapeutic and educative, and indeed how to prevent more people ever having to know it from inside. It was agreed that prison has an easy potential for 'making bad people worse'. There was, of course, also the sense that society must be protected, but on the whole society did not seem to be demanding retribution and vengeance. In 1994 the pendulum seems to have swung the other way. The ideas of 'back to basics', and 'condemn a bit more and understand a little less' seem almost to have provided a licence for an upsurge of retributive and punitive energy. The roots of this are complex and I cannot really take them further in this exploration; they must stem partly from a fear and a sense of threat that society as we know it could break down and plunge us all into primitive anarchy and violent chaos, but fear can make us savage.

I, in my turn, fear that unless we note such trends and try to understand them in ourselves and in society we could be carried where in the long term we would rather not go and into a culture that betrays the best in human nature; into a repressive society which has solved none of its ills but driven them underground, perhaps to lie dormant, perhaps to smoulder and perhaps to explode. Such extreme outcomes have prevailed in Nazi Germany or in oppressive Eastern Europe when we feel that the thing has been turned inside out in a deliberately perverse way. That which should be the safeguard of a benign but responsible individual and corporate sense of what people are aiming to be becomes the instrument of the unleashing of destructive, primitive power. Worse still, this power is virtually 'blessed' and sanctified. The process is deeply perverse because the bad and destructive is now perceived as benign and good.

The relation of all this to sin is very highly questionable. If we hang on to the sense that sin has an ultimate definition only in relation to God, then what is seen as sin will depend on the character of God as we perceive God. This is complicated by the claim of the preceding chapters that our perception of God must be deeply influenced by our individual and corporate psychological make-up and experience. So, God or the state are sometimes set up as alternative *externalizations* of an authority structure that has its roots *inside* us. Can we just *accept* these externalizations, or should we not *dialogue* with them so that their less humane elements can be modified and given a more compassionate face? This can be a very hard task, given that we also know that human beings are, on some level, primitive and fallible and are likely to resist such modifications.

Where is the corporate 'bedrock' for morality and sin? People will answer this question differently. Those who think like Maslow[6] would say: 'In a system which allows basic human needs to be met'. Christians—or some of them —would assert it is to be found in the primacy of love, though many would say that 'holiness' also play a part. Part of the problem is that I suspect that our world is always going to be in a state of some deprivation; there is too much need for it all to be met. Therefore there will always be the likelihood and danger of defences against deprivation— rage, self-seeking, exploitation, and greed—rearing their heads. There is need for altruism, for self-giving and self-transcendence, and there will almost inevitably be suffering and continuing deprivation. These will form part of the bedrock of experience which religious and non-religious people alike have to interpret and manage as best they can.

In this scenario our definitions both of morality and of what is sinful will come to represent the balance required by living in a society where there is too much need and too little resource. This balance tries to take into account the needs of the individual and the also inevitable need for structure and order. These different needs cannot all be met all of the time. The balance is always delicate and must often be seen as unfair.

The preceding chapters would seem to me to indicate that one of the surest safeguards that the balance is not destructive is the presence in *enough* people of the capacity for compassion and forgiveness—not just caring and pity, for these can be made defensive against the less acceptable and respectable parts of those exercising them. I am

thinking, rather, of people who—to paraphrase Christ—
know emotionally and intellectually 'what is in people',
and have in themselves worked through to enough resolution and balance of the 'good' and 'bad' so as to be able
to be realistic and kind towards others and to the world
in which we live.

As I write this I am struck by a stab of despair and a
fear that I am writing to a Utopian theme, because much
of the evidence suggests that there are *not* enough of such
people and there is *not* that balance. Love and compassion
do *not* rule. I am drawn back to one of my examples,
Margaret, who protested, 'Why do we pray for the peace
of the world; there never is any?' I have a memory that
psychoanalysis, at some point in its history, made a claim
that with enough psychoanalytic insight people and the
world would improve. Group analysts have been drawn into
similar hopes for our natural groupings and even society
itself. But such claims have not been able to produce the
goods; it doesn't seem to work like that.

So the concepts and practice of law and order, crime
and punishment, sin and righteousness continue to need
to exist, and be structured and codified. But in a strange
way the resulting structures—be they concepts, or even
the 'incarnation' of these concepts in our political and
economic institutions—are often a measure of our deficiencies, not our strength. They remain defences for us
against the full impact of ourselves, but, like all defences,
they are two-edged. They can be benign and facilitative,
or they can become oppressive and serve the reverse aim
of that for which they were designed. I cannot see how
we can do without them, but we need to be in constant
dialogue with them, seeking their reform and development,
and in this process remaining aware of our oscillations
between seeing their true purpose and making them into
instruments of oppression. The process is painfully and
sometimes frighteningly fallible.

This all sounds as if I think we are nothing but a
seething cauldron of primitive feelings just about kept at
bay and under control. Perhaps I have emphasized this
dimension because its reality tends to go unrecognized.
But there are other ways of looking at our development
which must be allowed to make their contribution.

First, there is the thrust in us towards cognitive development, explored pre-eminently in the work of Piaget.[7] Through his observations and controlled research into the cognitive development of children I think we can identify a move towards increasing stability and order. Children move from believing that an object isn't there because they cannot see it to a position where they 'know' it is still there and can tolerate the absence of perception. We become increasingly able both to accommodate ourselves to new raw experience and to assimilate it into our being in such a way that it does not overwhelm us. We are not all ultimately able to do this to the same degree, or at the same rate, neither do we grow up with equal capacity for problem solving and taking the initiative. This perhaps has to be accepted, but I think it is also true that our cognitive and intellectual development is itself in a delicate relationship with our emotional development.

A 'bad' external environment can delay intellectual development, but the exact relationship between the two is the subject of much past and ongoing research and conflict. All perhaps I can say here is that in our cognitive development there appears to be some thrust away from the purely primitive towards rationality, order, and a degree of helpful control. But the intellect *in isolation from the rest of our being* can render these very things— rationality and control—barren, founded on sand, and potentially agents of oppression. Who has not met the person of brilliant intellect who seems to have no heart, and whose human judgement is faulty because of this? So it must be a potential rather than a certainty that our cognitive and intellectual development will act to humanize us—it may not—but the potential is there. It is perhaps significant that the great scholastic theologians, Aquinas and others, saw God as supremely the author of order, meaning, and purpose, and themselves approached the study of God in the spirit of a rational exploration of a rational being.

Piaget also looked at the way in which an increasing sense of order becomes interpersonal as well as intra-personal. He observed that preschool children obeyed no rules when playing together. Between the ages of six and eight the rules of the game were set forth as inviolable, as if they came from heaven, even though they were in fact frequently broken as the children struggled to participate in the group activity. Inconsistencies like this pertained through to the ages of eleven to twelve, though there was a developing interest in codifying the rules and then revising the codes. Alongside this there is also a development of a sense of justice and of a degree of discrimination in matters of wrongdoing and punishment along the dimension of *intention*. At an earlier age punishment must fit the crime —'if you break more rules you should be punished more'. Later it depends much more on whether you *meant* to do the damage or whether it was an accident . . . foreshadowing adult dilemmas and conflicts between objective and subjective—'If you kill somebody, how important in the scheme of responsibility and punishment is it that you did or didn't mean to?' Is human error punishable?

Recent inquiries into accidents and disasters and indeed the 1991 British Road Traffic Act which concentrates on the actual standard of driving rather than the state of the driver's mind seems to be making human error more punishable, moving back from the subjective to the objective. It is a difficult area, but the fear must be that when we move strongly back towards the objective in such matters that we may be motivated by revenge, and that the painful way of forgiveness will in the end be superseded by the retaliatory principle.

Other psychologists have looked at our growth into morality and a sense of justice along different dimensions and parameters. Erikson[8] conceptualizes the process in terms of the unity that is or is not achieved within a developing ego or self. The development of ego-identity Erikson sees as the essential task of adolescence, laying the foundation for an inner strength and freedom as the basis of ethical action. Human freedom must involve the ability both to make choices and to take responsibility for them.

Kolhberg[9] went further along the road of a linear development in moral thinking, even though accepting that under certain kinds of stress we do not always act in accordance with our highest capacity. According to his theory, we develop from the need to keep rules in order to avoid punishment and pain and to satisfy our needs for acceptance and nourishment, through to the concept of loyalty to one's peer group and a sense of personal identity achieved through personal relationships. We utilize our new-developed selfhood first to win approval as part of our group, then to develop group goals, and then to maintain and develop the social order. In this we can see a progression from egocentricity to other-relatedness. Finally, we can move to the autonomous stage where we are free enough to make decisions without undue reference either to their personal consequences in terms of reward and punishment, or to a need for approval by the group, or even the desire to make a contribution to the group. There emerges the ability to work towards a 'higher' good and to live according to general principles such as 'love your neighbour as yourself', which embody universal processes of justice and respect. Not all of us reach this last stage and it seems to me also possible to appear to have reached true autonomy and still be ruled by something far less free inside ourselves.

It also seems to me that Kolhberg's theory reflects essentially a Western view of development. What of those systems in which adherence to group aims rather than to individual principles is regarded as the highest good? We see this, perhaps, in both Jewish and Islamic traditions in which adherence to the racial and religious culture is regarded as superior to individual identity and decisions.

Two questions emerge from all this. First, what happens in Piaget's, Erikson's or Kohlberg's terms when things 'go wrong' or appear to go wrong, when development for an individual or a group does not seem to proceed in an ordered way? Second, can there be any general and potentially universal theory of moral development—or indeed of sin—since the starting points and reference points of different natural groups and cultures vary so much?

Response to either of these questions can only, to my mind, be a matter of faith, not certainty. I am defining faith as that on which we bet our life; that is the bottom line or bedrock for each of us at any given moment. Therefore what I write now in considering these questions must be subjective.

In relation to the issue of when things 'go wrong' in moral or other development I cannot but say that I think it happens when earlier experience, insufficiently worked through and resolved, obtrudes into and makes impossible the negotiation of later developmental stages and hurdles. I cannot believe in the idea of 'monsters from birth' or freaks. I come back, therefore, to relying for explanatory power on the ideas and arguments advanced in earlier chapters of this book. Those chapters inevitably reflected my current valuing of insights from the psychoanalytic theory of development. I see it, rather like religious thinking on sin and forgiveness, as offering a way to include the *negative* dimension; it certainly addresses the question of what goes wrong and how this happens.

To value psychoanalytic *theory* for its explanatory power is not necessarily to claim that psychoanalytic *therapy* is the only way to *deal* with the situation. Psychotherapy is not for everyone and it can only be omnipotent to claim that it is. A more favourable environment, friendship, religion, or other forms of therapy may be preferable in any individual case. But that not everybody may be able to benefit from—or get access to—psychoanalytic therapy does not invalidate the insights I believe to come from the psychoanalytic way of looking at the world. And what psychoanalytic theory and the concept of sin have in common is that they take human beings as they actually are, and not as we would ideally like them to be.

I turn now to the second issue. In an many-cultured world can any value system claim pride of place? I find that I am prepared to give such primacy to the human concepts of compassion and forgiveness. In making this claim I think I am underpinned by both psychoanalytic thought and by the religious ideas of sin and forgiveness. Psychoanalytic thinking indicates that the capacity for concern, true guilt, and forgiveness lays the basis both for human development and fulfilment and the ability to give to as well as receive from society—as our portion of civilization understands that society. This is also the claim of Christianity—'faith, hope, love abide, these three; but the greatest of these is love.'[10] I would add this caveat; I am talking of that form of love which knows hurt and evil, which is strengthened by anger, and which gives birth to compassion and forgiveness. Indeed I would go further and claim that it is this constellation which actually *defines* love. Love is not an idyllic, one-dimensional conflict-free emotion.

But I am not sure how far this claim is bound to be culturally specific, and therefore in its turn really needs to be in dialogue with the findings of other cultures and other races which do not appear to give to compassion and forgiveness this pride of place. They in their turn might give the prize to survival, righteousness, purity of life or adherence to the laws of a transcendent God. All religions have to make sense of human history; most do not see the whole meaning of life as encapsulated in that history. In most religions the goal of happiness and fulfiment is not the sole arbiter of 'worthwhileness', meaning, and holiness. Moreover, there is a gap between the ideals of religions and their 'incarnation' in fallible human beings.

Many religions fill the gap with the equivalent of sin, though sin is sometimes seen as vested in the individual or sometimes in society, as in Islamic states in which the Islamic revolution heralds the return to the following of a hitherto-forsaken holy vocation. All suggest that a certain form of behaviour will help eradicate the gap. Christianity specifies that this should include increased compassion, forgiveness, and love. To be sure this is not all that Christianity specifies; we have also calls from within the Christian church for increased holiness, separation from the ways of the world, and for fundamentalism. In fact in many controversies within Christianity it has been hard to keep alive the dimensions of love, compassion, forgiveness, and concern for the social order and social values. There is a danger of the debate and conflict becoming monolithic; of righteousness winning out over mercy. Yet throughout the Old Testament the Hebrew concept of 'hesed'—or loving-kindness, or grace of God coexists with God's demand for righteousness and holiness. But we find it hard to keep a balance. The history of the church shows many periods of imbalance, in the community as a whole and within individuals.

Augustine stands as one great example of this. He seemed to oscillate in himself between a need for purity and holiness and a need to love and for love; his writings reflect this oscillation. Many rigorous movements in Christianity have claimed Augustine as their mentor but have not been able to stay with the sense of conflict and contradiction inherent in his thought. Of such movements in the church—past and present—there have been no lack, but in the movements, religious and secular, of the sixties and seventies we see an oversimplification in

the other direction; in these love alone was to be the true
arbiter of thinking and behaviour. But love without the
depth demanded through its clash with the universal
experience of sinfulness does not come out quite right. It
tends to provoke in its turn a backlash. Efforts to eradicate
sin and what we may call evil from the human book
ultimately always fail.

Guilt and forgiveness are central to religious thought
because what they represent is central to human nature.
They find their place in most, if not all of our human,
psychological, and religious languages. They have a currency in each of them, for whatever our chosen language
we find we cannot deny them or pretend that we have
never met them; we know we have. They may be hard to
understand; their *workings* remain to an extent deeply
mysterious, but we can accept, recognize, and intuitively
'own' them.

Sin, on the other hand, stands at the end of this book
—as at the beginning—as *the* mystery. Perhaps this is
because it is essentially what I think of as a second order
word. It does not immediately *describe* our experience,
rather it offers an *interpretative explanation* of that experience. I have tried to take its exploration a little further
and I have come to the conclusion that it represents *one
kind* of explanation of the *gap* between how we are and
how we think we should be, in relation to the values that
govern our existence when those values are formed from
our sense of God. I put it this way because sometimes we
do not want to be any different from the way we are.
Many people would not want to have to take on board the
current Christian understanding of what is sinful, even
though they do feel something of the gap. They may
feel this understanding to be oppressive and mistaken.
Something Christianity calls 'sin' may continue to have
meaning for many people, but they may be unwilling
and unable to define it more exactly and precisely.

We may want to reserve the right to re-evaluate what
exactly is sinful and what sorts of behaviour are sin(s).
Current debates on such issues as homosexuality, remarriage, and cohabitation reflect just this enterprise.
However, this does not mean throwing out the fundamental sense of sin—without an 's'—which I have come to
believe stands for the disordered and disturbed parts of

our being to which we can have only partial access and for which we can take only partial responsibility.

In the wake of this, the last word has to be not with sin alone, but with sin in the context of *redemption*. For it is redemption that sheds light on the mystery of sin and not the other way round. From the book of Exodus onwards with its great 'I am'[11] through to the claim of Jesus in St John's gospel: 'Before Abraham was, I am'[12] we come to be allowed to hope and think that the eternal nature of God is to be redemptive, to take on board in one fell swoop the mysteries of sin and forgiveness as two parts of the same whole. The Exodus revelation of the 'I am' of God shows that God is at his most 'am-ness' not when he stands alone in isolated majesty and omnipotence but when he is in a redemptive *relationship* with his oppressed creation.

Without the sense of relationship sin becomes sterile. Even the deep-rooted affliction of our disordered inner world that we have come to know as 'original sin' arises, or I have claimed it does, through deficiencies in relationship. When sin becomes codified as an end in itself instead of being seen as a part of relationship then it becomes divorced from forgiveness. Forgiveness is not just a way to repair breaks in a hypothesized perfect love, for there never was a perfect love in that sense. I end by claiming that human life and love—with or without the Christian God—are most authentically human not when sin is absent but when they are *defined* as a redemptive and reparative activity whose hallmarks are acceptance of sin—the gap, the disorder, the affliction, call it what we will—and concern, compassion, and forgiveness.

Notes

1. See, for example, Exodus 20; Deuteronomy 5.
2. Romans 13.1 (AV).
3. Matthew 22.21 (RSV).
4. For a summary, see J. N. D. Kelly, *Early Christian Doctrines* (A. and C. Black 1958), pp. 216–19 and 436–40.
5. C. Rycroft, *Critical Dictionary of Psychoanalysis* (Penguin 1972), pp. 160–1, and Chapter 3, Note 9.

6. See A. Maslow, *Motivation and Personality* (Harper and Row 1970), especially chapters 4–7 and 11–12.

7. Examples of J. Piaget's work are: *The Mental Development of the Child* in *Six Psychological Studies* (New York: Random House 1968), *The Child's Concept of Time* (London: Routledge and Kegan Paul 1969), *Play, Dreams and Imitation in Childhood* (New York: Norton 1951), *The Moral Judgement of the Child* (Glencoe Ill: The Free Press 1965), *The Language and Thought of the Child* (New York: Harcourt 1926). For an introduction to Piaget's work, see J. Radford and E. Govier (eds.), *A Textbook of Psychology* (Routledge 1991), chapters 16–18.

8. See E. Erikson, *Childhood and Society* (Penguin 1950), especially chapter 7.

9. L. Kohlberg, 'The Child as a Moral Philosopher', in J. Sants and H. J. Butcher (eds.), *Developmental Psychology: Selected Readings* (Penguin 1975), p. 441ff.

10. 1 Corinthians 13.13.

11. Exodus 3.6.

12. John 8.58.

Index